Data Analytics Using Splunk 9.x

A practical guide to implementing Splunk's features for performing data analysis at scale

Dr. Nadine Shillingford

BIRMINGHAM—MUMBAI

Data Analytics Using Splunk 9.x

Publishing Product Manager: Heramb Bhavsar
Senior Editor: Nathanya Dias
Technical Editor: Kavyashree K S
Copy Editor: Safis Editing
Project Coordinator: Farheen Fathima
Proofreader: Safis Editing
Indexer: Sejal Dsilva
Production Designer: Shankar Kalbhor
Marketing Coordinator: Nivedita Singh

First published: January 2023

Production reference: 2240123

Published by Packt Publishing Ltd.
Livery Place
35 Livery Street
Birmingham
B3 2PB, UK.

ISBN 978-1-80324-941-4

www.packt.com

Contributors

About the author

Dr. Nadine Shillingford is a certified Splunk Architect with 10 years of security consulting experience. She has installed, managed, and configured large-scale and large-volume Splunk deployments in the healthcare, retail, insurance, and federal spaces. In addition, Dr. Shillingford has teaching experience at the undergraduate and graduate levels. Dr. Shillingford holds a Ph.D. in computer science from the University of Notre Dame. She is an artist and the mother of a teenage daughter.

I want to thank the people who have supported me through this process, including my daughter Hailey, my friends, who gave moral support, and my reviewers and colleagues Duane and Mhike.

About the reviewers

Mhike Funderburk has been a member of the SplunkTrust for 3 years and is one of the foremost experts in the world on Splunk's SOAR technology. He has spent the last 10 years working in security engineering and incident response, primarily with Fortune 100 financial and technology companies. Mhike has had several opportunities to speak at conferences, including Splunk's .conf, on engineering logging and automation solutions within security operations, and he continues to work to educate and grow the community of Splunk users building security automation through SOAR.

Duane Waddle is currently employed as a principal cybersecurity architect at a large systems integrator. He holds a B.S. in computer science from Tennessee Technological University. With over 25 years of experience in the industry, spanning roles in system administration, LAN/WAN/SAN support, security engineering, and professional services consulting, he has seen much of today's technology up close. Duane is a long-time member of the SplunkTrust MVP program. Through the Splunk community, he has helped hundreds of organizations around the globe succeed with Splunk solutions.

Srikanth Yarlagadda is a SplunkTrust MVP and an expert in Splunk Enterprise, Enterprise Security, and SOAR products. With over 13 years of experience as an API developer, SOA developer, Splunk SME, and telecom messaging protocols implementation specialist, he has a wealth of knowledge and expertise in these fields. Srikanth is interested in cyber security, microservices, cloud computing, and web development. He likes reading the Head First Programming books and loves to spend time with his family. He also enjoys watching fiction movies.

Table of Contents

Part 2: Visualizing Data with Splunk

6

Creating Tables and Charts Using SPL   145

7

Creating Dynamic Dashboards   183

Part 3: Advanced Topics in Splunk

8

Licensing, Indexing, and Buckets   223

9

Clustering and Advanced Administration   243

10

Data Models, Acceleration, and Other Ways to Improve Performance
261

11

Multisite Splunk Deployments and Federated Search   285

12

Container Management   297

Index   307

Other Books You May Enjoy   316

Preface

I started working with Splunk in late 2013 when I joined the security team of a healthcare company. They were getting ready to migrate from a home-grown **Security Information and Event Management** (**SIEM**) system to Splunk. As part of the preparation, we did the Splunk Knowledge Manager, Admin, and Enterprise Security courses. They were very interesting, and I looked forward to working with the tool. Fast forward 9 years, and I have used Splunk on multiple contracts. The use cases have ranged from security, healthcare, retail, and education. I have incorporated Splunk into the courses that I teach. I became a member of SplunkTrust. So when the publishers approached me with the proposal to write a book on Splunk, I accepted.

This book is an introduction to Splunk. I will guide you through the main components of Splunk. You will learn about indexes, indexing, and indexers. You learn about search heads and clusters. You will get an introduction to the Splunk **Search Processing Language** (**SPL**) using logs and use cases from the BOTS dataset. Are you ready?

> **Note**
> Screenshots and code snippets are copyright Splunk Inc. Used with permission. All rights reserved.

Who this book is for

The book is for data analysts, data scientists, Splunk users, administrators, architects, product managers, and owners. You will have an understanding of Splunk fundamentals, at least at the Splunk administration certification level.

What this book covers

Chapter 1, Introduction to Splunk and its Core Components, is a discussion on the increase in Big data and how tools such as Splunk make it easier to deal with this data. The chapter discusses the basic Splunk components, such as indexers and search heads, and introduces the BOTS dataset, which will be used to learn Splunk SPL.

Chapter 2, Setting Up the Splunk Environment, provides step-by-step instructions on setting up Splunk components. It also includes an introduction to access management.

Chapter 3, Onboarding and Normalizing Data, provides step-by-step instructions on onboarding data into Splunk.

Chapter 4, Introduction to SPL, provides an introduction to the Splunk SPL, including different Splunk commands.

Chapter 5, Reporting Commands, Lookups, and Macros, is a continuation of the introduction to the Splunk SPL, including more advanced commands, lookups, and macros.

Chapter 6, Creating Tables and Charts Using SPL, provides step-by-step instructions on creating different visualizations in Splunk.

Chapter 7, Creating Dynamic Dashboards, builds on previous chapters and incorporates tables, charts, and other visualizations into dashboards.

Chapter 8, Licensing, Indexing, and Buckets, is an introduction to Splunk licensing and indexing. The discussion includes information about Splunk queues and pipelines.

Chapter 9, Clustering and Advanced Administration, is a discussion of Splunk indexer and search head clustering.

Chapter 10, Data Models, Acceleration, and Other Ways to Improve Performance, is an introduction to data models and how they improve search performance.

Chapter 11, Multisite Splunk Deployments and Federated Search, is an exploration of different Splunk deployments and concepts, including multisite deployments, hybrid search, and federated search.

Chapter 12, Container Management, is an introduction to the concept of container management, including Docker and Kubernetes. It includes an introduction to the Splunk add-ons and apps developed for getting container data into Splunk.

To get the most out of this book

You will need access to deploy **Amazon Web Services** (**AWS**) instances in *Chapter 2, Setting Up the Splunk Environment* and *Chapter 3, Onboarding and Normalizing Data*. You will also need a tool such as puTTY to connect to the servers via the **Secure Shell Protocol** (**SSH**). The instructions outlined in *Chapter 4* through to *Chapter 7* were executed in macOS but can be run on any machine where Splunk Enterprise is installed, including Linux, macOS, or Windows environments.

Software/hardware covered in the book	Operating system requirements
Splunk Enterprise	Windows, macOS, or Linux
Splunk apps and add-ons	
BOTS dataset	
AWS instances	
Amazon Web Services Account	

You will need an Amazon Web Services account to deploy the instances in *Chapter 2, Setting Up the Splunk Environment* and *Chapter 3, Onboarding and Normalizing Data*.

If you are using the digital version of this book, we advise you to type the code yourself or access the code from the book's GitHub repository (a link is available in the next section). Doing so will help you avoid any potential errors related to copying and pasting code.

Download the example code files

You can download the example code files for this book from GitHub at `https://github.com/PacktPublishing/Data-Analytics-Using-Splunk-9.x`. If there's an update to the code, it will be updated in the GitHub repository.

We also have other code bundles from our rich catalog of books and videos available at `https://github.com/PacktPublishing/`. Check them out!

Conventions used

There are a number of text conventions used throughout this book.

`Code in text`: Indicates code words in text, database table names, folder names, filenames, file extensions, pathnames, dummy URLs, user input, and Twitter handles. Here is an example: "Find the `[general]` stanza and replace the `serverName` value with `forwarder1`."

A block of code is set as follows:

```
index=botsv1 earliest=0
index=botsv1 sourcetype=iis http_referer=*
index=botsv1 earliest=0 sourcetype=suricata
| eval bytes=bytes_in+bytes_out
index=botsv1 earliest=0 sourcetype=iis referer_domain=*
| table _time, cs_Referer, referer_domain
index=botsv1 earliest=0 sourcetype="WinEventLog:Security"
| stats count by Account_Name
```

When we wish to draw your attention to a particular part of a code block, the relevant lines or items are set in bold:

```
index=botsv1 earliest=0 sourcetype=iis c_ip="23.22.63.114" OR
c_ip="52.23.25.56"
| <transforming commands>
| search...
```

Any command-line input or output is written as follows:

```
/opt/splunk/bin/splunk set servername indexer
/opt/splunk/bin/splunk set default-hostname indexer
/opt/splunk/bin/splunk restart
```

Bold: Indicates a new term, an important word, or words that you see onscreen. For instance, words in menus or dialog boxes appear in **bold**. Here is an example: "Click on the orange **Confirm Changes** button to continue."

> **Tips or important notes**
> Appear like this.

Get in touch

Feedback from our readers is always welcome.

General feedback: If you have questions about any aspect of this book, email us at customercare@ packtpub.com and mention the book title in the subject of your message.

Errata: Although we have taken every care to ensure the accuracy of our content, mistakes do happen. If you have found a mistake in this book, we would be grateful if you would report this to us. Please visit www.packtpub.com/support/errata and fill in the form.

Piracy: If you come across any illegal copies of our works in any form on the internet, we would be grateful if you would provide us with the location address or website name. Please contact us at copyright@packt.com with a link to the material.

If you are interested in becoming an author: If there is a topic that you have expertise in and you are interested in either writing or contributing to a book, please visit authors.packtpub.com.

Share Your Thoughts

Once you've read *Exploring Data with Splunk*, we'd love to hear your thoughts! Scan the QR code below to go straight to the Amazon review page for this book and share your feedback.

https://packt.link/r/1-803-24941-2

Download a free PDF copy of this book

Thanks for purchasing this book!

Do you like to read on the go but are unable to carry your print books everywhere? Is your eBook purchase not compatible with the device of your choice?

Don't worry, now with every Packt book you get a DRM-free PDF version of that book at no cost.

Read anywhere, any place, on any device. Search, copy, and paste code from your favorite technical books directly into your application.

The perks don't stop there, you can get exclusive access to discounts, newsletters, and great free content in your inbox daily

Follow these simple steps to get the benefits:

1. Scan the QR code or visit the link below

https://packt.link/free-ebook/978-1-80324-941-4

2. Submit your proof of purchase
3. That's it! We'll send your free PDF and other benefits to your email directly.

Part 1: Getting Started with Splunk

In this part we will look at the need for Splunk and Splunk's core components. We will set up a simple deployment and follow the steps to add and normalize data in Splunk.

This part comprises the following chapters:

1

Introduction to Splunk and its Core Components

A few years ago, I was hired by the IT security team of a large healthcare company to work as a security engineer. At the time, the company had a homegrown **Security Information and Event Management** (**SIEM**) system and was at the initial stages of rolling in a brand new Splunk deployment. Physical servers were ordered and scheduled to be delivered and licensing paperwork was completed. A Splunk Education instructor conducted on-site core Splunk and Splunk Enterprise Security training, and we were ready to go. The thought of working with Splunk was so exciting. At the time, we were getting ready to install Splunk 6.x with one of the earlier releases of Splunk Enterprise Security. Before my arrival, the team had worked with Splunk Professional Services to estimate storage and license requirements. The next step was to focus on the data. "How do you get value from data? How do you configure Splunk Enterprise to get value from your company's data?" We will explore how to use Splunk Enterprise to gain insight into your data in this book. In this chapter, we will introduce how the big data tool called Splunk Enterprise can be used to explore data.

In this chapter, we will cover the following topics:

- Splunking big data

- Exploring Splunk components

- Introducing the case study – splunking the BOTS Dataset v1

Splunking big data

Splunk is a big data tool. In this book, we will introduce the idea of using Splunk to solve problems that involve large amounts of data. When I worked on the IT security team, the problem was obvious – *we needed to use security data to identify malicious activity*. Defining the problem you are trying to solve will determine what kind of data you collect and how you analyze that data. Not every problem requires a big data solution. Sometimes, a traditional database solution might work just as well and with less cost. So, how do you know if you're dealing with a big data problem? There are three *V's* that help define big data:

- **High Volume**: A big data problem usually involves large volumes of data. Most times, the amount of data is greater than what can fit into traditional database solutions.

- **High Velocity**: Traditional database solutions are usually not able to handle the speed at which modern data enters a system. Imagine trying to store and manage data from user clicks on a website such as amazon.com in a traditional database. Databases are not designed to support that many operations.

- **High Variety**: A problem requiring analysis of big data involves a variety of data sources of varying formats. An IT security SIEM may have data being logged from multiple data sources, including firewall devices, email traces, DNS logs, and access logs. Each of these logs has a different format and correlating all the logs requires a heavy-duty system.

Here are some cases that can be solved using big data:

- A retail company wants to determine how product placement in stores affects sales. For example, research may show that placing packs of *Cheetos* near the **Point Of Sale** (**POS**) devices increases sales for customers with small children. The target assigns a guest ID number to every customer. They correlate this ID number with the customer's credit card number and transactions.

- A rental company wants to measure the times of year that are busiest to ensure that there is a sufficient inventory of vehicles at different locations. Even so, they may realize that a certain type of vehicle is more suitable for a particular area of town.

- A public school district wants to explore data pulled from multiple district schools to determine the effect of remote classes on certain demographics.

- An online shop wants to use customer traffic to determine the peak time for posting ads or giving discounts.

- An IT security team may use datasets containing firewall logs, DNS logs, and user access to hunt down a malicious actor on the network.

Now, let's look at how big data is generated.

How is big data generated?

Infographics published by **FinancesOnline** (https://financesonline.com) indicated that humans created, captured, copied, and consumed about *74 zettabytes* of data in 2021. That number is estimated to grow to 149 zettabytes in 2024.

The volume of data seen in the last few years can be attributed to increases in three types of data:

- **Machine data**: Data generated by machines such as operating systems and application logs
- **Social data**: Data generated by social media systems
- **Transactional data**: Data generated by e-commerce systems

We are surrounded by digital devices, and as the capacity and capabilities of these devices increase, the amount of data generated also increases. Modern devices such as phones, laptops, watches, smart speakers, cars, sensors, POS devices, and household appliances all generate large volumes of machine data in a wide variety of formats. Many times, this data stays untouched because the data owners do not have the ability, time, or money to analyze it.

The prevalence of smartphones is possibly another contributor to the exponential increase in data. IBM's Simon Personal Communicator, the first mainstream mobile telephone introduced in 1992, had very limited capability. It cost a whopping $899 with a service contract. Out of the box, a user could use the Simon to make calls and send and receive emails, faxes, and pages. It also contained a notebook, address book, calendar, world clock, and scheduler features. IBM sold approximately 50,000 units (`https://time.com/3137005/first-smartphone-ibm-simon/`).

Figure 1.1 shows the first smartphone to have the functions of a phone and a **Personal Digital Assistant (PDA)**:

Figure 1.1 – The IBM Simon Personal Communicator released in 1992

The IBM Simon Personal Communicator is archaic compared to the average cellphone today. Apple sold 230 million iPhones in 2020 (`https://www.businessofapps.com/data/apple-statistics/`). iPhone users generate data when they browse the web, listen to music and podcasts, stream television and movies, conduct business transactions, and post to and browse social media feeds. This is in addition to the features that were found in the IBM Simon, such as sending and receiving emails. Each of these applications generates volumes of data. Just one application such as Facebook running on an iPhone involves a variety of data – posts, photos, videos, transactions from Facebook Marketplace, and so much more. *Figure 1.2* shows data from OurWorldData.org (`https://ourworldindata.org/internet`) that illustrates the rapid increase in users of social media:

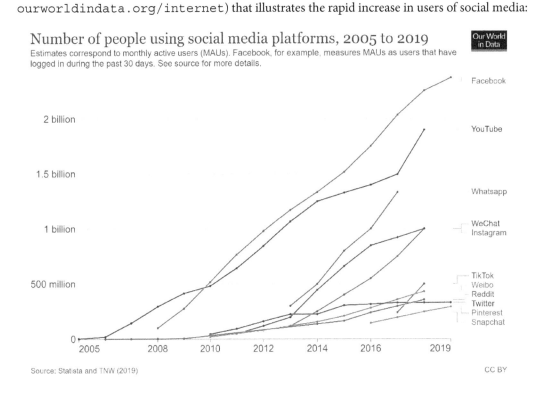

Figure 1.2 – Number of people using social media platforms, 2005 to 2019

In the next section, we'll explore how we can use Splunk to process all this data.

Understanding Splunk

Now that we understand what big data is, its applications, and how it is generated, let's talk about Splunk Enterprise and how Splunk can be used to manage big data. For simplicity, we will refer to *Splunk Enterprise* as *Splunk*.

Splunk was founded in 2003 by Michael Baum, Rob Das, and Erik Swan. Splunk was designed to search, monitor, and analyze machine-generated data. Splunk can handle *high volume*, *high variety* data being generated at *high velocity*. This makes it a perfect tool for dealing with big data. Splunk works on various platforms, including Windows (32- and 64-bit), Linux (64-bit), and macOS. Splunk can be installed on physical devices, virtual machines such as VirtualBox and VMWare, and virtual cloud instances such as **Amazon Web Services** (**AWS**) and Microsoft Azure. Customers can also sign up for the Splunk Cloud Platform, which supplies the user with a Splunk deployment hosted virtually. Using AWS instances and Splunk Cloud frees the user from having to deploy and maintain physical servers. There is a free version 60-day trial of Splunk that allows the user to index 500 MB of data daily. Once the user has used the product for 60 days, they can use a perpetual free license or purchase a Splunk license. The 60-day version of Splunk is a great way to get your feet wet. Traditionally, the paid version of Splunk was billed at a volume rate – that is, the more data you index, the more you pay. However, new pricing models such as workload and ingest pricing have been introduced in recent years.

In addition to the core Splunk tool, there are various free and paid applications, such as Splunk Enterprise Security, Splunk Soar, and various observability solutions such as Splunk **User Behavior Analytics** (**UBA**) and Splunk Observability Cloud.

Splunk was designed to index a variety of data. This is accomplished via pre-defined configurations that allow Splunk to recognize the format of different data sources. In addition, `splunkbase.com` is a constantly growing repository of 1,000+ apps and **Technical Add-Ons** (**TAs**) developed by Splunk, Splunk partners, and the Splunk community. One of the most important features of these TAs includes configurations for automatically extracting fields from raw data. Unlike traditional databases, Splunk can index large volumes of data. A dedicated Splunk Enterprise indexer can index over 20 MB of data per second or 1.7 per day. The amount of data that Splunk is capable of indexing can be increased with additional indexers. There are many use cases for which Splunk is a great solution.

Table 1.1 highlights how Splunk improved processes at The University of Arizona, Honda, and Lenovo:

Use Case	Company	Details
Security	The University of Arizona	The University of Arizona used **Splunk Remote Work Insights** (**RWI**) to help with the challenges of remote learning during the pandemic (`https://www.splunk.com/en_us/customers/success-stories/university-of-arizona.html`)
IT Operations	Honda	Honda used predictive analytics to increase efficiency and solve problems before they became machine failures or interruptions in their production line (`https://tinyurl.com/5n7f7naz`)
DevOps	Lenovo	Lenovo reduced the amount of time spent in troubleshooting by 50% and maintained 100% uptime despite a 300% increase in web traffic (`https://tinyurl.com/yactu398`)

Table 1.1 – Examples of success stories from Splunk customers

We will look at some of the major components of Splunk in the next section.

Exploring Splunk components

A Splunk deployment consists of three key components:

- Forwarders
- Indexers
- Search heads

Forwarders are the data consumers of Splunk. Forwarders run on the source of the data or an intermediate device. Configurations on the forwarder device collect data and pass them on to the indexers. There are two types of forwarders – **universal** and **heavy forwarders**. Universal forwarders merely pass on the data to the indexers. Heavy forwarders, however, perform additional tasks, such as parsing and field extractions.

The **indexer** is the component responsible for indexing incoming data and searching indexed data. Indexers should have a good input/output capacity as they do a lot of reading and writing from disk. Multiple indexers can be combined to form clusters to increase data availability, data fidelity, data recovery, disaster recovery, and search affinity. Users access data in Splunk using **search heads**. They access data indexed by Splunk by running search queries using a language called **Search Processing Language (SPL)**.

Search heads coordinate searches across the indexers. Like indexers, multiple search heads can be combined to form search head clusters. There are other roles that devices can play in a Splunk deployment. These include deployment servers, deployers, license masters, and cluster masters. The Splunk forwarders send data to the indexers. It's a one-way transfer of data. The search head interacts with the indexers by sending search requests in the form of bundles. The indexers find the data that fits the search criteria and send the results back to the search heads. *Figure 1.3* shows how the three main components interact in a Splunk deployment:

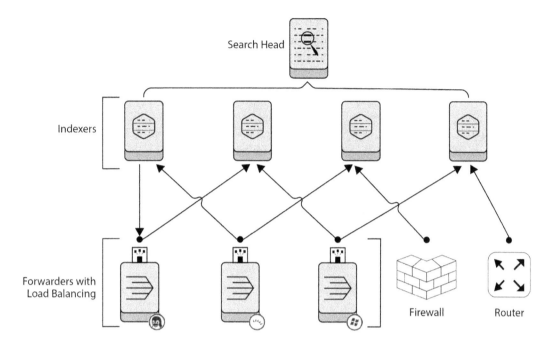

Figure 1.3 – The major Splunk components

We will discuss the different Splunk components in detail in the following sections.

Forwarders

A Splunk deployment can have the magnitude of tens of thousands of universal forwarders. As mentioned in the *Exploring Splunk components* section, there are two kinds of forwarders – the lightweight universal forwarders and the heavy forwarders. Both universal and heavy forwarders perform the following tasks:

- Assign metadata to incoming data (source, sourcetype, and host)
- Buffer and compress data
- Run local scripted inputs
- Break the data into 64 KB blocks

The universal forwarder is a low-footprint process that is used to forward raw or unparsed data to the indexer layer. However, if you need to do any filtering of the data before it arrives at the indexer layer, it is best to use a heavy forwarder. In a single instance of a Splunk deployment, the forwarder sits on the same device as the indexer and search head.

The universal forwarder can be installed on multiple platforms, including Windows (32- and 64-bit), Linux (64-bit, ARM, s390x, and PPCLE), macOS (Intel and M1/Intel), 64-bit FreeBSD, Solaris (Sparc and 64-bit), and AIX. Heavy forwarders run on the same platforms as Splunk Enterprise. You can install a universal forwarder using a `universal forwarder install` file, while heavy forwarders are installed using the regular `Splunk Enterprise install` file.

Both universal and heavy forwarders collect data by using `inputs`. A Splunk administrator configures inputs using the CLI commands, by editing a configuration file called `inputs.conf`, or by using Splunk Web (**Settings | Add Data**). A Splunk forwarder can be configured to accept the following inputs using different settings, such as the following:

- **Files and directories**: Monitor new data coming into files and directories. Splunk also has an upload or one-shot option for uploading single files.

- **Network events**: Monitor TCP and UDP ports, syslog feeds, and SNMP events.

- **Windows sources**: Monitor Windows Event Logs, Perfmon, WMI, registries, and Active Directory.

- **Other sources**: Monitor **First In, First Out** (**FIFO**) queues, changes to filesystems, and receive data from APIs through scripted inputs.

> **Important note**
> **HTTP Event Collectors** (**HEC**) inputs allow users to send data events over HTTP and HTTPS using a token-based authentication model. This does not require a Splunk forwarder.

The following code shows a sample of the `inputs.conf` file from the Splunk add-on for Microsoft Windows:

```
###### OS Logs ######
[WinEventLog://Application]
disabled = 1


###### DHCP ######
[monitor://$WINDIR\System32\DHCP]
disabled = 1
whitelist = DhcpSrvLog*
[powershell://generate_windows_update_logs]
script =."$SplunkHome\etc\apps\Splunk_TA_windows\bin\
powershell\generate_windows_update_logs.ps1"
schedule = 0 */24 * * *
```

```
[script://.\bin\win_listening_ports.bat]
disabled = 1
## Run once per hour
interval = 3600
sourcetype = Script:ListeningPorts
```

Data from the forwarders are sent to the indexers. We will explore indexers in the next section.

Indexers

Splunk forwarders forward data to Splunk indexers. Think of the indexer as the brain of the Splunk deployment. It is the heavy input/output device that not only transforms and stores data but also searches the data based on queries passed down by the search heads. Indexers transform data into Splunk events. These events are then stored in an **index**, a repository for Splunk data. There are two types of indexes – *events* and *metrics*.

Splunk indexes *time series data* either by extracting timestamps from data or assigning a current datetime. A **Splunk index** is a collection of directories and subdirectories on the filesystem. These subdirectories are referred to as *buckets*. Data that arrives at an indexer is passed through *pipelines and queues*. A **pipeline** is a thread running on the indexer, while a **queue** is a memory buffer that holds data between pipelines.

We access data indexed on the indexers using search heads. We will look at search heads in the next section.

Search heads

A **search head** is a Splunk instance that allows users to search events indexed on *the indexers* (*also referred to as search peers*). The average user only interacts with the search head on a Splunk deployment. The user accesses the search head using a browser interface called **Splunk Web**. Users access data in Splunk using search queries in the Splunk search bar or view dashboards, reports, and other visualizations.

Figure 1.4 is an example of a Splunk bar graph:

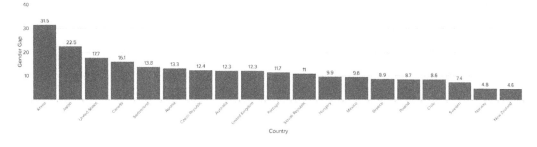

Figure 1.4 – Sample Splunk bar graph

Search heads do not index data. Rather, search heads distribute searches to the indexers. The search head parses search queries and decides what accompanying files, called *knowledge objects*, need to be sent to the indexers. Why is this important? Some files may exist only on the search head. By combining all these files into a *knowledge bundle*, the search head equips the indexer with all the information (configuration files and assets) it needs to perform the search. It's almost like the search head offloads its work to the indexers and says, "here are the files that you need to get the work done." Sometimes, the knowledge bundle contains almost all the search head's apps. The indexers search their indexes for the data that match the search query and send the results back to the search heads. The search heads then merge the results and present them to the user.

Search queries are written with Splunk's SPL. *Figure 1.5* shows a screenshot of an SPL query typed in the Splunk search bar:

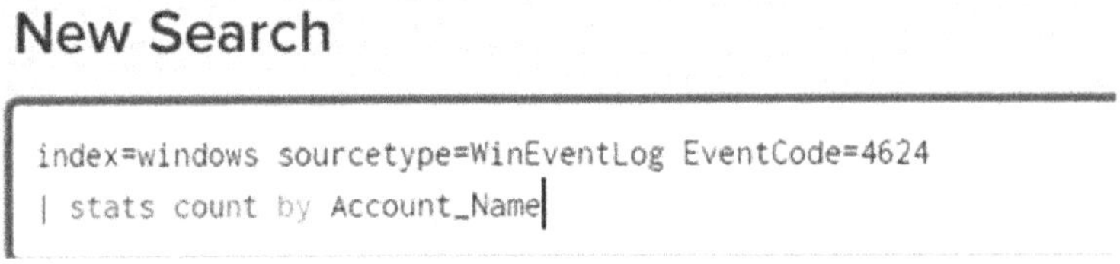

New Search

```
index=windows sourcetype=WinEventLog EventCode=4624
| stats count by Account_Name
```

Figure 1.5 – An SPL query

In the next section, we'll talk about the BOTS Dataset v1, which we will use throughout this book.

Introducing the case study – splunking the BOTS Dataset v1

In this section, we will introduce the case study that we will use throughout this book. We will explore logs in BOTS Dataset v1. **Boss of the SOC (BOTS)** is a blue-team **capture-the-flag** competition held during the annual *Splunk .conf* conference (https://tinyurl.com/39ru8d4b). Participants are given access to realistic network security logs to investigate real-world cybersecurity attacks. The nature of the attacks or the exact attack sequence is beyond the scope of this book. However, the dataset is a collection of data that we can use to explore some of the rich features of Splunk. BOTS Dataset v1 was compiled by Ryan Kovar, David Herrald, and James Brodsky in 2016.

The setup

A fictional company, ABC Inc., has observed unusual activity on its network. They think that the problem is centered around three Windows devices (*we8105desk*, *de9041srv*, and *we1149srv*). The very cyber-conscious ABC Inc. also has several network security solutions installed on their network as part of their security infrastructure:

- **Suricata**: An open source intrusion detection system and intrusion prevention system (https://suricata.io)

- **Fortigate**: A next-generation firewall (`https://www.fortinet.com`)

- **Internet Information Services (IIS)**: An extensible web server software created by Microsoft (`https://www.iis.net/`)

- **Nessus**: A proprietary vulnerability scanner developed by Tenable (`https://www.tenable.com/products/nessus`)

- **Splunk Stream**: A wire data capture solution built into Splunk (`https://splunkbase.splunk.com/app/1809/`)

The company would like you to investigate an incident that occurred in August 2016. What abnormal activity will you discover?

Our solution is to use Splunk to investigate the logs generated in August 2016. To get the full experience of installing Splunk, we will first deploy a Splunk environment to simulate the environment that generated `BOTS Dataset v1`. The environment will consist of the following components:

- Three Splunk forwarders running on Windows devices (*we8105desk*, *de9041srv*, and *we1149srv*) deployed using AWS instances

- A dedicated indexer (Splunk Enterprise installed on an AWS instance running Red Hat Linux)

- A dedicated search head (Splunk Enterprise installed on an AWS instance running Red Hat Linux)

- A deployment server (Splunk Enterprise installed on an AWS instance running Red Hat Linux)

This will give us an environment that we can use to explore the important process of setting up and configuring Splunk in *Chapter 2, Setting Up the Splunk Environmentment*. This case study will require access to an AWS account, so you should sign up for an account using the AWS Management Console (`https://aws.amazon.com/console/`) if you do not have one. This case study does not require advanced knowledge of AWS, but it may be helpful to read a tutorial on AWS Cloud such as Learn the Fundamentals (`https://tinyurl.com/2p8aj7b7`) or watch a YouTube video (`https://www.youtube.com/watch?v=r4YIdn2eTm4`). You will also need a Splunk account to download the Splunk installation file and Splunk apps (`https://www.splunk.com`).

`BOTS Dataset v1` is available for download from the Splunk **Git** repository (`https://github.com/splunk/botsv1`). We will use the dataset containing only *attack* logs due to space limitations of the free license of Splunk Enterprise. The dataset comes in the form of a Splunk app, which will install on our dedicated search head. Once we have installed and configured the Splunk deployment, we will design a series of Splunk queries, dashboards, reports, and alerts as we investigate the logs.

For this case study, we are assuming that Alice has an established security infrastructure that includes firewalls and other security devices. However, monitoring those devices does not fall under the scope of the project.

Once we have deployed and configured the Splunk environment, we will install BOTS Dataset v1 as an app on the search head and continue our exploration on the search head. The dataset consists of various machine and network logs generated by the appliances mentioned in the *The setup* section.

Now, let's summarize what we have learned in this chapter.

Summary

Corporations are discovering the value of analyzing big data to give insight into users behavior. This analysis has yielded results that have proven useful in various fields, including education, medicine, and computer security. In this chapter, we explored the use of Splunk to tackle big data problems. We looked at how data generation has changed over time. We looked at how Splunk has been used in organizations to solve problems. We also reviewed the key components of Splunk – forwarders, indexers, and search heads. We learned that forwarders send data to the indexers, which index the data. Users use Splunk search heads to create search queries in SPL. These search heads create knowledge bundles that they send to the indexers. The indexers search their indexes for data that match the queries. They return the results to the search heads. These components work together to give powerful results.

Finally, we introduced our BOTS dataset v1 dataset, which was generated for the Splunk BOTS competition and is a rich dataset for this exercise. We will use examples from this dataset throughout the rest of this book.

We will deploy our Splunk environment in *Chapter 2, Setting Up the Splunk Environment*, which will consist of a search head, an indexer, a deployment server, and three forwarders.

2

Setting Up the Splunk Environment

To fully appreciate the capabilities of Splunk, we will set up a Splunk Enterprise deployment in this chapter. We will use **Amazon Web Services** (**AWS**) instances to deploy three forwarders, an indexer, a search head, and a deployment server. As we learned in *Chapter 1, Introduction to Splunk and its Core Components*, the indexer is the Splunk server responsible for the storage of the data in a format that is easily searchable. The search head is used to search the data by sending requests to the indexers. In addition, in this chapter, we will install a deployment server used to deploy configurations throughout the deployment. Remember that Splunk can be installed on a standalone server to run the case study, however, we are including this chapter to give you hands-on experience of installing and configuring Splunk. Understanding the different components and how they are set up will be very useful as we move through the rest of this chapter.

In this chapter, we will cover the following topics:

- Installing Splunk Enterprise
- Setting up Splunk forwarders
- Setting up Splunk deployment servers
- Setting up Splunk indexers
- Setting up Splunk search heads
- Installing additional Splunk add-ons and apps
- Managing access to Splunk

Congratulations! You have completed the installation of your Splunk deployment, configured the different servers, installed apps, and run your first Splunk search query. But we before we conclude this chapter, let's take a brief look at access management in Splunk.

Technical requirements

Before you begin, you will need the following:

- Access to the AWS Management Console (`https://aws.amazon.com/console/`). This requires Amazon login credentials. The AWS **Elastic Compute Cloud** (**EC2**) instances that will host the Splunk deployment server, indexer, and search head are `c5.large` (Splunk-recommended) instances. They will incur a cost of about $0.085/hr at the time of writing this book. Be careful to turn off the servers once you are finished with the case study to avoid additional costs.

- You will need an **SSH** client to access the Linux-based AWS instances (deploymentserver, searchhead, and indexer). We use the **Terminal** application on a **Macbook** in this chapter. You can use a SSH client such as **PuTTY** (`https://www.putty.org`) if you are using a Microsoft Windows device.

- You will access AWS EC2 instances using *key pairs*. You will generate a key pair when you launch an instance. You can use one key pair across your different EC2 instances. You will need to remember where you store the private key to access an EC2 instance via *SSH*. Refer to `https://tinyurl.com/yt4nwysf` for more information on generating key pairs.

- You will need a **Remote Desktop Protocol** (**RDP**) application such as *Microsoft Remote Desktop* (`https://bit.ly/3PK24tQ`) (`we8105desk, de9041srv, we1149srv`).

- You will need to keep track of your passwords for the different devices. A tool such as *KeePass* (`https://keepass.info/`) may come in handy. Best practices recommend that we create new users and disable the default `admin` username and passwords. For simplicity and consistency, the instructions in this book use the default credentials for accessing the AWS EC2 instances via SSH, RDP, and Splunk Web.

- To keep the installation instructions in this chapter as simple as possible, more advanced security hardening steps are not implemented. Be sure to read up on hardening your servers on the Splunk website (`https://splk.it/3zc2HFd`).

Installing Splunk Enterprise

In this chapter, we will install and deploy Splunk instances to simulate the environment used to generate the `BOTS Dataset v1` app in our case study. Our deployment will consist of one deployment server, one indexer, one search head, and three forwarders. We will utilize AWS EC2 instances for each of the components. *Figure 2.1* shows the main components. We will deploy the *AWS EC2 Splunk Enterprise* **Amazon Machine Image** *(AMI)* to host the deployment server (`deploymentserver`), search head (`searchhead`), and indexer (`indexer`). These devices are represented as orange rectangles in *Figure 2.1*. The forwarders (`forwarder1, forwarder2, and forwarder3`) are AWS EC2 instances running Windows Server 2019. The forwarders in the `BOTS Dataset v1` app are named `we8105desk, de9041srv, and we1149srv`, but we will use a simple naming convention (`forwarder1`, `forwarder2`, and `forwarder3`) in the instructions. They are represented as blue rectangles here:

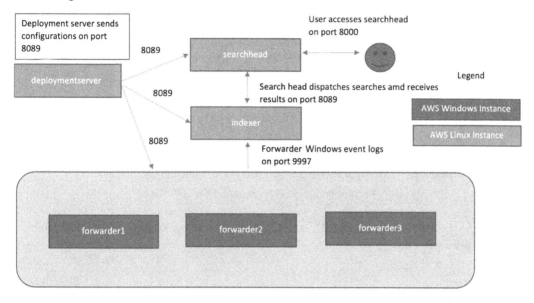

Figure 2.1 – Windows event logging case study: Splunk deployment

Let's install AWS Splunk instances!

Deploying AWS EC2 instances with the Splunk Enterprise AMI

In this section, we will deploy the AWS EC2 Splunk Enterprise AMI. This will be used for the deployment server, indexer, and search head. This AMI allows for quick deployment of Splunk. Other options include installing a regular *Amazon Linux 2 Kernel 5.10 AMI* and installing Splunk manually. We will use this method when we deploy the forwarders:

1. Browse to the AWS Management Console and log in to your AWS account. Type `EC2` in the search bar in the top left-hand corner. Click on **EC2** in the results to navigate to the **EC2** dashboard. This initial dashboard will give you a summary of the instances deployed in your environment. It also shows you the number of key pairs, security groups, and volumes in your account. If this is the first time you are using AWS, these numbers will all be zero. Click on the orange **Launch instances** button (see *Figure 2.2*) and click on **Launch an instance**:

Figure 2.2 – Launch instances button

2. Enter the name `deploymentserver` in the **Name** field.

Enter the word `Splunk` in the search bar for **Application and OS Images (Amazon Machine Image)** (see *Figure 2.3*):

Figure 2.3 – Entering the word Splunk in the Application and OS Images
(Amazon Machine Image) search bar to find the Splunk AMI

3. Click on the **AWS Marketplace AMIs** tab and click on the orange **Select** button next to **Splunk Enterprise** (see *Figure 2.4*):

Figure 2.4 – Selecting the Splunk Enterprise AMI

Review the information about the Splunk AMI, including the version, operating system, and pricing per hour. Click the orange **Continue** button (see *Figure 2.5*):

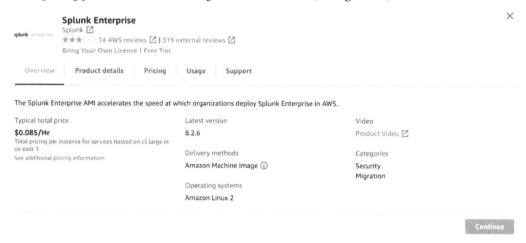

Figure 2.5 – The Splunk Enterprise AMI running Splunk version 8.2.6

4. Click on the orange **Confirm Changes** button to continue. Note that this AMI uses a `c5.large` instance type with two **Virtual CPUs (vCPUs)** and four GiB of memory. This is the recommended instance type from Splunk, but you may add additional resources; however, bear in mind that this will incur more charges.

5. Create a new *key pair* if you do not have one already. Click on the **Create new key pair** link under the **Key pair (login)** section. You will need your private key to log into the AWS instances. AWS will store a copy of your public key on the new instance. Use a key pair name that is easy to remember and note the location when the private key is downloaded to your local machine. Note that this is the only chance to store your private key so keep it safe. *Figure 2.6* shows that we created an *RSA* key pair named *book1* in `.pem` format:

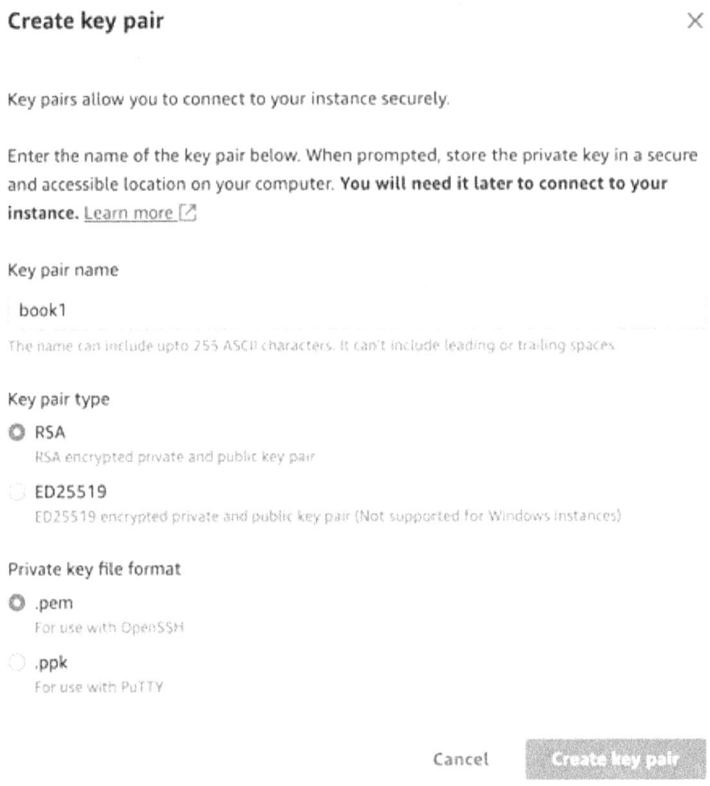

Create key pair   ✕

Key pairs allow you to connect to your instance securely.

Enter the name of the key pair below. When prompted, store the private key in a secure and accessible location on your computer. **You will need it later to connect to your instance.** Learn more ⬀

Key pair name

book1

The name can include upto 255 ASCII characters. It can't include leading or trailing spaces.

Key pair type

◉ RSA
   RSA encrypted private and public key pair

○ ED25519
   ED25519 encrypted private and public key pair (Not supported for Windows instances)

Private key file format

◉ .pem
   For use with OpenSSH

○ .ppk
   For use with PuTTY

                                    Cancel   Create key pair

Figure 2.6 – Create a new key pair.

The new private key is automatically downloaded when you click the orange **Create key pair** button.

6.   Select your IPv4 address in the **Allow SSH traffic from** dropdown (see *Figure 2.7*) to prevent access from other devices. Note that leaving the address as **0.0.0.0/0** will allow anyone to access your device:

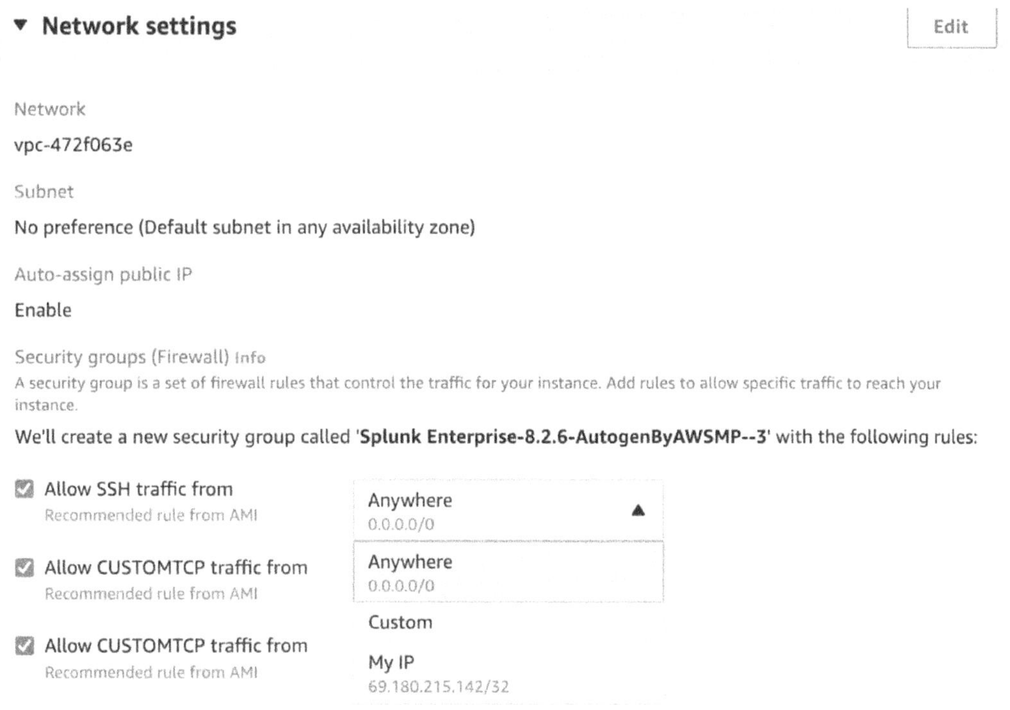

▼ **Network settings**   Edit

Network

vpc-472f063e

Subnet

No preference (Default subnet in any availability zone)

Auto-assign public IP

Enable

Security groups (Firewall) Info
A security group is a set of firewall rules that control the traffic for your instance. Add rules to allow specific traffic to reach your instance.

We'll create a new security group called '**Splunk Enterprise-8.2.6-AutogenByAWSMP--3**' with the following rules:

☑ Allow SSH traffic from   Anywhere   ▲
   Recommended rule from AMI   0.0.0.0/0

☑ Allow CUSTOMTCP traffic from   Anywhere
   Recommended rule from AMI   0.0.0.0/0

☑ Allow CUSTOMTCP traffic from   Custom
   Recommended rule from AMI
                                            My IP
                                            69.180.215.142/32

Figure 2.7 – Modifying your network settings to protect your instance

7.   Click the **Launch instance** button on the bottom right (see *Figure 2.8*):

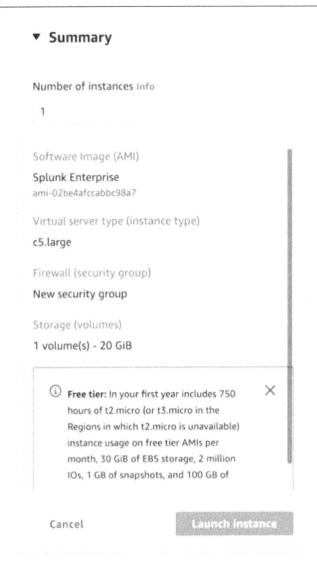

Figure 2.8 – Launching your new instance

8.   Repeat *steps 1-7* to create AWS instances for the search head and indexer.

Now that we have installed the Linux instances, let's install our AWS Windows instances.

Deploying AWS EC2 instances with the Windows Server 19 Base AMI

In this section, we will use AWS EC2 instances to install Windows Splunk forwarders. We will install the **Microsoft Windows Server 2019 Base** (64-bit x86) AMI and use a remote desktop application to log in to the servers. We will go through the following steps to install the instances:

1. Log in to your AWS account and navigate to the **EC2** dashboard. Click on the **Launch instances** button in the upper right-hand corner, which we saw in *Figure 2.2*:

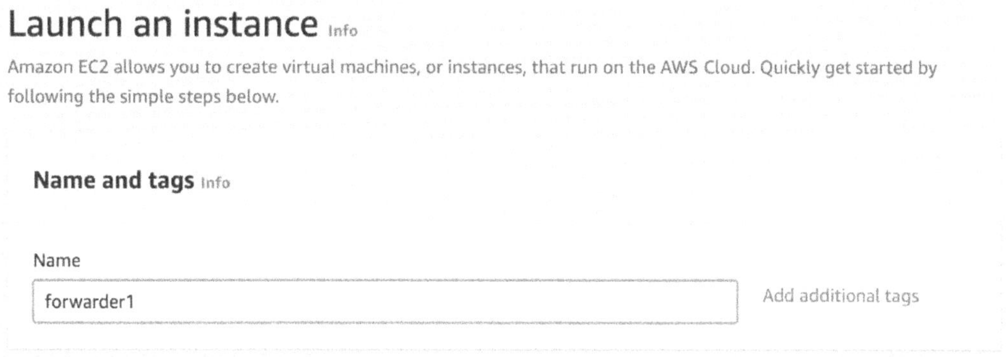

Launch an instance Info

Amazon EC2 allows you to create virtual machines, or instances, that run on the AWS Cloud. Quickly get started by following the simple steps below.

Name and tags Info

Name

| forwarder1 | Add additional tags |

Figure 2.9 – Launching a Windows instance called forwarder1

2. Choose the Microsoft Windows AMI. Notice that this AMI is a **Microsoft Windows Server 2019 Base** (64-bit x86) AMI, as shown in *Figure 2.10*:

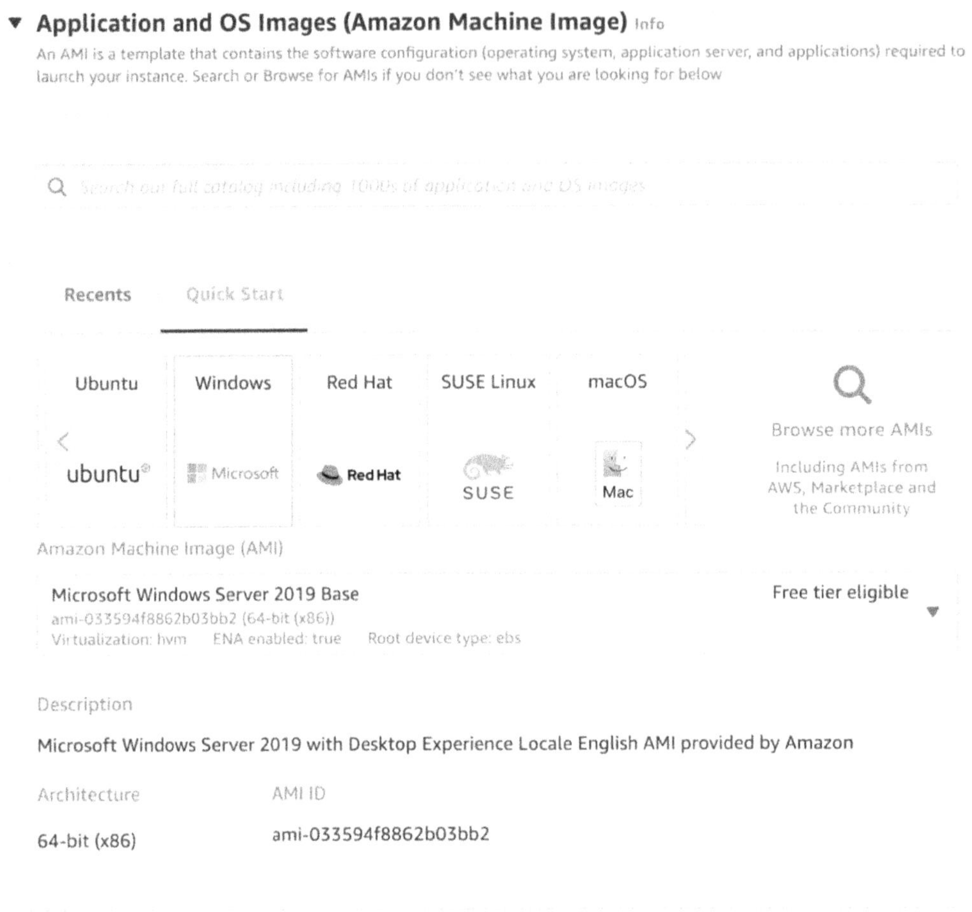

Figure 2.10 – Choosing the Microsoft Windows AMI

The **Microsoft Windows Server 2019 Base** AMI uses the `t2.micro` instance type, which has 1 vCPU and 1 GiB of memory. The on-demand Windows pricing is set at $0.0162 per hour at the time of writing this book.

3. Create a new key pair if you do not have one already. You can also reuse the key pair you created when you deployed the AWS EC2 Splunk Enterprise AMIs from the *step 5* in the *Deploying AWS EC2 instances with the Splunk Enterprise AMI* section (see *Figure 2.6*).

4. We will use an RDP application to access the Windows-based servers. Select your IPv4 address in the **Allow RDP traffic from** dropdown to restrict RDP traffic to only your device (see *Figure 2.11*):

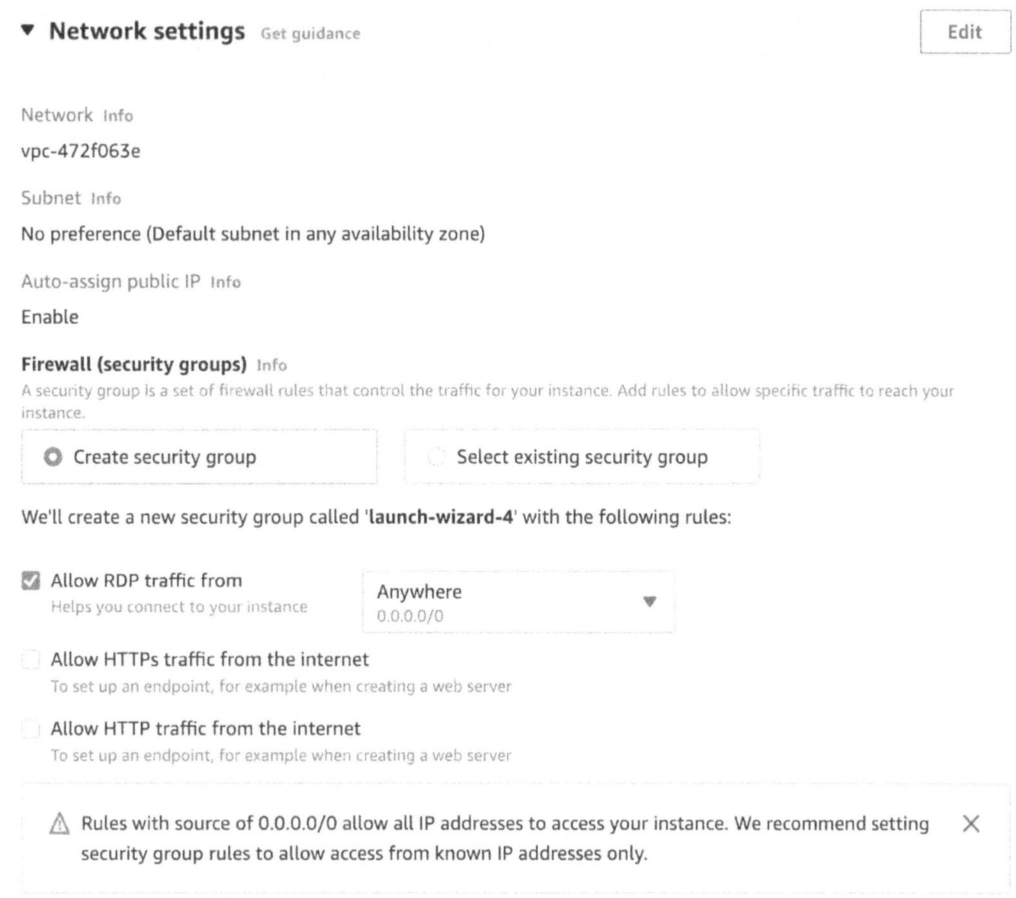

▼ **Network settings** Get guidance

Edit

Network Info

vpc-472f063e

Subnet Info

No preference (Default subnet in any availability zone)

Auto-assign public IP Info

Enable

Firewall (security groups) Info
A security group is a set of firewall rules that control the traffic for your instance. Add rules to allow specific traffic to reach your instance.

| ⊙ Create security group | ○ Select existing security group |

We'll create a new security group called '**launch-wizard-4**' with the following rules:

☑ Allow RDP traffic from
   Helps you connect to your instance

   | Anywhere   ▼ |
   | 0.0.0.0/0 |

☐ Allow HTTPs traffic from the internet
   To set up an endpoint, for example when creating a web server

☐ Allow HTTP traffic from the internet
   To set up an endpoint, for example when creating a web server

△ Rules with source of 0.0.0.0/0 allow all IP addresses to access your instance. We recommend setting ✕
   security group rules to allow access from known IP addresses only.

Figure 2.11 – Selecting your IPv4 address to allow RDP traffic from only your IPv4 address

5. Leave the other settings at their default values.

6. Click the orange **Launch instance** button on the bottom right, as shown in *Figure 2.12*:

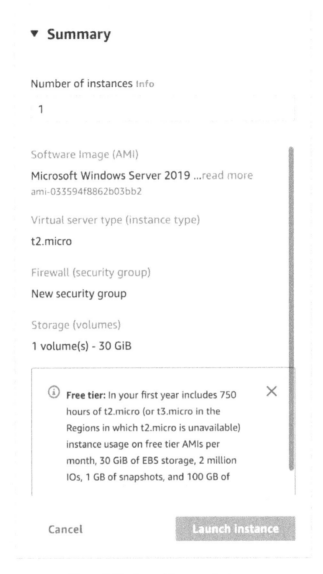

Figure 2.12 – Launching your instance

7.   Repeat *steps 1-7* to create instances for the `forwarder2` and `forwarder3` servers.

    I.   *Figure 2.13* shows the instances generated in the last two sections. Observe the **Instance type** column and ensure that the instance types listed match the instance types in your environment. It also shows an example of the AWS console after all the servers have been deployed.

II. Note that each of your instances is currently in the **Running** state. Take note of the addresses in the Public IPv4 address column of each instance. You will need them later when we set up the Splunk servers. If you decide to stop the instance, select **Instance state | Stop instance**. You will lose the IPv4 address for that instance. Keep that in mind as you move on to the next section:

Instances (6)   Info

	Name	▽	Instance ID	Instance state	▽	Instance type	▽
	indexer ⬕		i-05b35f70fb5352e2a	⊘ Running	⊕⊖	c5.large	
	deploymentserver		i-0b2d3a512d8863e43	⊘ Running	⊕⊖	c5.large	
	searchhead		i-090d70af0467e7da7	⊘ Running	⊕⊖	c5.large	
	forwarder1		i-07c0647a6da0c7183	⊘ Running	⊕⊖	t2.micro	
	forwarder2		i-002f6b28717dff1bc	⊘ Running	⊕⊖	t2.micro	
	forwarder3		i-0501713e7e2dfac14	⊘ Running	⊕⊖	t2.micro	

Instance state = running ✕   Clear filters

Figure 2.13 – List of devices in the test environment displayed in the AWS console

Now that we have deployed our instances, it's time to set up our individual Splunk components. We will first install and configure our Splunk forwarders on our Windows instances, and then we will configure the deployment server, indexer, and search head on the Linux instances. We can use multiple ways to configure a Splunk instance. Let's look at three methods before continuing to the section on installing and configuring Splunk forwarders. The three methods are as follows:

- **Using the Splunk Web interface**: Once Splunk is installed, we can log on to Splunk Web in a browser and use the **Settings** menu to make changes to the default configurations

- **Using the Command Line Interface** (**CLI**): Splunk has a collection of CLI commands that can be used to create, modify, or remove configurations

- Editing the configuration files using your favorite text editor such as **vim** or **Notepad**

We will use each of these methods at different times during our Windows event logging case study. We have deployed our AWS instances for our search head, indexer, deployment servers, and forwarders. The search head, indexer, and deployment servers use the Splunk Enterprise AMI, so they're ready to go. We will install and configure Splunk on our forwarders in the next section.

Setting up Splunk forwarders

In this section, we will set up the Splunk forwarders. Remember that the forwarders will collect Windows event logs and send them on to the indexer. First, let's use the following steps to install and configure Splunk on the three Windows-based AWS instances to host our forwarders:

1. Before we can access the Windows-based instances, we will need to generate a password.

2. Click on the `forwarder1` Windows-based AWS instance in your AWS console.

3. Click on the white **Connect** button at the top of the page. The **Connect to instance** page tells us how to access the instance.

4. Navigate over to the **RDP client** tab. Download the remote desktop file to set up your RDP session. You will need the *public DNS* or *IPv4 address*, the *Administrator* username, and the password.

5. Click on **Get password** (see *Figure 2.14*) to retrieve the password. Click the yellow **Decrypt password** button:

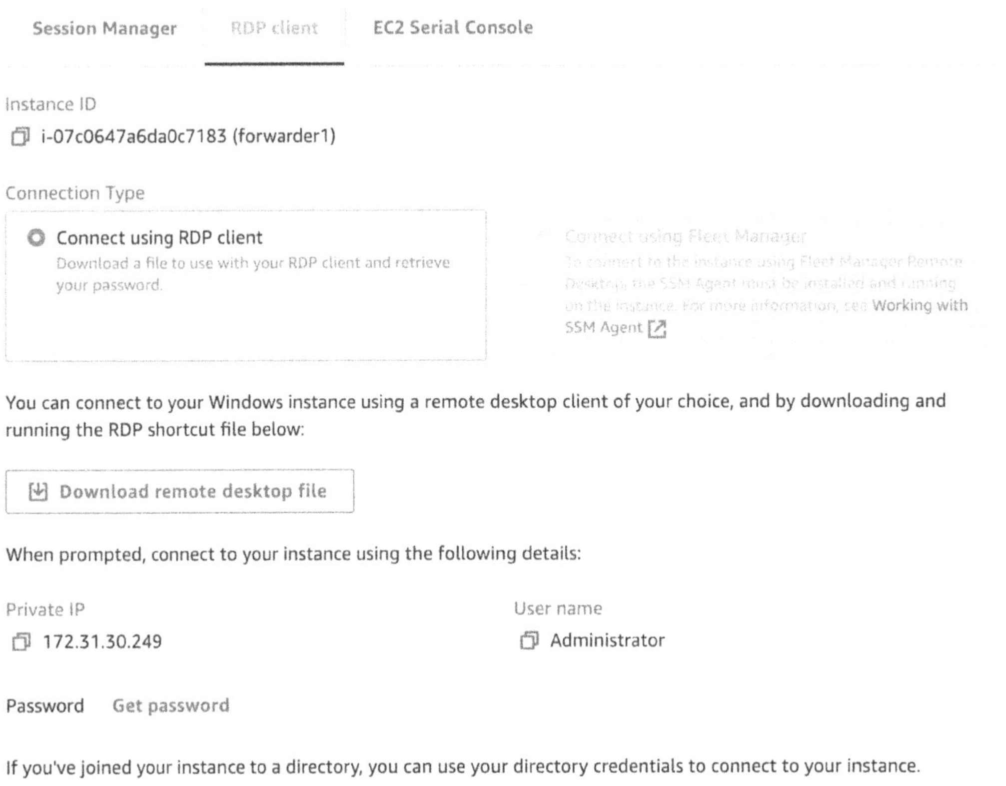

Session Manager | RDP client | EC2 Serial Console

Instance ID

☐ i-07c0647a6da0c7183 (forwarder1)

Connection Type

◉ Connect using RDP client
Download a file to use with your RDP client and retrieve your password.

Connect using Fleet Manager
To connect to the instance using Fleet Manager Remote Desktop, the SSM Agent must be installed and running on the instance. For more information, see **Working with** SSM Agent ☑

You can connect to your Windows instance using a remote desktop client of your choice, and by downloading and running the RDP shortcut file below:

⤓ Download remote desktop file

When prompted, connect to your instance using the following details:

Private IP   User name
☐ 172.31.30.249   ☐ Administrator

Password   Get password

If you've joined your instance to a directory, you can use your directory credentials to connect to your instance.

Figure 2.14 – Get password screen for connecting to your forwarders using RDP

6. Browse your filesystem to find the key pair (.pem) file (see *Figure 2.15*) that you created in *step 5* of *Deploying AWS EC2 instances with the Splunk Enterprise AMI*:

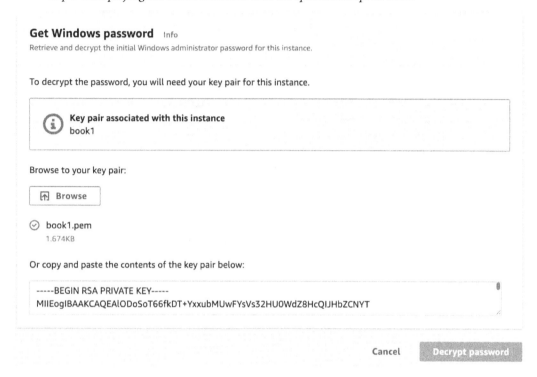

Figure 2.15 – Selecting your key pair and clicking Decrypt password on the bottom right

7. Log in to the forwarder1 Windows-based AWS instance using your favorite RDP application. Use the *Administrator* username and the password generated in *step 6*.

8. Now that you have logged on to the forwarder1 instance, we will need to install the Splunk forwarder. Download the Splunk forwarder .msi file from the Splunk website (https://splk.it/3S78XqI).

9. Double-click on the .msi file that you downloaded from the Splunk website and follow the prompts:

    I. Accept the license agreement by checking the checkbox at the top of the dialog box. Select an **on-premises Splunk Enterprise** instance and click **Next**.

II.   Create a username and password for your Splunk *Administrator* account. Remember that the **Administrator** user should not be used in a production environment. Splunk recommends that you disable this account and create another user with admin privileges for production environments. Refer to `https://splk.it/3oz9J1Q` for further information. Click **Next**.

III. Enter the IPv4 address for the deployment server in the **Hostname** or **IP** field. Refer to your list of IPv4 addresses that you compiled when you launched your AWS instances. Enter the default port `8089` in the Port field (see *Figure 2.16*). Note that entering the deployment server IPv4 creates a file called `deploymentclient.conf`. We will use the deployment server to send configurations to the forwarders. Click **Next**:

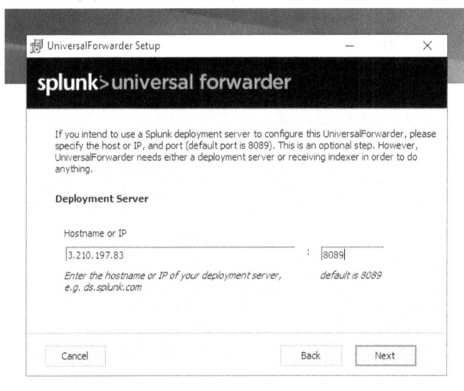

Figure 2.16 – Entering the IPv4 address for the deployment server and port 8089

IV.   Enter the IPv4 address for the indexer in the **Hostname** or **IP** field. Enter the default port 9997 in the **Port** field (see *Figure 2.17*). Click **Next**:

Figure 2.17 – Entering the IPv4 address for the indexer and port 9997

10. Click **Install** to complete your installation.

11. Your forwarder has been installed. Navigate to **Windows Administrative Tools | Services** to see that the SplunkForwarder service is running.

12. The Splunk forwarder install process in Windows allows us to set up configurations such as the deployment server and indexer IPv4 address. However, we will need to make a few adjustments to our configurations. Let's modify our installation to give the forwarder a hostname and server name that matches the name of the corresponding AWS instance. You're probably wondering why it is important that we change these names. The hostnames generated when we create our AWS instances are random and rather long, such as EC2AMAZ-MQSGTHU. Changing the hostnames to something simple such as forwarder1 makes it easier for us to administer Splunk in the *Setting up Splunk deployment servers* section.

13. Let's use the Splunk configuration files to make these changes.

14. Use Windows Explorer to navigate to the following folder: `C:\Program Files\SplunkUniversalForwarder\etc\system\local`.

15. Double-click on the `inputs.conf` file. Don't see an `inputs.conf` file in that folder? Create a new text file named `inputs.conf` and enter the following stanza in the file using your favorite editing tool such as **Notepad**. Splunk uses the term *stanza* to refer to the configuration groupings in the configuration files. A stanza begins with a stanza name in square brackets such as `[default]` and contains one or more configurations in the form `key = value` such as `host = forwarder`:

    ```
    [default]
    host = forwarder1
    ```

16. Next, double-click on the `server.conf` file in the same directory. Find the `[general]` stanza and replace the `serverName` value with `forwarder1`:

    ```
    [general]
    serverName = forwarder1
    ```

17. Next, double-click on the `deploymentclient.conf` file in the same directory. Find the `[general]` stanza and replace the `clientName` value with `forwarder1`:

    ```
    [deployment-client]
    clientName = forwarder1
    ```

18. Navigate to **Windows Administrative Tools** | **Services** to restart the `SplunkForwarder` service. Click **Restart** (see *Figure 2.18*):

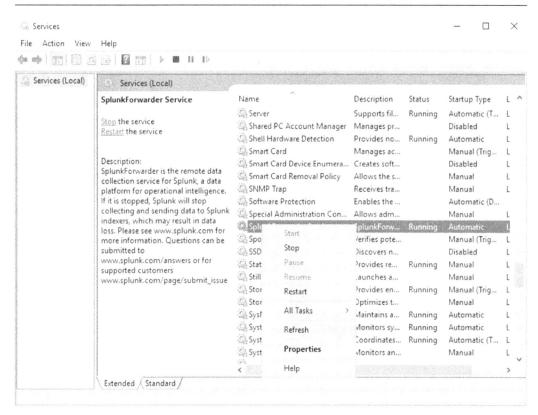

Figure 2.18 – Restarting the SplunkForwarder service to execute
the changes made to the configuration files

19. Repeat *steps 1-9* to configure `forwarder2` and `forwarder3`. *Figure 2.19* shows the RDP
console with our three forwarders:

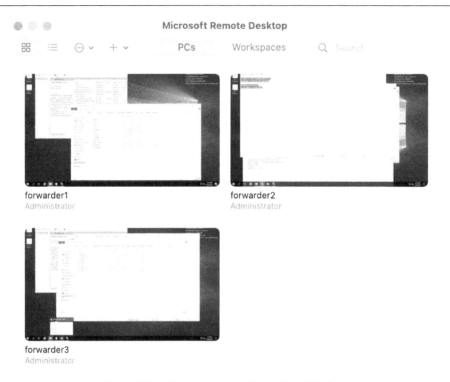

Figure 2.19 – The three forwarders in the RDP client

We have installed our Splunk forwarders. We will set up the deployment server in the next section.

Setting up Splunk deployment servers

In this section, we will set up the deployment server. We already have the three forwarders listening for configurations from the deployment server. We will need to configure the deployment server so that we can manage the forwarders, indexer, and search head from Splunk Web. But first, we must figure out how to log in to the server. We need the key pair—more specifically, the .pem file that we downloaded when we set up the key pair in *step 5* of *Deploying AWS EC2 instances with the Splunk Enterprise AMI*. Let's take the following steps:

1. Using the Terminal application in MacOS, navigate to the folder where you downloaded your .pem file. Remember that we used MacOS for these instructions but you can use a SSH client such as PuTTY on Microsoft Windows as well. Refer to https://tinyurl.com/k8d84p8w for setup instructions if necessary. Log into your *deploymentserver* instance using a *SSH* client and enter *yes* to the authenticity prompt:

   ```
   ssh -i "<your private key>.pem" ec2-user@<your EC2
   Instance name or IPv4>
   ```

You will need the `.pem` file and the **public IPv4 address** of the server. This can be found in the Public IPv4 address column of the **Instances** panel of your AWS console (see *Figure 2.13*). For example, the following command will log into a host with the IPv4 address of 55.55.55.55 using the `book1.pem` private key we downloaded:

```
ssh -i "book1.pem" ec2-user@55.55.55.55
```

Use the following command to update the server:

```
sudo yum update
```

A user account called `splunk` was created when we launched the Splunk AMI. This user is the owner of all the Splunk files and configurations. We will use this user whenever we log in to the deployment server, indexer, and search head. Use the `sudo` command to change from `ec2-user` to the `splunk` user. The `sudo` command gives the `splunk` user the ability to run Splunk-based commands on the command line:

```
sudo -i -u splunk
```

Note the change in the prompt (see *Figure 2.20*):

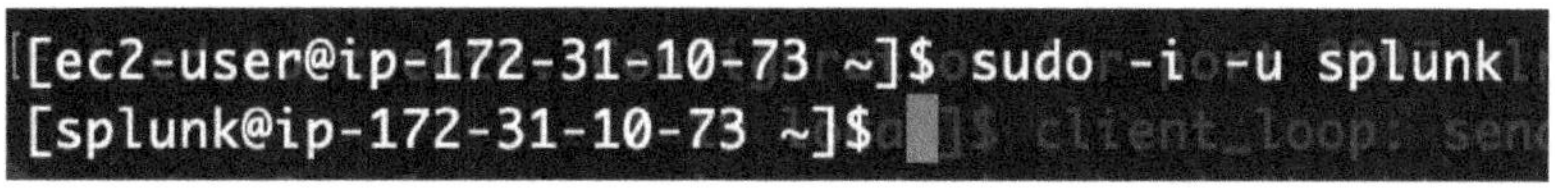

Figure 2.20 – Change to the splunk user from the ec2-user using sudo -i -u splunk

Use the following command to check that Splunk is running:

```
/opt/splunk/bin/splunk status
```

Figure 2.21 shows that Splunk is running:

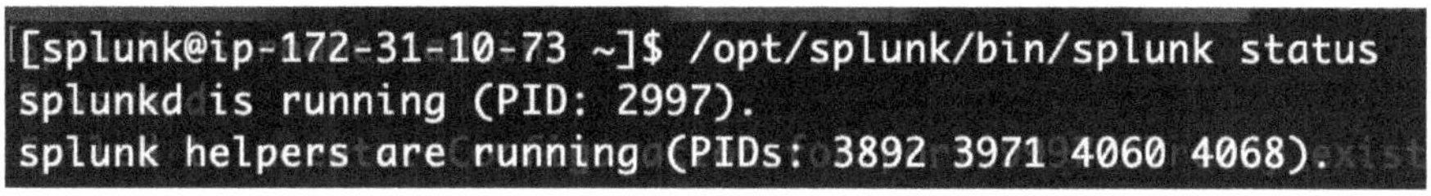

Figure 2.21 – Checking whether Splunk is running by using the status command

2. Now, let's set up our deployment server. First, we will start by changing the `hostname` and `servername` values, as we did for the forwarders. Use the following command to change the `hostname` and `servername` values:

```
/opt/splunk/bin/splunk set servername deploymentserver
/opt/splunk/bin/splunk set default-hostname
deploymentserver
/opt/splunk/bin/splunk restart
```

3. Log in to Splunk Web by typing the following in your browser window: `http://<your deployment server IPv4 address>:8000`.

    Note that Splunk Web runs on port `8000`. Use the following credentials to log in:

    -   **User**: `admin`

    -   **Password**: *SPLUNK-<the AWS instanceid>*

    The instance ID can be found in the **Instance ID** column of the **Instances** panel of your AWS console (see *Figure 2.13*). For example, the login credentials for the deploymentserver instance in *Figure 2.13* would be the following:

    -   **User**: *admin*

    -   **Password**: *SPLUNK-i-0b2d3a512d8863e43*

    Figure 2.22 shows the Splunk login page:

Figure 2.22 – The login page for the deployment server

4. Once you've logged in, navigate to the **Forwarder Management** dashboard by clicking on the **Settings** menu in the top right-hand corner of Splunk Web. Click **Forwarder management** on the right-hand side under **DISTRIBUTED ENVIRONMENT** (see *Figure 2.23*):

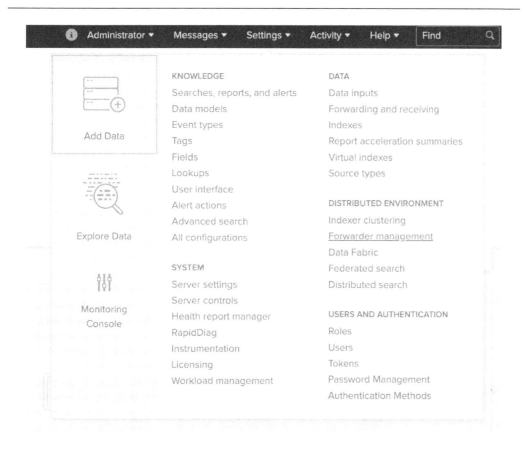

Figure 2.23 – The Settings menu showing the link to the Forwarder Management dashboard

The **Forwarder Management** dashboard is used to manage the clients and apps that are deployed from the deployment server. It shows us the number of clients that have phoned home to the deployment server in the last 24 hours, the number of clients with deployment errors, and the number of apps downloaded in the last hour.

There are three tabs on the **Forwarder Management** dashboard. Navigate the tabs to see the **Apps**, **Server Classes**, and **Clients** tabs. You should see forwarder1, forwarder2, and forwarder3 in the **Clients** tab (see *Figure 2.24*). The dashboard lists the client hostname, client name, instance name, IPv4 address, machine type (windows-x64), number of apps deployed, and the last time the client has phoned home to the deployment server. The machine type is useful because it allows us to deploy machine-specific apps to different clients. For example, we may deploy the Microsoft Windows add-on for Splunk to only the Windows clients. The **Phone Home** column is very useful when debugging missing data. It could indicate that a forwarder is down and/or is unable to access the deployment server due to networking issues.

5. Check that the hostnames and server names are correct:

Figure 2.24 – Forwarder Management dashboard showing the three forwarders

6. Let's create our first **serverclass**. A serverclass is a set of configurations that determine which apps a client receives. A serverclass stanza can contain one or more apps and one or more clients. First, we will illustrate how to construct a serverclass by deploying **Splunk Add-on for Microsoft Windows** (see *Figure 2.25*) to the Windows-based forwarders. This app has out-of-the-box configurations for indexing and manipulating Windows event logs:

Figure 2.25 – Downloading Splunk Add-on for Microsoft Windows from Splunkbase.com

7. First, download **Splunk Add-on for Microsoft Windows** from Splunkbase (`https://splunkbase.splunk.com/app/742/`).

8. Once you have downloaded the app from Splunkbase, transfer the file to your deployment server instance using a **Secure Copy** (**SCP**) client such as *WinSCP*. You can also use **yum** to download the file directly on the deployment server.

9. SSH to the deployment server and **untar** the `splunk-add-on-for-microsoft-windows*.tgz` file that you downloaded. Use the following command to expand the add-on into the `deployment-apps` folder. In this example, we extract version 8.5.0 of the add-on to the `deployment-apps` folder on the deployment server. Be sure to include the `-C` flag in the command:

```
tar xzf splunk-add-on-for-microsoft-windows_850.tgz  -C /
opt/splunk/etc/deployment-apps/
```

Navigate to the `/opt/splunk/etc/deployment-apps` folder on the deployment server. You should see the extracted app in this folder. Splunk practitioners sometimes use the terms *add-on* and *app* interchangeably. Usually, an add-on is a set of configurations that does not have a visible interface—that is, there are no views and dashboards associated with an add-on. Splunk apps usually have a visible interface. However, both add-ons and apps are referred to as apps in the deployment server environment. Unfortunately, this is often confusing to new Splunk users.

10. Log in to the deployment server in Splunk Web. Do you see **Splunk Add-on for Microsoft Windows** listed in the **Apps** tab of the **Forwarder Management** dashboard? (see *Figure 2.26*):

Figure 2.26 – The Splunk_TA_windows app in the Apps tab of the Forwarder Management dashboard

11. Now that we have installed the Windows app in the `deployment-apps` folder and it is displayed on the **Forwarder Management** dashboard, let's finish setting up the serverclass. Let's set it up using the **Forwarder Management** dashboard in Splunk Web.

12. Navigate to the **Forwarder Management** dashboard in Splunk Web and click on the **Server Classes** tab. Click the green **New Server Class** button (see *Figure 2.27*). Name your serverclass `forwarders` since we will use this configuration to send apps to the forwarders. Note that serverclasses can be created for different components including indexers and search heads, but we will only need to send **Splunk Add-on for Microsoft Windows** (`https://splunkbase. splunk.com/app/742/`) to the forwarders for the purpose of this case study:

Figure 2.27 – Creating a new serverclass by clicking on the green New Server Class button

13. Click on the **Add Apps** button (see *Figure 2.28*):

Figure 2.28 – An empty serverclass

14. Drag the Splunk_TA_windows app from the **Unselected Apps** box to the **Selected Apps** box. Click the green **Save** button in the top right-hand corner (*see Figure 2.29*):

Figure 2.29 – Dragging Splunk_TA_windows to Selected Apps

15. Click on the **Add Clients** button. Enter the forwarder* wildcard in the **Include** textbox. Note that we could also use windows-x64 since all our forwarders are Windows-based.

However, we want to restrict this app to just the forwarders, and we do not want to accidentally send it to another Windows-based component such as a search head. This is not applicable in our case, but is worth mentioning.

16. Click on the **Preview** button and select **Matched**. Note that there is a checkmark next to each of the forwarders. Click the green **Save** button (*see Figure 2.30*):

Figure 2.30 – Using a wildcard to add forwarders to the serverclass

17. The deployment server will dispatch the `Splunk_TA_windows` app to each forwarder. Sometimes, we will need to restart Splunk after a new app is deployed to a server or a new configuration change is completed. Refer to the Splunk docs to determine which configuration changes require a restart (`https://splk.it/3PIeOkt`). If new configuration changes in the app require a restart, click on the app name (for example, `Splunk_TA_windows`) and click **Restart Splunkd** in the **App** setup dashboard (see *Figure 2.31*):

Figure 2.31 – Using the Restart Splunkd checkbox to restart Splunk after a new app is installed

Figure 2.32 shows that the `Splunk_TA_windows` app has been installed on the forwarder:

This PC › Local Disk (C:) › Program Files › SplunkUniversalForwarder › etc › apps ›

Name	Date modified	Type
introspection_generator_addon	5/22/2022 8:56 PM	File folder
learned	5/22/2022 8:57 PM	File folder
search	5/22/2022 8:56 PM	File folder
splunk_httpinput	5/22/2022 8:56 PM	File folder
splunk_internal_metrics	5/22/2022 8:56 PM	File folder
Splunk_TA_windows	5/26/2022 12:36 AM	File folder
SplunkUniversalForwarder	5/22/2022 8:56 PM	File folder

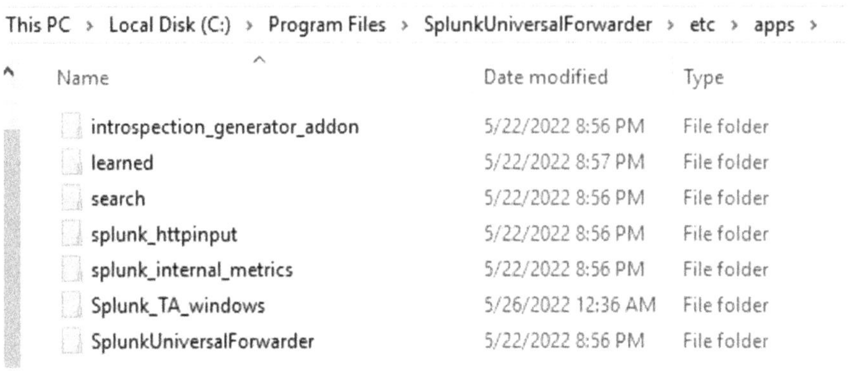

Figure 2.32 – Splunk Add-on for Microsoft Windows installed on the forwarder

18. Use a *SSH* client to connect to the deployment server and view the new serverclass configuration in the `/opt/splunk/etc/system/local/serverclass.conf` folder on the deployment server:

```
[serverClass:forwarders]
whitelist.0 = forwarder*

[serverClass:forwarders:app:Splunk_TA_Windows]
restartSplunkWeb = 0
restartSplunkd = 0
stateOnClient = enabled
```

19. Restart Splunk using the following command:

`/opt/splunk/bin/splunk restart`

Your deployment server is now set up. It's important to note that since our environment is small, we could have completed each of these tasks without the deployment server. However, the deployment server makes it easier for us when we make configurations across multiple servers. Once we have installed serverclass apps, making changes require only a change to the apps in the `deployment-apps` folder on the deployment server and a reload using the following `reload` command:

`/opt/splunk/bin/splunk reload deploy-server`

Enter the administrator username and password when prompted to complete the reload.

The deployment server is up and running. We have successfully installed the `Splunk_TA_windows` add-on on the forwarders. Now, let's set up the indexer.

Setting up Splunk indexers

We already configured our forwarders to send data to the indexer. Now, we need to ensure that the indexer is listening for the forwarded data. We will use a series of CLI commands to accomplish this in this section. Follow these steps:

1. Log in to your indexer using an *SSH* client. Refer to *step 1* of the *Setting up Splunk Deployment Servers* section for information on logging in to SSH. Enter *yes* to the authenticity prompt:

    ```
    ssh -i "<your private key>.pem" ec2-user@<your EC2
    Instance name or IPv4>
    ```

2. Use the `sudo` command to change from `ec2-user` to the `splunk` user:

    ```
    sudo -i -u splunk
    ```

    Use the following command to check that Splunk is running:

    ```
    /opt/splunk/bin/splunk status
    ```

3. We will start by changing the hostname and servername, as we did for the forwarders and deployment server. Use the following command to change the `default-hostname` and `servername` values:

    ```
    /opt/splunk/bin/splunk set servername indexer
    /opt/splunk/bin/splunk set default-hostname indexer
    /opt/splunk/bin/splunk restart
    ```

4. Not every Splunk server needs access to Splunk Web. We don't want anyone to access Splunk Web on our indexer, so let's turn off Splunk Web by running the following command:

    ```
    /opt/splunk/bin/splunk disable webserver
    ```

5. We may need to deploy configurations later when we want to use the deployment server. Let's create that configuration by typing the following command:

    ```
    /opt/splunk/bin/splunk set deploy-poll <your deployment
    server IPv4 address>:8089
    ```

6. Indexers listen for incoming data on port `9997`. Run the following command to turn on this listening feature of our indexer:

    ```
    /opt/splunk/bin/splunk enable listen 9997
    ```

7. Restart Splunk using the following command:

    ```
    /opt/splunk/bin/splunk restart
    ```

Your indexer is now set up. We will install the search head in the next section.

Setting up Splunk search heads

The last component that we will set up is the search head. Remember that the search head is how users access Splunk Web. Follow these steps:

1. Log in to your `deploymentserver` instance using an *SSH* client. Refer to *step 1* of the Setting up Splunk Deployment Servers section for information on logging in to SSH. Enter yes to the authenticity prompt:

   ```
   ssh -i "<your private key>.pem" ec2-user@<your EC2
   Instance name or IPv4>
   ```

   Use the `sudo` command to change from `ec2-user` to the `splunk` user:

   ```
   sudo -i -u splunk
   ```

   Use the following command to check that Splunk is running:

   ```
   /opt/splunk/bin/splunk status
   ```

2. Now, let's set up our search head. First, we will start by changing the hostname and server name, as we did for the forwarders, deployment server, and indexer. Use the following command to change the hostname and server name:

   ```
   /opt/splunk/bin/splunk set servername searchhead
   /opt/splunk/bin/splunk set default-hostname searchhead
   /opt/splunk/bin/splunk restart
   ```

3. Log in to Splunk Web by typing the following in your browser window: `http://<your search head IPv4 address>:8000`.

   Note that Splunk Web runs on port `8000`. Use the following credentials to log in:

   - **User**: *admin*

   - **Password**: *SPLUNK-<the AWS instanceid>*

   - The AWS instance ID is in the list of AWS instances in the AWS console (see examples in *Figure 2.13*).

4. Navigate to the distributed search dashboard by clicking on the **Settings** menu in the top right-hand corner. Select **Distributed search** from the **DISTRIBUTED ENVIRONMENT** menu (see *Figure 2.33*):

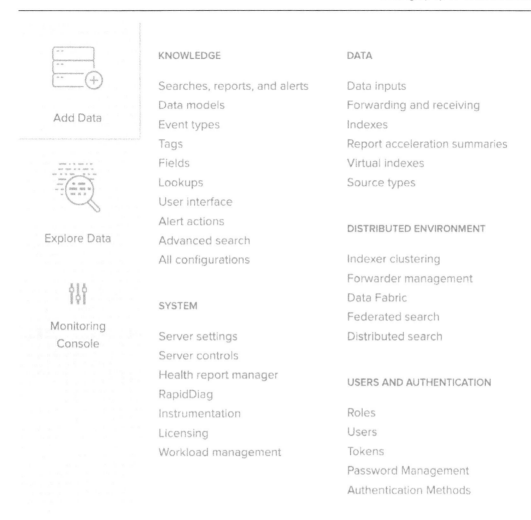

KNOWLEDGE

Searches, reports, and alerts

Data models

Event types

Tags

Fields

Lookups

User interface

Alert actions

Advanced search

All configurations

SYSTEM

Server settings

Server controls

Health report manager

RapidDiag

Instrumentation

Licensing

Workload management

DATA

Data inputs

Forwarding and receiving

Indexes

Report acceleration summaries

Virtual indexes

Source types

DISTRIBUTED ENVIRONMENT

Indexer clustering

Forwarder management

Data Fabric

Federated search

Distributed search

USERS AND AUTHENTICATION

Roles

Users

Tokens

Password Management

Authentication Methods

Add Data

Explore Data

Monitoring
Console

Figure 2.33 – The Settings menu showing the link to the Distributed Search dashboard

5. Click on the green **New Search Peer** button in the top right-hand corner.

6. Enter the IPv4 address of the indexer in the **Peer URI** textbox. Enter the indexer's admin username and password in the **Remote username** and **password** textboxes. Click **Save**, as shown in *Figure 2.34*:

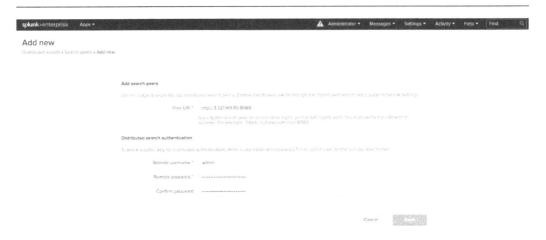

Figure 2.34 – Enabling a search peer by entering the peer URI and credentials

7.   The indexer is now saved as a search peer to the search head. Ensure that the status says **Healthy** in the **Health status** column (see *Figure 2.35*):

Figure 2.35 – Search peers dashboard showing the indexer

Our search head installation is complete. We will install the necessary add-ons and apps in the next section. We will also install the BOTS Dataset v1 app on the search head.

Installing additional Splunk add-ons and apps

Now that we have our components installed, let's revisit the BOTS Dataset v1 app. In order to use the dataset, we will need to install some additional Splunk add-ons and apps. Download the following add-ons and apps from Splunkbase:

- **Fortinet FortiGate Add-On for Splunk** (https://splunkbase.splunk.com/app/2846/)

- **TA for Suricata** (https://splunkbase.splunk.com/app/4242/)

- **Splunk Add-on for Stream Wire Data** (https://splunkbase.splunk.com/app/5234/)

- **Nessus** (https://splunkbase.splunk.com/app/5918/)

It's important to note that some apps may contain configurations that require them to be installed on different Splunk components. **Splunk Add-on for Windows**, which we deployed to the forwarders, is one of those apps. The add-on is needed on the Splunk forwarders because of the input configurations—that is, a set of configurations that tell Splunk how to find the data sources that we will be ingesting. However, the add-on is also needed on the indexers (for configurations that instruct Splunk to perform tasks such as line breaking) as well as the search heads (for configurations such as field extractions). We will deploy this add-on along with the add-ons in the previous list, as well as **Splunk Add-on for Windows**, to the indexers and search heads.

Repeat the steps in the *Setting up Splunk deployment servers* section, to create a new serverclass called `bots_addons`. Use this serverclass to deploy **Splunk Add-on for Windows**, **Splunk Add-on for Stream Wire Data**, **Nessus**, **TA for Suricata**, and **Fortinet FortiGate Add-on for Splunk** to the indexer and search head.

Installing the BOTS Dataset v1 app

Now that we have explored the `inputs.conf` file, we will *ingest* our data from the BOTS Dataset v1 app (`https://github.com/splunk/botsv1`). Just a reminder that the logs in the dataset were generated from actual and simulated malicious activity. The dataset is organized into an app called `botsv1_data_set`. We will install the dataset on `searchhead1`. The app can run on a standalone Splunk instance as well, so feel free to install it on your laptop if you have Splunk installed on it.

Use the following instructions to install the app:

1. Download the compressed `botsv1-attack-only.tgz` file (`https://github.com/splunk/botsv1`).

2. Log on to Splunk Web on the search head that you installed in the *Setting up Splunk search heads* section.

3. Click on the gear icon next to **Apps** in the top left-hand corner (see *Figure 2.36*):

Figure 2.36 – Accessing Apps

4. This displays a list of apps installed on the Splunk instance. Click on the **Install app from file** button on the top right-hand side (see *Figure 2.37*):

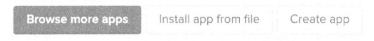

Figure 2.37 – Install app from file button

5. Click on the **Choose File** button and navigate to the `botsv1-attack-only.tgz` file that you downloaded in *step 1* (see *Figure 2.38*):

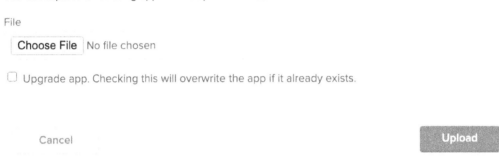

Figure 2.38 – Navigating to botsv1-attack-only.tgz file

6. Restart the search head by navigating to **Settings | Server controls** and clicking the **Restart Splunk** button.

7. Click on the gear next to **Apps** in the top left-hand corner and ensure that the `botsv1_data_set` app is installed on the search head (see *Figure 2.39*):

Figure 2.39 – botsv1_data_set installed

8. Open the **Search and Reporting** app and enter the following Splunk query in the search bar to view the logs:

    ```
    index=botsv1 earliest=0
    ```

9. Explore the results using the field explorer on the left-hand side of the screen. We will further explore the **Search and Reporting** app in *Chapter 4, Introduction to SPL*.

Congratulations! You have completed the installation of your Splunk deployment, configured the different servers, installed apps, and run your first Splunk search query. But we before we conclude this chapter, let's take a brief look at access management in Splunk.

Managing access to Splunk

Most modern computer systems have mechanisms to control who has access to the systems (authentication) and what functions they are authorized to perform. For example, most users can access a website online but only the site administrators and/or developers are able to access the backend systems that drive the website, such as databases. In addition, most systems are designed to support multiple users at one time. Likewise, administrators in Splunk can control who has access to Splunk and what features they are able to use once they have logged on to the system. We will explore the concept of access control in Splunk in this section. We will discuss the concept of Splunk *roles* that can be assigned to users to assign *permissions* and *capabilities*. A user's **permissions** defines their level of access to Splunk. Each knowledge object in Splunk has two possible permissions:

- **read** – The user can view the knowledge object
- **write** – The user can view and edit the knowledge object

A **capability** defines what a user can do in Splunk. A Splunk administrator can make changes to capabilities via Splunk Web or by editing the `authorize.conf` file on the filesystem. There are several predefined capabilities available in Splunk.

Table 2.1 shows a sample of the capabilities available in Splunk:

Capability	Description
`change_own_password`	Allows the user to change their password
`edit_deployment_server`	Allows the user to edit deployment server settings
`edit_indexer_cluster`	Allows the user to edit the indexer cluster settings
`edit_sourcetypes`	Allows the user to edit source types
`list_indexer_cluster`	Allows the user to view information about the indexer cluster
`list_inputs`	Allows the user to list data inputs
`restart_splunkd`	Allows the user to restart Splunk
`schedule_search`	Allows the user to schedule searches
`search`	Allows the user to run a search

Table 2.1 – Sample Splunk capabilities

Now, let's look at the different types of roles, users, and authentication schemes available in Splunk.

Roles

A fresh installation of Splunk has one user – *admin*. As expected, this user has all the access and capabilities required to configure the Splunk deployment. Splunk best practice suggests that the Splunk administrator create a new user with admin privileges and then disable the default admin user as a security measure. Before we can do that, we need to understand the different roles available in Splunk.

There are five main predefined roles in Splunk:

1. **admin** – A role assigned to Splunk administrators that gives the widest access to Splunk knowledge objects. An example of a user with the admin role is the initial admin account created during Splunk installation. A user with the admin role needs to have a strong understanding of Splunk to avoid catastrophic mistakes.

2. **power** – A role assigned to users with fewer privileges than the admin user but who can still edit shared knowledge objects such as saved searches, tags, alerts, and dashboards. Such users would need to have a good understanding of Splunk but may not be trusted to perform more important administrative tasks.

3. **user** – A role assigned to users who can create, edit, and delete their own knowledge objects. A user with the user role can basically change their Splunk environment but has no access to others.

4. **can_delete** – A user with this role can use the *delete* keyword. As you can imagine, this role should not be assigned to anyone. This means the user can use the `delete` keyword in the search bar. The `delete` keyword will search for any data specified in the search and delete it permanently. This role should be assigned with caution.

5. **sc_admin** – This role is assigned in Splunk Cloud to allow users to create other users and roles.

In a small Splunk deployment, the Splunk administrator may choose to assign users to these basic roles. However, we are not limited to these roles – we can create custom roles by modifying the basic roles. New roles inherit from the *predefined roles* and can be used to limit access to indexes, restrict search results, modify capabilities, and limit the number and type of searches that the user can run. For example, we can create a role called *iis_team* that inherits the capabilities of the **power** role but only has access to the *iis* logs in our dataset. For this to work, we would need to ensure that the *iis* logs are ingested into an *iis* index. Unfortunately, it is not possible to restrict permissions to source types.

Users

The admin user is probably the only user that most Splunk novices encounter when experimenting with Splunk. This account is part of the Splunk Enterprise installation and usually has the password `changeme`. The user is prompted to change to a more secure password at first login. This can be done in Splunk Web or on the command line with the following CLI command:

```
splunk edit user admin -password newSecurePassword  -auth
admin:changeme
```

This command can be used to change any user's password as long as the account executing the command has admin rights.

Splunk Web has a **Users** dashboard for managing users. We can access this dashboard by accessing the **Settings** menu and clicking on **Users** in the bottom-right corner. This dashboard shows information about all the users that have access to Splunk, including the following:

- **Name** – The username assigned to the user
- **Actions** – A dropdown of possible actions that you can perform on the user account
- **Authentication system** – The system that authenticates the user such as Splunk or **Lightweight Directory Access Protocol (LDAP)** authentication
- **Full name** – The user's full name
- **Email address** – The user's email address
- **Time zone** – The user's time zone
- **Default app** – The default application context when a user logs in
- **Default app inherited from** – The default app of the user's role.
- **Roles** – Roles assigned to the user
- **Last login** – The last recorded login timestamp for the user
- **Status** – Whether the account is active or not

Users can be created and assigned roles by clicking on the green **New User** button on the **Users** dashboard. Note that you cannot directly assign capabilities to a new user. Instead, you will need to create a role, if one does not exist, that has the capabilities and assign the user to the new role.

A brief note on authentication schemes: the basic authentication scheme in Splunk is Splunk authentication. This means that you create a user in Splunk and Splunk authenticates the user on login. This is the case for the default admin account created during a new Splunk installation. However, Splunk allows different authentication schemes such as **Lightweight Directory Access Protocol (LDAP)** and **Security Assertion Markup Language (SAML)**. More recent versions of Splunk have also introduced **Multifactor Authentication (MFA)** systems such as *Duo Security* and *RSA Security*. A Splunk administrator can create LDAP groups in Active Directory and create LDAP strategies in Splunk. LDAP strategy configuration requires information such as the Active Directory *host name*, *port*, *bind DN*, *user base DN*, and a *bind DN* password.

Splunk also allows a Splunk administrator to configure password policy management settings, but this only works with Splunk authentication.

This has been a brief discussion on Splunk access management. For most Splunk users, this is sufficient for dealing with basic Splunk deployments. However, the reader is encouraged to dig deeper in the Splunk documentation if further administrative knowledge is required.

Summary

In this chapter, we deployed a simple Splunk environment. The environment included a search head, indexer, deployment server, and three forwarders. We used a combination of the CLI, configuration file changes, and Splunk Web to configure each of these components. Our three Windows-based forwarders are managed by the deployment server. We then used the deployment server to install add-ons to different Splunk instances. The forwarders are configured to send data to the indexer and the search head is configured to send search requests to the indexer. Finally, we discussed the different concepts in Splunk access management including capabilities, roles, users, and authentication schemes. Splunk provides us with pre-defined roles that come with a set of capabilities. A Splunk administrator can create new roles that inherit from these existing roles and assign the roles to users. In addition, we can choose to use authentication schemes such as LDAP and SAML instead of the basic Splunk authentication scheme.

In the next chapter, we will explore the process of onboarding and normalizing data.

3

Onboarding and Normalizing Data

Splunk refers to the process of configuring new data sources as **onboarding**. Onboarding can be accomplished using the Splunk **Graphical User Interface** (**GUI**) (commonly known as **Splunk Web**) and Splunk **Command Line Interface** (**CLI**) commands, as well as by editing configuration files. The term **normalizing** data refers to the action of ensuring that the data is Splunk meets a **Common Information Model** (**CIM**). This is a very important step in using Splunk. In this chapter, we will explore the way data is onboarded and how we can extract fields. First, we will explore the way data is onboarded in the default `inputs.conf` file in the **Splunk Add-on for Microsoft Windows**. Then, we will use Splunk Web and configuration files to extract fields. Finally, we will explore event types and tags in the add-ons and apps that we installed in *Chapter 2, Setting Up the Splunk Environment*. We will create new event types and tags. We will also be executing simple **Search Processing Language** (**SPL**) queries throughout this chapter as we add new configurations. However, do not focus too much on the structure of the queries. We will learn how to write proper SPL queries in *Chapter 4, Introduction to SPL*.

In this chapter, we will cover the following topics:

- Exploring inputs.conf using the Splunk Add-on for Microsoft Windows
- Extracting fields using Splunk Web
- Extracting fields using props.conf and transforms.conf
- Creating event types and tags

Exploring inputs.conf using the Splunk Add-on for Microsoft Windows

To appreciate the power of Splunk, we have to first ingest data. This data can come from various sources using various methods. However, we will need to tell Splunk how to ingest this data. This process of creating new configurations that instruct Splunk on where to find the new data is called onboarding. It can be accomplished by modifying configuration files, running commands using the Splunk CLI, or by using readymade forms or widgets in Splunk Web. In this section, we will investigate how Splunk inputs can be configured by modifying the Splunk `inputs.conf` configuration file. Every app in Splunk has a basic structure (`bin`, `etc`, and `default` folders). Remember that the default configuration files can be found in the `default` directory. However, we should never make changes within this directory. Instead, any new configurations or modifications should be made in the `local` directory. Therefore, the default `inputs.conf` file can be found in `<app_name>/default/inputs.conf`. Custom `inputs.conf` configurations can be found in `<app_name>/local/inputs.conf`. We will explore the filesystem in the next subsection, *Understanding the filesystem of a Splunk add-on*.

There are multiple ways to ingest logs and various configurations to accomplish this. In this section, we will explore the default `inputs.conf` file found in the **Splunk Add-on for Microsoft Windows**, which we installed in *Chapter 2, Setting Up the Splunk Environment*. This add-on is especially useful since it has a wide variety of inputs, including configurations for monitoring files and directories and running scripts. We will first look at the Splunk filesystem to properly navigate the configuration files.

Understanding the filesystem of a Splunk add-on

Throughout the remaining chapters, we will refer to different types of configuration files. It is important to understand where these files are located on the Splunk filesystem. Most add-ons and apps have the same filesystem. Therefore, we will use the Splunk Add-on for Microsoft Windows to illustrate where certain files are located.

Figure 3.1 shows the standard folders in a Splunk add-on/app:

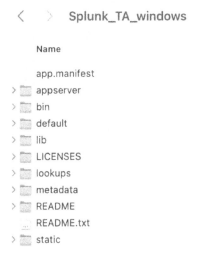

Figure 3.1 – The file structure of a Splunk add-on

The following is a list of some of the folders and files found in the **Splunk Add-on for Microsoft Windows**. The other folders are beyond the scope of this book. Feel free to browse the Splunk documentation to understand the purpose of some of the other folders:

- `bin`: This folder contains the scripts that Splunk uses to implement some of the functionality of the app/add-on. In some cases, an app may not contain any scripted inputs, so this folder will be empty. The `bin` folder of the **Splunk Add-on for Microsoft Windows** contains several `.bat`, PowerShell, and Python scripts such as `win_installed_apps.bat` and `Invoke-MonitoredScript.ps1`.

- `default`: This folder holds the default configurations for working with Windows Event Logs. We will find the `inputs.conf` file in this folder. However, we should never change configurations in this folder. Instead, we must create a new folder called `local`, create a new version of the configuration file (for example, `inputs.conf`), and enter the new configurations there. *Figure 3.2* shows an example of a filesystem after the local folder has been created. In some cases, the `local` folder is created when modifications are made on the CLI or the GUI:

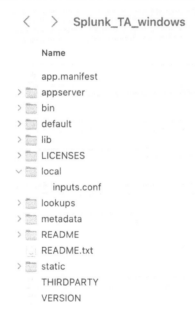

Figure 3.2 – The file structure of a Splunk add-on after the local directory has been created

- `lookups`: A lookup is a `.csv` file that can be used to enrich ingested data. For example, the `windows_actions.csv` file contains two fields (**Type** and **action**). When invoked, this lookup will create a new **action** field in the ingested Windows Event Logs based on the **Type** field found in the logs. For example, if the **Type** field that's ingested is an **audit failure**, then the **action** field will be a **failure**. We will explore lookups further in *Chapter 5, Reporting Commands, Lookups, and Macros. Figure 3.3* shows a section of `windows_actions.csv`:

windows_actions

Type	action
audit failure	failure
Audit Failure	failure
AUDIT_FAILURE	failure
failure audit	failure
Failure Audit	failure
FAILURE_AUDIT	failure
audit success	success
Audit Success	success

Figure 3.3 – The windows_action.csv lookup for mapping Type in
the raw Windows Event Logs to the new action field

Now that we are familiar with the add-on's file structure, let's look at the `inputs.conf` file.

Exploring inputs.conf

There are multiple types of input stanzas in the `inputs.conf` file. Exploring the **Splunk Add-on for Microsoft Windows** is a great way of exploring a variety of input types. The following is a list of input types:

- The `WinEventLog` inputs are scripted inputs that correspond to scripts in the `bin` folder. These correspond to the three types of Windows logs that can be ingested (`Application`, `Security`, and `System`):

  - Every configuration stanza in Splunk has a **stanza heading**. A **stanza heading** is a group of configuration lines that start with a stanza name enclosed in square brackets (`[]`). The name of the stanza also indicates the type of input it is. For example, `[WinEventLog://Security]` tells us that this is a scripted input for Windows security logs.

  - The configurations that follow the stanza heading are in the form of *key-value* pairs. For example, `disabled = 1` indicates that the stanza is disabled. This means that Splunk will not ingest Windows security logs by default when the add-on is first installed.

Let's explore the `WinEventLog` configurations by enabling three different inputs.

Enable the three `WinEventLog` inputs (`Security`, `Application`, and `System`) by following these steps:

1. Create a new folder called `local` in your filesystem using Windows Explorer. Refer to *Figure 3.2* to see where the folder should be located.

2. Create a new file called `inputs.conf` in that folder. Be sure that it is in the right place. Enter the following in your new `local/inputs.conf` file:

    ```
    [WinEventLog://Security]
    disable = 0
    [WinEventLog://Application]
    disable = 0
    [WinEventLog://System]
    disable = 0
    ```

The `blacklist*` configurations are interesting. They tell Splunk that we want to index all Windows security logs except the logs that match the regex specified in the list of `blacklist*` *key-value* pairs. For example, the following configuration indicates that we do not want to index Windows security logs with an `EventCode` of `4662` or `566`:

```
blacklist1 = EventCode="4662" Message="Object Type:(?!\
s*groupPolicyContainer)"
blacklist2 = EventCode="566" Message="Object Type:(?!\
s*groupPolicyContainer)"
```

Blacklist the Windows `EventCode` `4776` by adding the following `blacklist3` line to the `[WinEventLog://Security]` stanza of your `local/inputs.conf` file. We are using `blacklist3` because the default configuration in `default/inputs.conf` already contains `blacklist1` and `blacklist2`:

```
[WinEventLog://Security]
disable = 0
blacklist3 = EventCode="4776"
```

Now, let's look at `inputs.conf` from Splunk Web:

1. Navigate to **Settings | Add Data** from the left-hand side of the **Settings** menu (see *Figure 3.4*):

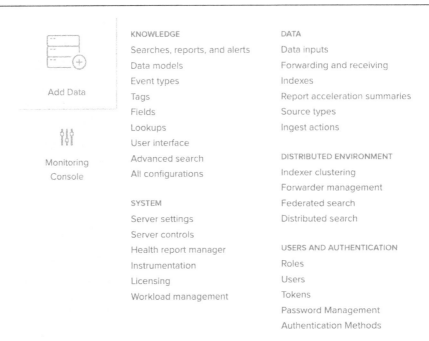

Figure 3.4 – Clicking on Add Data in the Settings menu

Explore the different types of input types available on the **Data inputs** page. *Figures 3.5* shows options for **Cloud computing**, **Networking**, **Operating System**, and **Security** data sources:

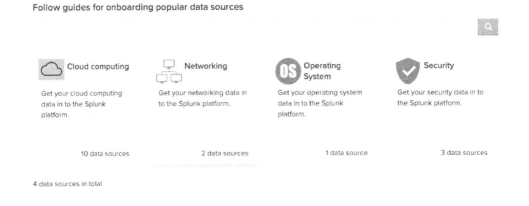

Figure 3.5 – Popular data source types

Figures 3.6 shows three types of inputs – that is, **Upload**, **Monitor**, and **Forward**:

Or get data in with the following methods

Figure 3.6 – Use the Upload, Monitor, and Forward methods for data inputs.

2.   Click on the **Upload** icon. This method of ingesting files is called a **oneshot**. It allows you to upload a single file to Splunk. You have the option to drag and drop the file onto the screen or use the **Select File** button to select a file on your device. The maximum file size that can be uploaded is 500 MB (see *Figure 3.7*):

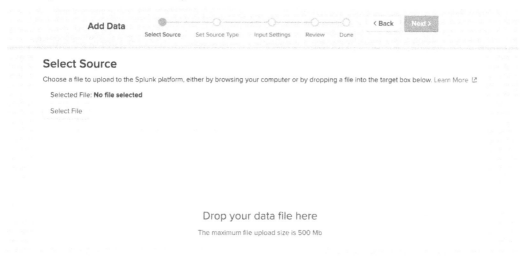

Figure 3.7 – Adding oneshot data by dropping a file or selecting a file on your device

We have selected a `.csv` file containing a sample log from BOTS Dataset v1. Splunk automatically detects that it is a `.csv` file and assigns the **sourcetype** as .csv. Splunk also uses the `.csv` headers as field names. There are also options on the left for creating additional extractions, which we will discuss in the next section, *Extracting fields using Splunk Web*. *Figure 3.8* shows the next page in the process:

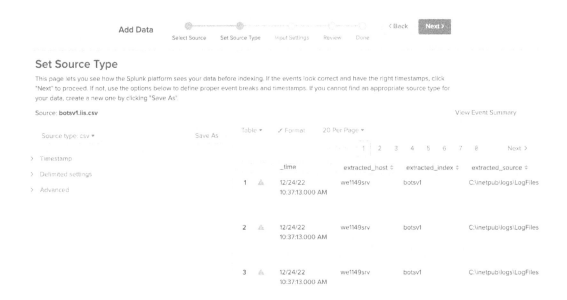

Figure 3.8 – The Set Source Type screen for selecting a sourcetype when creating a data input

Figure 3.9 shows the **Input Settings** step, where you can specify the **hostname** and **index**:

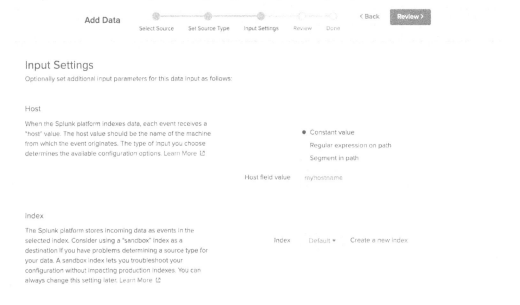

Figure 3.9 – The Input Settings step allows you to select the host and index

The final step involves reviewing the input settings you just created. It shows the **Input Type**, **File Name**, **Source Type**, **Host**, and **Index** properties. *Figure 3.10* shows an example:

Figure 3.10 – The Review page of the input settings

3. Next, we will explore the **Monitor** option on the **Add Data** screen. Go to **Settings | Add Data**, scroll to the bottom of the page, and click on **Monitor**.

    Figure 3.11 shows the page for the **Files & Directories** option. We can choose a file or directory to monitor by using the **Browse** button. Clicking **Index Once** is the equivalent of doing a **oneshot** input. Clicking **Continuously Monitor** tells Splunk to monitor files and directories for new data. You can also specify a **Whitelist** and **Blacklist**:

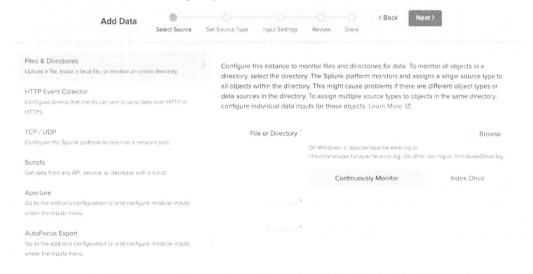

Figure 3.11 – The different types of inputs that can be monitored showing the Files & Directories option

Another input option is the **HTTP Event Collector (HEC)**. *Figure 3.12* shows how to create an HEC input. This HEC input allows you to configure a **token** that clients can use to send data to the server over HTTP or HTTPS:

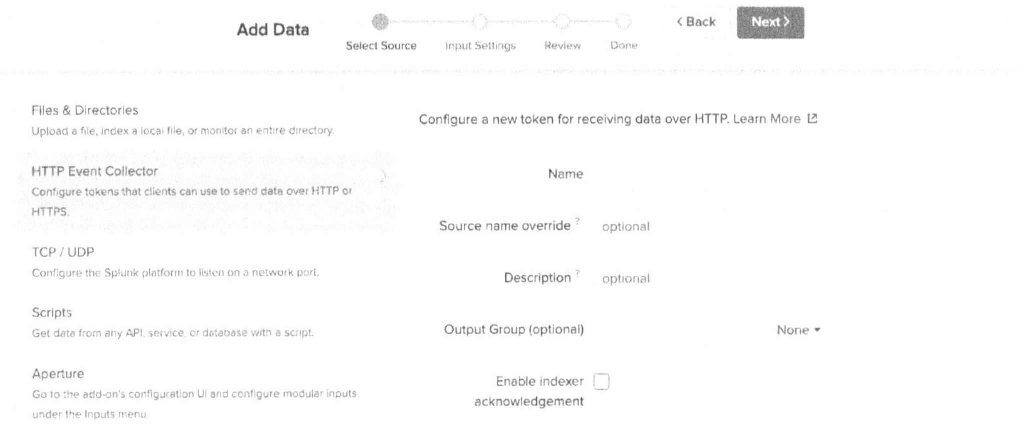

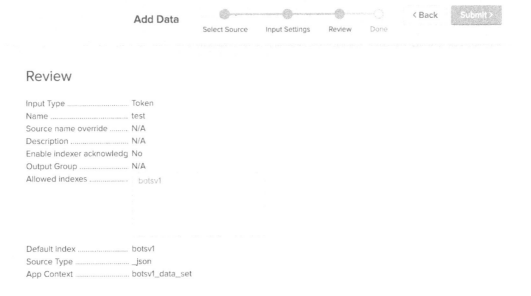

Figure 3.12 – Setting up an HEC input

Figure 3.13 shows the **Review** page for an HEC input called **test**, which will be stored in the **botsv1** index, stored in the **botsv1_data_set** app, and has a **_json** sourcetype:

Figure 3.13 – The Review page showing the settings for a new HEC input called test

Figure 3.14 shows the HEC token that was generated. This HEC token can be sent to the data source owner, along with the *servername* for the server:

Figure 3.14 – The token created for the new HEC input

Figure 3.15 shows the input type used to configure a **Transmission Control Protocol/User Datagram Protocol (TCP/UDP)** input. This tells Splunk to listen on a network port. We can select the transport protocol type (TCP or UDP) as well as the port. For example, a data owner can send syslog to this Splunk server by selecting UDP and port **514**:

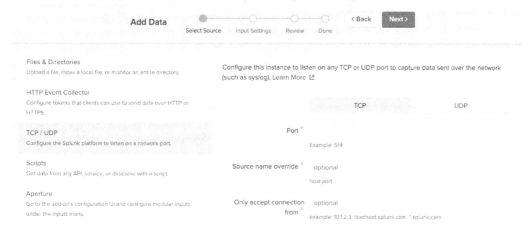

Figure 3.15 – Configuring a Splunk input to listen on a network port

Figure 3.16 shows an example of a syslog input configured to send **cisco:asa** logs to the **botsv1** index over **UDP Port** number **514**:

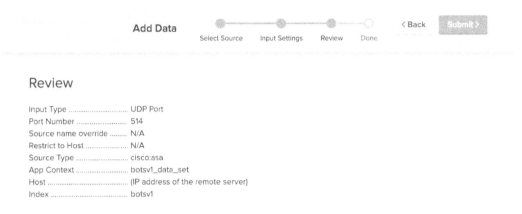

Figure 3.16 – The settings to listen on UDP port 514 for a cisco:asa log feed

The last input type we will look at is *script* input. We can configure Splunk to execute a script and send the output to a Splunk index. To set this up, we will need the following:

- **Script Path**: A link to the script. This can be a **Bash** or **Python** script in `<app_name>/bin`.

- **Command**: This allows you to specify any arguments that need to be included when the script is executed.

- **Interval**: This tells Splunk how often the script should be run in seconds.

Let's look at the setup in *Figure 3.17*:

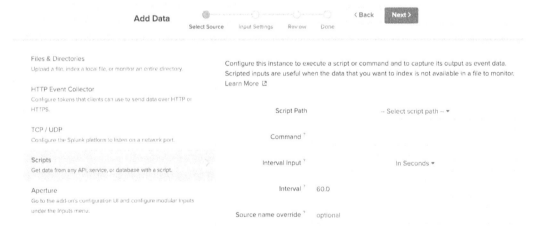

Figure 3.17 – The information needed to set up a scripted input

Figure 3.18 shows an example of a script input showing the monitoring process for the `external_lookup.py` script:

Configure this instance to execute a script or command and to capture its output as event data. Scripted inputs are useful when the data that you want to index is not available in a file to monitor. Learn More

Script Path	$SPLUNK_HOME/etc/system/bin ▼
Script Name	external_lookup.py ▼
Command ?	$SPLUNK_HOME/etc/system/bin/external_lookup.py
Interval Input ?	In Seconds ▼
Interval ?	60.0

Figure 3.18 – An example of the external_lookup.py script that will run every 60.0s

Now that we have learned how to create inputs in Splunk, let's look at how we can extract fields from the data.

Extracting fields using Splunk Web

We have onboarded the data and it's flowing into Splunk. Our next step is to determine whether all the fields are being extracted properly in the data. What does that mean? Every data source contains information that we want to easily search. We can write configurations so that Splunk will pull out specific parts of the data being ingested and label them with field names. This will make it much easier to write efficient Splunk queries. In the following subsections, we will use the logs in BOTS Dataset v1, which we installed in *Chapter 2, Setting Up the Splunk Environment*. We will use Splunk Web to create new *field aliases*, *calculated fields*, and *field extractions*.

Field aliases

As the name suggests, we can use a *field alias* to assign a new name to a field. This makes a field name easier to read. Field aliases also allow us to ensure that field names are the same across data sources. For example, a field may be called client_ip in one data source and src in another data source. Renaming the fields so that they are both named src makes it easy to correlate data between data sources. Before we can create a new field alias, let's explore the data in the botsv1 dataset:

1. Log on to the search head and navigate to the **Searching and Reporting** app. Enter the following SPL query in the search bar:

    ```
    index=botsv1 earliest=0.
    ```

2. Click on **All Fields** to see all the fields available in the dataset (see *Figure 3.19*):

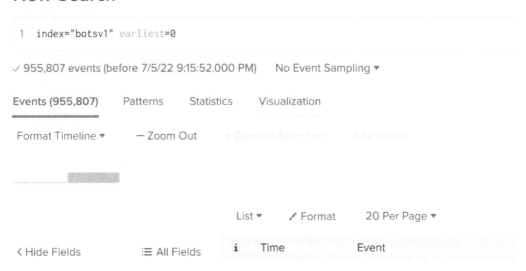

New Search

```
1   index="botsv1" earliest=0
```

✓ 955,807 events (before 7/5/22 9:15:52.000 PM)   No Event Sampling ▾

Events (955,807)   Patterns   Statistics   Visualization

Format Timeline ▾   — Zoom Out   + Zoom to Selection   × Deselect

List ▾   ✎ Format   20 Per Page ▾

‹ Hide Fields   ≔ All Fields   **i**   Time   Event

Figure 3.19 – Clicking on All Fields to browse through all the fields in the dataset

3. Enter the term `refer` in the filter box at the top of the **All Fields** page. Why are there three variations of the **HTTP referer** field? Remember that this dataset contains data from multiple log types. In this example, `cs_Referer` is the name that was assigned to the field in the **Internet Information Services (IIS)** logs, `http.http_refer` is a field in the `suricata` logs, while `http_referrer` is a field in the stream logs. Sometimes, when dealing with big data, we may discover that multiple names have been assigned to the same data.

4. This is a good opportunity to create a field alias. Splunk has a framework called the **Splunk Common Information Model**, which is a semantic model for extracting value from data (`https://docs.splunk.com/Documentation/CIM/5.0.1/User/Overview`). Suppose we wanted to write SPL to query data from the three different data sources – `IIS`, `suricata`, and `stream` logs. It would be confusing to remember what each field is called in each log type. This would be tiresome. Instead, Splunk gives us the ability to rename fields. Let's normalize the `*refer*` fields so that they are all called `http_referer`.

5. Navigate to **Settings** | **Fields** | **Field aliases**.

6. Click the + **Add New** button. Enter the values shown in *Figure 3.20* in the **Add new** dialog box and click **Save**:

Add new

Fields » Field aliases » Add new

Destination app	botsv1_data_set
Name *	http_refer_rename
Apply to	sourcetype named * iis
Field aliases	cs_Referer = http_referer Delete
	+ Add another field
	☐ Overwrite field values

Cancel   Save

Figure 3.20 – Creating a new field alias called http_referer_rename that renames cs_Referer as http_referer

Most knowledge objects in Splunk belong to either a user (**Private**), an app (**App**), or everyone (**Global**). We created the new field alias in the **botsv1_data_set** app; however, the new configuration is still **Private**. This means that it will not be visible to other apps. Therefore, we will need to alter the permissions.

7. Click on the **Permissions** link under the **Sharing** column (see *Figure 3.21*):

Field aliases

Fields » Field aliases

Showing 1-1 of 1 item

App   Splunk Boss of the SO... ▾   Created in the App ▾   filter   🔍   25 per page ▾

Name ⬍	Field aliases ⬍	Owner ⬍	App ⬍	Sharing ⬍	Status ⬍	Actions
iis : FIELDALIAS-http_refer_rename	cs_Referer ASNEW http_referer	admin	botsv1_data_set	Global ¦ Permissions	Enabled	Clone ¦ Move ¦ Delete

Figure 3.21 – The newly created field alias, http_referer_rename, is set to Private

8. Click the **All apps (system)** checkbox under **Object should appear** in **Options**. Click **Save**. See *Figure 3.22*:

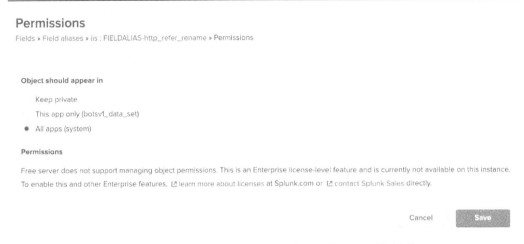

Figure 3.22 – Changing permissions on the newly created field alias

9.   Browse back to the search bar and enter the following query:

```
index=botsv1 sourcetype=iis http_referer=*
```

10. You should see the **http_referer** field listed under **Interesting fields** on the left-hand side of the screen. Is the field listed in **Interesting fields**? Sometimes, it may take a few seconds or minutes for the change to propagate. *Figure 3.23* shows the new **http_referer** field:

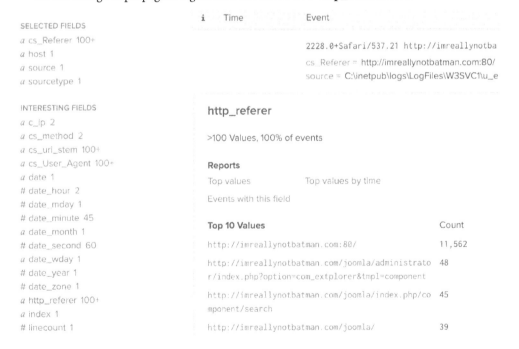

Figure 3.23 – List of fields showing the newly created http_referer alias

We created a field alias to rename a field in the previous example. However, there are several other options for creating and modifying fields, as shown in *Figure 3.24*:

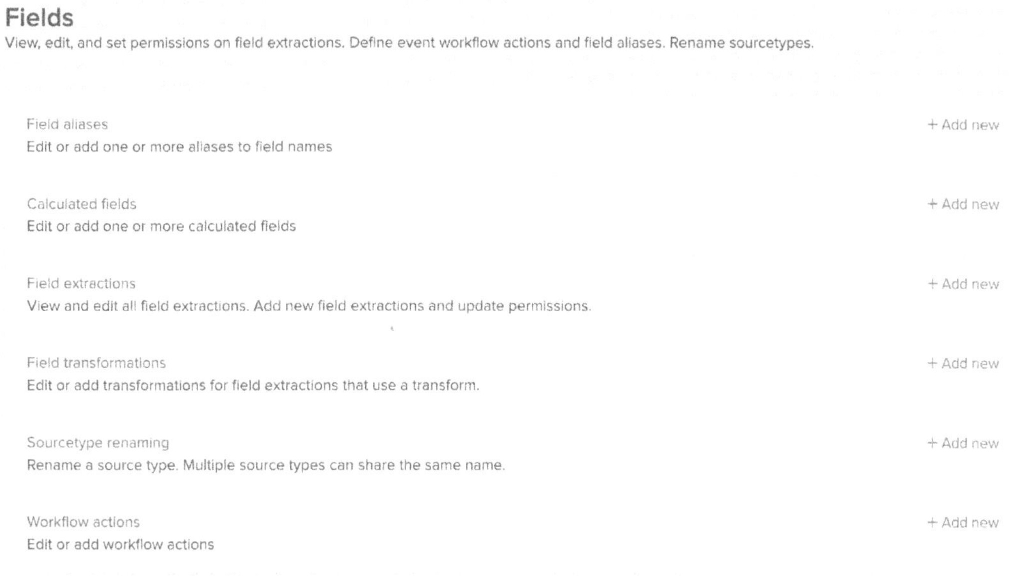

Fields

View, edit, and set permissions on field extractions. Define event workflow actions and field aliases. Rename sourcetypes.

Field aliases Edit or add one or more aliases to field names	+ Add new
Calculated fields Edit or add one or more calculated fields	+ Add new
Field extractions View and edit all field extractions. Add new field extractions and update permissions.	+ Add new
Field transformations Edit or add transformations for field extractions that use a transform.	+ Add new
Sourcetype renaming Rename a source type. Multiple source types can share the same name.	+ Add new
Workflow actions Edit or add workflow actions	+ Add new

Figure 3.24 – Options for creating new field configurations

We will continue exploring field configurations in the next subsection by creating calculated fields.

Calculated fields

The field alias that we created in the previous example renamed the existing `cs_Referer` field in the `iis` logs and created a new field called `http_referer`. The two fields contain the same values. A *calculated field*, on the other hand, is usually configured when we want to create a new field based on a combination or a reformatting of other fields. For example, there are two fields called `bytes_in` and `bytes_out` in the `suricata` logs. If we wanted to display the total number of `bytes`, we could add a clause to our Splunk query to perform the calculation, like so:

```
index=botsv1 earliest=0 sourcetype=suricata
| eval bytes=bytes_in+bytes_out
```

The alternative would be to create a calculated field called `bytes` that we can use in searches without having to add that extra line in the search query. Navigate to **Settings** | **Fields** | **Calculated fields** and input and save the values shown in *Figure 3.25* on the **Add new** page. Be sure to modify the permissions on the new calculated field to make the field **Global**:

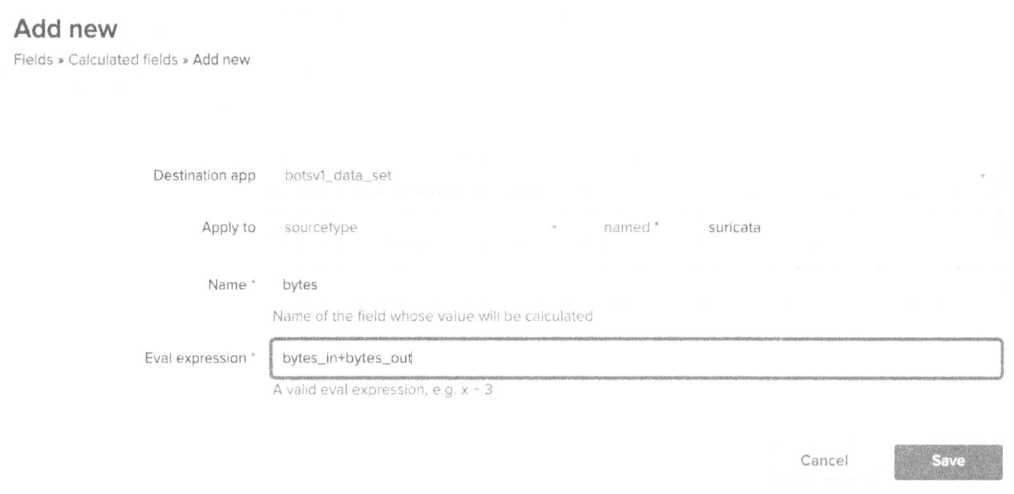

Add new

Fields » Calculated fields » Add new

Destination app	botsv1_data_set
Apply to	sourcetype ▾ named * suricata
Name *	bytes
	Name of the field whose value will be calculated
Eval expression *	bytes_in+bytes_out
	A valid eval expression, e.g. x + 3

Cancel   **Save**

Figure 3.25 – Creating a calculated field called bytes that is the sum of bytes_in and bytes_out

Next, we will look at how to create a new field by extracting parts of an existing field or a raw log.

Field extractions

Sometimes, we want to extract parts of a raw event or field. We can do this by using the **Field Extractions** option. Consider the `cs_Referer` field in the `IIS` logs, which contains values such as the following:

- `http://71.39.18[.]126/?BVw=2x9zYDwKMPFpiCM2CSgY`
- `http://imreallynotbatman[.]com/joomla/media`

Now, suppose we wanted to extract the highlighted portion of the `cs_Referer` field, which corresponds to the `domain` portion of this field. Why is this important? Sometimes, a security analyst wants to detect if there is a lot of traffic to a particular domain. We can create a new field extraction called `referer_domain`. To get this field extraction to work, we will use `regex`. Are you familiar with regex? If not, it's a great skill to have when working with Splunk. A website such as `https://regexr.com` is a great resource for learning how to write regex.

The following search query extracts the domain portion of the `cs_Referer` field into a field called `referer_domain`:

```
index=botsv1 earliest=0 sourcetype=iis cs_Referer=*
| rex field=cs_Referer "http://(?<referer_domain>(\w+\.\w+|\
d+\.\d+\.\d+\.\d+))\/"
```

Let's explore this regex:

- \w+: Matches one or more alphanumeric characters
- \ . : Matches a period character
- | : Indicates an OR operation
- \d+\ . \d+\ . \d+\ . \d+: Matches an IP address
- \/: Matches a forward slash

Let's create a field extraction in Splunk Web. Go to **Settings | Fields | Calculated Extractions** and enter the values shown in *Figure 3.26*:

Add new

Fields » Field extractions » **Add new**

Destination app	botsv1_data_set
Name *	referer_domain
Apply to	sourcetype named * iis
Type *	Inline
Extraction/Transform *	http://(?<referer_domain>(\w+\.\w+|\d+\.\d+\.\d+\.\d+))\/

If the field extraction is inline, provide the regular expression. If the field extraction uses a transform, specify the transform name.

Cancel   Save

Figure 3.26 – Creating a new field extraction using the GUI

Enter the following in the search bar to view the newly extracted field:

```
index=botsv1 earliest=0 sourcetype=iis referer_domain=*
| table _time, cs_Referer, referer_domain
```

Don't see the new `referer_domain` field? Ensure that you entered the right regex. Be sure that you did not leave the quotes around the regex. Finally, be sure that the permissions on the new field extraction are set to **Global**.

Now that we have learned how to create and modify fields using Splunk Web, let's look at how we can create fields using the `props.conf` and `transforms.conf` configuration files.

Extracting fields using props.conf and transforms.conf

So far, we have created field aliases, calculated fields, and field extractions using Splunk Web. These changes can also be made using configuration files. Let's look at the changes in the configuration files that occurred when we created the `http_referer` and `referer_domain` fields in the previous section, *Extracting fields using the GUI*. Use a *ssh* client to connect to `searchhead1` and browse to `/opt/splunk/etc/apps/botsv1_data_set/local/props.conf`. You should see the following configurations under the `[iis]` and `[suricata]` stanzas:

```
[iis]
FIELDALIAS-http_refer_rename = cs_Referer ASNEW http_referer
EXTRACT-referer_domain = http://(?<referer_domain>(\w+\.\w+|\
d+\.\d+\.\d+\.\d+))\/


[suricata]
EVAL-bytes = bytes_in + bytes_out
```

Since the field alias (`http_referer`) and the field extraction (`referer_domain`) are associated with the IIS sourcetype, they are inserted under the `[iis]` stanza. The calculated field (`bytes`) was created for the `suricata` data, so it is under the `[suricata]` stanza. A field alias generates a line in `props.conf` that starts with the **FIELDALIAS** keyword. We can see the use of the **ASNEW** keyword to rename `cs_Referer` to `http_referer`. Similarly, the field extraction that we created for the IIS sourcetype creates a new configuration **Calculated Fields** option that begins with the **EVAL** keyword. You can see the calculation that we entered when upon creation that starts with the **EXTRACT** keyword. The `bytes` field that we created using the new field is on the right-hand side of the equals sign.

Don't see all the configurations? Go back to the **Fields** menu (**Settings | Fields**) in Splunk Web and look for the missing knowledge objects that you just created. Use the filter box at the top of the **Fields** page to search for the field. Check that the new configuration is in the `botsv1_data_set` app and that the permissions are set to **Global**.

Let's create a few new fields. We will start with a new field for the *Fortigate* firewall traffic. First, enter the following query in the search bar using Splunk Web on the search head:

```
index=botsv1 earliest=0 sourcetype=fgt_traffic
```

Look at the fields under **Interesting fields**. Do you see the `rcvdbyte` and `sendbyte` fields? Let's use the configuration files to create a new calculated field similar to the one we created in the *Calculated fields* subsection.

Return to the *ssh* session on your search head and navigate to `/opt/splunk/etc/apps/ botsv1_data_set/local/props.conf`. Use a text editor such as *vi* or *nano* to enter the following code in `props.conf`:

```
[fgt_traffic]
EVAL-bytes = sendbyte + rcvdbyte
```

Save the file and return to Splunk Web on the search head. Rerun the `fgt_traffic` search query shown here:

```
index=botsv1 earliest=0 sourcetype=fgt_traffic
```

Do you see your new `bytes` field?

Let's see the configuration for a calculated field. Take a look at `Account_Name` in the `WinEventLog:Security` logs:

```
index=botsv1 earliest=0 sourcetype="WinEventLog:Security"
|         stats count by Account_Name
```

Some of the account names are lowercase, some are uppercase, and some are mixed case. Let's create a calculated field to format the `Account_Name` field so that all the values are in uppercase. Add this stanza to the end of the `/opt/splunk/etc/apps/botsv1_data_set/local/props. conf` file on the search head:

```
[WinEventLog:Security]
EVAL-Account_Name = upper(Account_Name)
```

Explore the calculated fields, field extractions, and field aliases in the *Installing additional Splunk add-ons and apps* section in *Chapter 2, Setting Up the Splunk Environment*. Remember that the default configurations will be found in the default folder in `etc/apps/<addon name>/default`.

Next, we will learn how to create event types and tags so that we can easily find data in our logs.

Creating event types and tagging

An **event type** is a way of categorizing data to make it easier to search. For example, we might want to get all authentication-type events from multiple log sources or we may tag all error messages with an *error* tag. In this section, we will explore event types for our `BOTS Dataset v1`.

An event type is a Splunk query. It is similar to the queries that we have executed so far in this chapter. Let's look at an example. Suppose we wanted to get all authentication logs from our `BOTS Dataset v1`. Where would we find those logs?

1. We can search our dataset by using the `tag` keyword. Enter the following Splunk query in the search bar:

    ```
    index=botsv1 earliest=0 tag=authentication
    ```

2. Click on the **sourcetype** field in **Interesting fields** on the left of the page. We will see that most of the authentication events come from the Windows logs (see *Figure 3.27*):

Figure 3.27 – Using tag=authentication in a search of the botsv1 data

3. How do we know that the events are authentication events? Click on the **signature** field in **Interesting fields** to view the signatures for the logon events (see *Figure 3.28*):

Figure 3.28 – Using tag=authentication shows all the signatures for the logon events

4. Now, click on the **EventCode** field and note the different Windows EventCodes listed (see *Figure 3.29*). Do the numbers in *Figure 3.28* and *Figure 3.29* match up?

Figure 3.29 – The EventCodes that correspond to tag=authentication

So, why are we looking at this? A Windows log has an **EventCode** that tells us what type of event has occurred. For example, **EventCode 4624** indicates a successful login.

5. Look at an event with this **EventCode** by typing the following query in the search bar:

```
index=botsv1 earliest=0 tag=authentication
sourcetype=wineventlog EventCode=4624
```

Figure 3.30 shows a sample log for a successful login:

```
8/24/16          08/24/2016 11:27:24 AM
1:27:24.000 PM   LogName=Security
                 SourceName=Microsoft Windows security auditing.
                 EventCode=4624
                 EventType=0
                 Type=Information
                 ComputerName=we9041srv.waynecorpinc.local
                 TaskCategory=Logon
                 OpCode=Info
                 RecordNumber=1116706
                 Keywords=Audit Success
                 Message=An account was successfully logged on.
```

Figure 3.30 – A successful login Windows event

Now that we have explored the idea of **EventCodes**, let's get back to understanding how event types and tags work.

6. To get the `tag` keyword to work in the search bar, we need to create a knowledge object called a **tag**. A tag is associated with an **event type**. Let's look at the **authentication** tag.

7. Navigate to **Settings | Event types** and enter the values shown in *Figure 3.31* into the input boxes at the top of the page. Notice that we are looking at event types that were created in the **Splunk Add-on for Microsoft Windows** and which have the **authentication** and **success** search keys. We are looking for the event types that categorize successful authentication logon events. We can see that there is a **windows_logon_success** event type. This event type contains another event type called **wineventlog_security**:

Figure 3.31 – The windows_logon_success event type search string

The **wineventlog_security eventtype** represents any event logs from the Windows Security logs (see *Figure 3.32*):

wineventlog_security   source=WinEventLog:Security OR   os windows
                                                            source=WMI:WinEventLog:Security
                                                            OR
                                                            source=XmlWinEventLog:Security

Figure 3.32 – The wineventlog_security event type search string

But let's look at the rest of the **windows_logon_success** event type in *Figure 3.32*. What else does it tell us?

(EventCode=4624 OR EventCode=528 OR EventCode=540)

We can see that it specifies that a successful windows logon event could be one of three Windows EventCodes (4624, 528, or 540). You can learn more about Windows EventCodes at https://www.ultimatewindowssecurity.com/securitylog/encyclopedia/default.aspx. The definition of **windows_logon_success** also shows us that any event that meets this criterion is assigned the **authentication** tag. This is why we can see the event with the 4624 EventCode in our search results.

8. Explore the other *event types* in **Splunk Add-on for Microsoft Windows**, such as **windows_logon_failure** in *Figure 3.33*. What EventCodes are associated with this event type? Besides the event codes, what defines a Windows logon failure?

| windows_logon_failure | eventtype=wineventlog_security
((EventCode=4625 AND
ta_windows_action!=error) OR
EventCode=529 OR
EventCode=530 OR
EventCode=531 OR
EventCode=532 OR
EventCode=533 OR
EventCode=534 OR
EventCode=535 OR
EventCode=536 OR
EventCode=537 OR
EventCode=539) | authentication | No
owner | Splunk_TA_windows | Global \| Permissi |

Figure 3.33 – The windows_logon_failure event type search string

9. Now that we've explored some of the existing Windows event types and tags, let's create a new event type for our `Fortigate` traffic logs. Enter the following Splunk query in the search bar:

```
index=botsv1 earliest=0 sourcetype=fortigate_traffic
  | stats count by srccountry
```

10. Don't worry if you see any new Splunk keywords such as **stats** that you don't recognize. We will go over them in *Chapter 5, Reporting Commands, Lookups, and Macros. Figure 3.34* shows part of the output of this search query. The results show the country of origin of the **Fortigate** traffic:

Events (55,279)   Patterns   Statistics (84)   Visualization

100 Per Page ▼   ✎ Format   Preview ▼

srccountry ⇕	count ⇕
Afghanistan	1
Algeria	2
Argentina	23
Armenia	1
Australia	1
Azerbaijan	4
Bahrain	1
Belgium	3
Bolivia	4

Figure 3.34 – The output of the query displays the country of origin of the Fortigate traffic

11. What if we wanted to display all the traffic except the traffic from the United States and Canada? Modify your search query so that it includes a condition that exempts these two countries:

```
index=botsv1 earliest=0 sourcetype=fortigate_traffic
srccountry!="United States" srccountry!="Canada"
```

The results show all the international countries where traffic originated.

Now, let's create an **event type** to represent international countries:

12. Navigate to **Settings | Event types** and click on the green **New Event Type** button.

13. Enter the values shown in *Figure 3.35* and click the green **Save** button.

14. We are creating this new event type in the **botsv1_data_set** app. We will call it **fortigate_international_traffic** and we will specify the condition that this traffic is coming from the **fortigate_traffic** logs, as well as that we are including all countries except the United States and Canada.

15. We will also remove any events where **srccountry** is set to **Reserved**.

16. We will also assign the **international_traffic** tag to these logs.

You may be wondering why we are tagging the data. The **international_traffic** tag will include all traffic sources, not just **Fortigate** logs. The event type may be different. For example, **Palo Alto** traffic logs from international countries may be called **pa_international_traffic** but have the **international_traffic** tag. Remember, we are categorizing our data. So, if we were to search for **tag=international_traffic** in the search bar, we would get *all* international traffic logs, including those from the **Fortigate** and **Palo Alto** logs:

fortigate_international_traffic

Event types » fortigate_international_traffic

Figure 3.35 – The new fortigate_international_traffic event type

17. Modify the permissions so that the event type is **Global**. Enter the following search query in the search bar to view all international traffic in the `botsv1` dataset:

```
index=botsv1 earliest=0 eventtype=fortigate_
international_traffic
```

18. Click on the **src_country** field in **Interesting fields** and view the countries listed. Test out your event type by entering the following search query in the search bar:

```
index=botsv1 earliest=0 eventtype=fortigate_
international_traffic srccountry="Canada"
```

Figure 3.36 shows that there are no logs that match the **fortigate_international_traffic** events from **Canada**:

Figure 3.36 – There are no fortigate_international_traffic events that originate from Canada

We created field aliases, calculated fields, and field extractions in this section. These new configurations allowed us to make our data easier to search using Splunk queries.

Summary

In this chapter, we explored the process of onboarding data and creating configurations that will allow us to search more efficiently. We covered the basic structure of a Splunk add-on and app, including the main folders such as bin, default, local, and lookups. Each of these folders has a specific purpose. We looked at different ways of inputting data that exist in the **Splunk Add-on for Microsoft Windows**. We learned that the `inputs.conf` file is the file where we store input configurations. The default `inputs.conf` file in the **Splunk Add-on for Microsoft Windows** contains file monitors and scripts that allow us to ingest **Microsoft Windows** logs. We enabled configurations in the add-on to ingest Microsoft Windows `Security`, `Application`, and `System` logs. We also learned how to use

Splunk Web to create new inputs. Next, we went through a series of examples of renaming fields (field aliases), creating calculated fields, and extracting fields using regex. Finally, we reviewed some of the event types and tags in the **Splunk Add-on for Microsoft Windows**. We also practiced creating new event types and tags. Now, we understand how these configuration steps can help us search more efficiently in Splunk.

We will continue our Splunk journey by learning how to write Splunk queries in *Chapter 4, Introduction to SPL*.

Part 2: Visualizing Data with Splunk

This part will explore the Splunk **Search Processing Language (SPL)** by introducing features such as commands, lookups, and macros. We will also use SPL to create tables and charts and insert these visualizations into dashboards.

This part comprises the following chapters:

- *Chapter 4, Introduction to SPL*
- *Chapter 5, Reporting Commands, Lookups, and Macros*
- *Chapter 6, Creating Tables and Charts Using SPL*
- *Chapter 7, Creating Dynamic Dashboards*

4
Introduction to SPL

The **Search Processing Language** (**SPL**) is a language written by Splunk that allows indexed data to be searched. SPL includes a variety of commands and functions based on the Unix pipeline and **Sequential Query Language** (**SQL**). SPL allows us to perform a variety of actions on data. We can search, filter, manipulate, and even delete information from Splunk events. We will introduce some of these actions in this chapter. But first, we will explore the Splunk search interface and understand how parts of the interface can be used to compose search queries. For example, the time picker can be used to narrow down search periods. We will also look at commands such as `eval`, which can be used to manipulate and modify data in an event using mathematical and string functions. Let's get started!

In this chapter, we will explore the following topics:

- Understanding the Splunk search interface
- Dissecting a Splunk query
- Formatting and transforming data

Understanding the Splunk search interface

Now that we've understood how Splunk stores indexed data, it's time to delve into the mechanics of the Splunk query language. We saw examples of simple queries in *Chapter 3, Onboarding and Normalizing Data*. Some of the queries we wrote in *Chapter 3, Onboarding and Normalizing Data*, searched the botsv1 index and used keywords such as **sourcetype** and **earliest**. Examples included the following:

```
index=botsv1 earliest=0
index=botsv1 sourcetype=iis http_referer=*
index=botsv1 earliest=0 sourcetype=suricata
| eval bytes=bytes_in+bytes_out
index=botsv1 earliest=0 sourcetype=iis referer_domain=*
| table _time, cs_Referer, referer_domain
index=botsv1 earliest=0 sourcetype="WinEventLog:Security"
| stats count by Account_Name
```

In this section, we will write some basic Splunk queries, but first, let's look at the Splunk search interface:

1. We will type up our Splunk search queries using the **Search and Reporting** app.

2. Open the Splunk search head where you have installed **Bots Dataset v1**.

3. Click the **Apps** dropdown at the top left of the browser window.

4. Click on the **Search and Reporting** app. Let's look at the different parts of this window.

    Figure 4.1 shows the **Search and Reporting** app after a search has run:

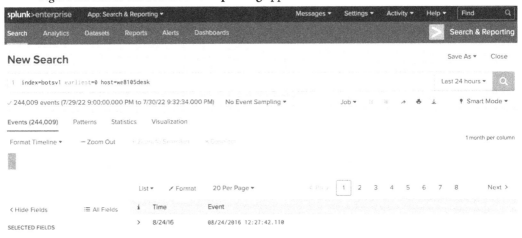

Figure 4.1 – The Splunk search interface

Let's look at the different parts of the window:

5. **Search bar**: This multi-line white text box is directly under the **New Search** label. We will use this text box to type up search queries. Pressing the *Enter* key on your keyboard executes the search query typed in the search bar. Pressing *Shift + Enter* places the cursor on a new line. *Ctrl + * formats the search query. Later, in *Chapter 5, Reporting Commands, Lookups, and Macros*, when we explore macros, we will learn how to expand macros by pressing *Ctrl + Shift + E*. Common practice is to start each new clause of a search on a new line (see the example in *Figure 4.2*):

New Search

```
1    index=botsv1 earliest=0 sourcetype="stream:tcp"
2    | stats sum(bytes) as bytes by dest_ip, dest_port
3    | eval KB=bytes/(1024)
4    | table dest_ip, dest_port, KB
```

Figure 4.2 – A multi-line search query

6. **Time picker**: Splunk events are all timestamped. Therefore, the time picker is an important part of the search. The time picker provides several different options for specifying search periods. Let's explore some of these options. *Figure 4.3* shows the first option, which is the **Presets** menu:

Figure 4.3 – Time picker showing presets

This menu gives a set of *real-time*, *relative*, and *other* preset search periods. Real-time searches allow us to see the results as the data is being indexed. This is useful for seeing immediate results as the data comes in. However, we should be very careful with the real-time searches as they incur more load on the servers. We should also be careful about running **All time** searches in a production environment. **All time** searches the entire index and can cause serious issues. We can set the default setting on the time picker by navigating to **Settings** | **Server settings** | **Search preferences**. Then, select your default setting, as indicated in *Figure 4.4*:

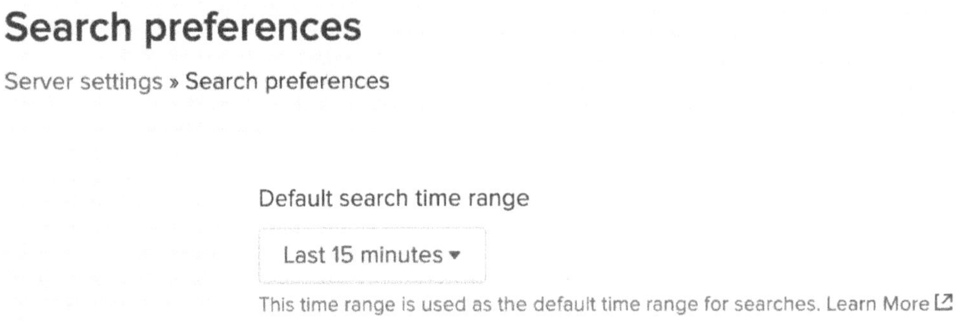

Search preferences

Server settings » Search preferences

Default search time range

Last 15 minutes ▼

This time range is used as the default time range for searches. Learn More ↗

Figure 4.4 – Setting the default time range to the last 15 minutes

Some other interesting options include the **Relative** option and the **Date & Time Range** option. The **Relative** option allows you to be more flexible with search periods. For example, we can specify how many seconds, minutes, hours, or years the search period should cover.

Figure 4.5 shows the time picker set to search the last 30 minutes:

Figure 4.5 – The Relative option on the time picker showing the setting for the last 30 minutes

7. The **Date Range** and **Data and Time Range** menus allow us to specify specific periods such as *January 15, 2006*, at *4:56 P.M.* to *January 27, 2006*.

    Figure 4.6 shows the time picker for a search during this period:

Figure 4.6 – The time picker showing a time range

8. Event count, which is located right below the search bar on the left, displays the number of events and the time range of the search query results. The event count in *Figure 4.1* shows that there were **244,009** events matching the search query.

There are three search modes in Splunk, as shown in *Figure 4.7*:

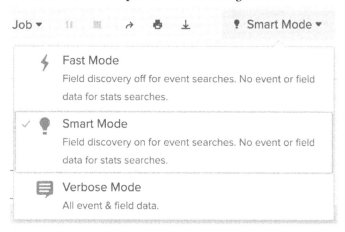

Figure 4.7 – The three Splunk search modes

Now, let's look at these search modes briefly:

A. **Fast Mode**: As its name implies, this search is the fastest because no fields are extracted at search time. *Figure 4.8* shows the fields returned when using **Fast Mode**. The fields listed (**host**, **source**, **sourcetype**, **index**, **linecount**, and **splunk_server**) are the fields that are extracted when the data is first indexed. Fields that we have instructed Splunk to extract at search time are not extracted:

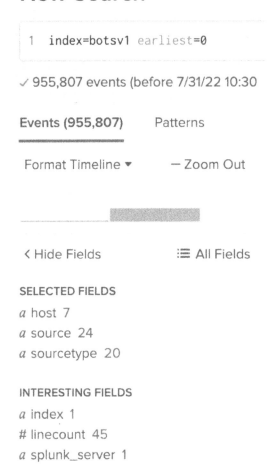

Figure 4.8 – The fields returned when using Fast Mode

B.   **Smart Mode**: This mode is the most used because it is more efficient. It includes field discovery for event searches. However, if we use reporting commands such as stats and tables (to be discussed in *Chapter 5*, *Reporting Commands, Lookups, and Macros*), the search results will only include the fields that we specify. The raw data will not be returned. *Figure 4.9* shows the result of running the search from *Figure 4.8* in **Smart Mode**. Notice the fields displayed on the left:

Figure 4.9 – Search query results when run in Smart Mode

Figure 4.10 shows the results when a reporting command (**stats**) is added to the query.

The results show only the action field in tabular format; no events are returned. If we wanted to see other fields along with this tabular result, we would need to run the search in **Verbose Mode**:

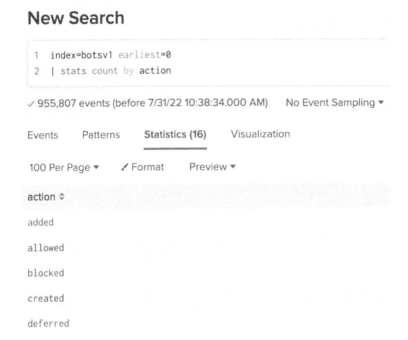

Figure 4.10 – Search query results for a Smart Mode search with a reporting command (stats)

C. **Verbose Mode**: This mode is the slowest because it returns all data that meets the search query, extracts fields, and performs any reporting commands such as stats. This is very useful when we are still exploring data. For example, in *Figure 4.10*, we displayed the action field, but we may want to add a new field to the results. In this case, we would click on the **Events** tab and explore the raw events. Once we find the field or value we need, we can make changes to the search and rerun the query. *Figure 4.11* shows our example search run in **Verbose Mode**. Note that the **Events** tab lists the number of events. By default, the formatted results will be displayed in the **Statistics** tab; however, clicking on the **Events** tab will reveal all the logs returned from the search query. Compare the results in this figure to the ones in *Figure 4.10*:

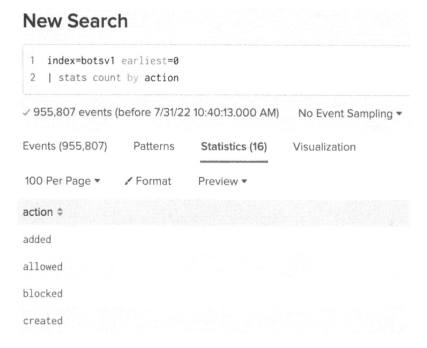

Figure 4.11 – Sample search run in Verbose Mode

9. **Timeline:** This shows the event count over time. Each column represents the number of events over a period. Splunk automatically adjusts the timeline depending on the time range requested using the time picker. *Figure 4.12* shows the results of a search for all logs in the **botsv1** index on *August 24, 2016*. Note the bars displayed in the timeline:

Figure 4.12 – The timeline shows a cluster of events around 11 A.M. on 8/24/2016

10. **Search results:** This part of the window shows the query results. The format of the data displayed in this section depends on the way the data was indexed and whether the search query included reporting commands. For example, *Figure 4.13* shows one event from the **fortigate_traffic** logs. This log was indexed as key/value pairs, such as **dstcountry="United States"**. The event includes the event timestamp on the left (**8/24/16 1:27:44.000 PM**). It includes the raw event, which starts with the date **Aug 24** and ends with **crlevel=high**. The event also includes **host (192.168.250.1)**, **source (udp:514)**, and **sourcetype (fortigate_traffic)**:

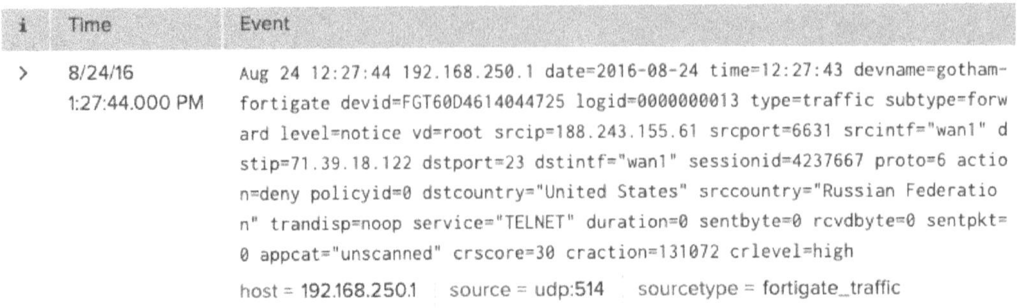

i	Time	Event
>	8/24/16 1:27:44.000 PM	Aug 24 12:27:44 192.168.250.1 date=2016-08-24 time=12:27:43 devname=gotham-fortigate devid=FGT60D4614044725 logid=0000000013 type=traffic subtype=forward level=notice vd=root srcip=188.243.155.61 srcport=6631 srcintf="wan1" dstip=71.39.18.122 dstport=23 dstintf="wan1" sessionid=4237667 proto=6 action=deny policyid=0 dstcountry="United States" srccountry="Russian Federation" trandisp=noop service="TELNET" duration=0 sentbyte=0 rcvdbyte=0 sentpkt=0 appcat="unscanned" crscore=30 craction=131072 crlevel=high
		host = 192.168.250.1 source = udp:514 sourcetype = fortigate_traffic

Figure 4.13 – A fortigate_traffic event in the botsv1 dataset

We can explore the fields returned from a search run in **Smart Mode** or **Verbose Mode** by clicking on the > icon on the left-hand side. *Figure 4.14* shows the expanded fields view showing the fields for the **fortigate_traffic** event in *Figure 4.13*:

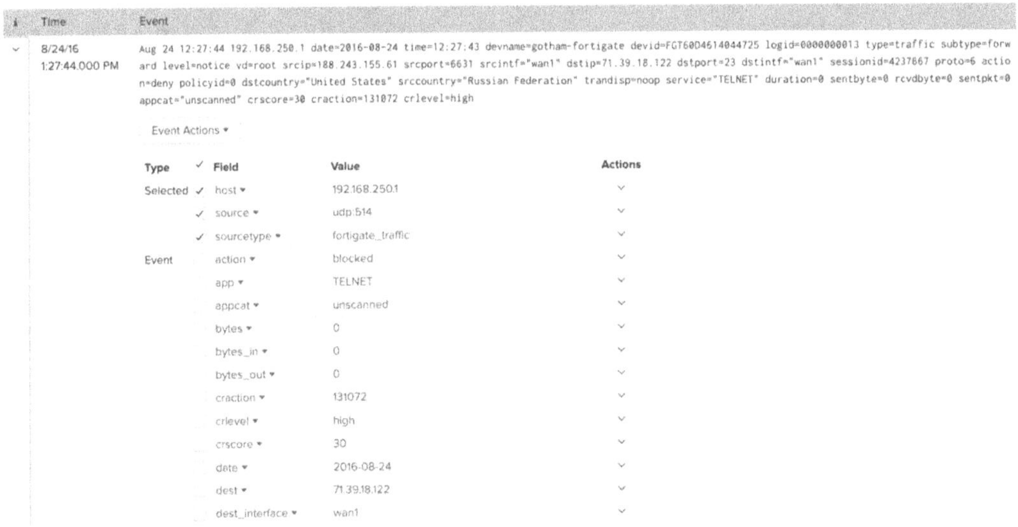

Figure 4.14 – The expanded fields list for a fortigate_traffic event

Note that we can add fields to the selected fields by clicking on a field and using the **Selected** button on the top right of the dialog window. *Figure 4.15* shows this dialog window:

transport   ☒

6 Values, 48.057% of events   Selected | Yes | No |

Reports

Top values   Top values by time   Rare values

Events with this field

Values	Count	%	
tcp	186,441	55.786%	
udp	62,178	18.605%	
UDP	56,422	16.882%	
TCP	29,159	8.725%	
ICMP	4	0.001%	
icmp	2	0%	

Figure 4.15 – Setting the Selected button to Yes to include the transport field in the list of selected fields

Splunk indexes events in multiple formats. *Figure 4.16* shows a **stream:dns** event in **JSON** format:

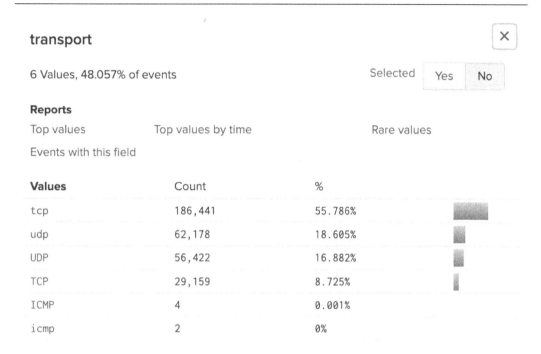

```
>    8/24/16        { [-]
     1:27:43.227 PM    bytes: 50
                       bytes_in: 50
                       bytes_out: 0
                       dest_ip: 8.8.8.8
                       dest_mac: 08:58:0E:93:92:AF
                       dest_port: 53
                       endtime: 2016-08-24T18:27:43.227000Z
                       message_type: [ [+]
                       ]
                       query: [ [+]
                       ]
                       query_type: [ [+]
                       ]
                       src_ip: 192.168.250.40
                       src_mac: 00:0C:29:C6:3B:0F
                       src_port: 53273
                       time_taken: 7
                       timestamp: 2016-08-24T18:27:43.227893Z
                       transaction_id: 29967
                       transport: udp
                     }
                     Show as raw text
                     host = splunk-02    source = stream:dns    sourcetype = stream:dns
```

Figure 4.16 – A stream:dns event in JSON format

Right below the time picker and to the left of the search modes dropdown are a series of buttons that can be used to perform multiple operations:

Figure 4.17 – Miscellaneous utilities

11. **Job**: Splunk refers to the process of executing a search query as a job. The **Job** dropdown allows us to **Edit Job Settings**, **Send Job to Background**, **Inspect Job**, and **Delete Job**. *Figure 4.18* shows the options available in the **Job** dropdown:

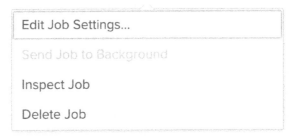

Figure 4.18 – The Job dropdown

The **Edit Job Settings** option allows us to change settings such as *read permission* and the *lifetime* of the job (how long search results will be available after the search runs). Perhaps the most used feature on the **Job** dropdown is **Inspect Job**. This option lets you explore the execution of the search query. The **Inspect Job** window includes information such as the duration of the search and the number of events scanned and returned. It also gives us a link to the **search. log**, which we can peruse to find a use for debugging. The **Inspect Job** window also displays the execution costs of the multiple components in the Splunk queueing process, such as the time it took to execute **command.search.index** or how long it took to dispatch the search to the indexer (dispatch). The **Search job properties** section of the **Inspect Job** window is a breakdown of the search, including metrics such as the normalized and optimized version of the search, the **dispatchState** (whether the search is running, done, and so on), and the **diskUsage**. Overall, the **Inspect Job** window is very useful for debugging and optimizing Splunk searches. *Figure 4.19* shows the first part of the **Inspect Job** window, including the search summary at the top and the execution costs of the search:

Search job inspector

This search has completed and has returned **1,000** results by scanning **74,720** events in **3.942** seconds

(SID: 1659294878.282) search.log

∨ **Execution costs**

Duration (seconds)		Component	Invocations	Input count	Output count
	0.00	command.fields	21	74,720	74,720
	3.46	command.search	21	-	74,720
	0.08	command.search.calcfields	19	74,720	74,720
	0.06	command.search.expand_search	2	-	-
	0.00	command.search.expand_search.calcfield	2	-	-
	0.00	command.search.expand_search.fieldaliaser	2	-	-
	0.00	command.search.expand_search.kv	2	-	-
	0.00	command.search.expand_search.lookup	2	-	-
	0.02	command.search.expand_search.sourcetype	2	-	-
	0.12	command.search.fieldalias	19	74,720	74,720
	0.05	command.search.index	21	-	-
	0.03	command.search.filter	19	-	-
	0.00	command.search.index.usec_1_8	354	-	-
	0.00	command.search.index.usec_512_4096	1	-	-
	0.00	command.search.index.usec_64_512	70	-	-
	0.00	command.search.index.usec_8_64	70	-	-
	1.05	command.search.kv	19	-	-
	0.97	command.search.lookups	19	74,720	74,720
	0.70	command.search.typer	19	74,720	74,720
	0.26	command.search.rawdata	19	-	-
	0.12	command.search.tags	19	74,720	74,720

Figure 4.19 – The Inspect Job window showing the search summary and execution costs

Figure 4.20 shows the **Search job properties** section of the job inspector:

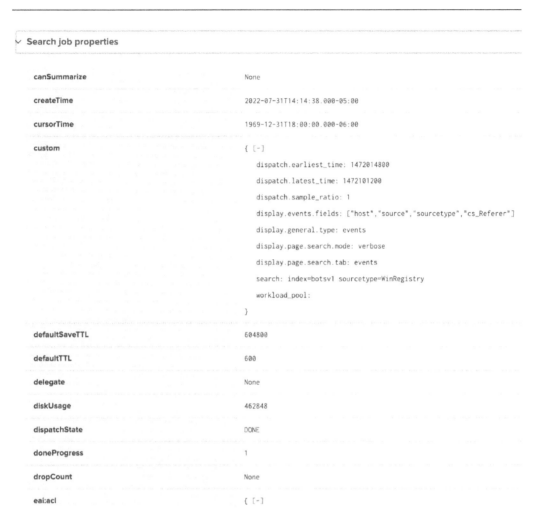

Figure 4.20 – The search job properties section of the Inspect Job window

The other buttons near the **Job** dropdown include the pause and stop buttons, share (right-facing curvy arrow), print (printer), and export (down arrow) buttons. These buttons are self-explanatory.

In this section, we explored the different parts of a search page in Splunk. Now, let's start running Splunk queries!

Dissecting a Splunk query

A Splunk query consists of different clauses separated by the pipe symbol (|), as seen in Unix commands. For example, we can list the files in a folder and search for the inputs.conf filename all at once using the following command on a Unix command line:

```
$ ls -l | grep inputs.conf
-rw-------    1 botsuser     botsuser    123 Jul    9 13:15
inputs.conf
```

The ls -l command lists all the files in the folder. The result of this command is passed to the grep command and tells us whether the inputs.conf file is included in the list.

Let's look at another example. The following command determines whether the Splunk process is running on a Splunk server by running the ps command (left-hand side of the pipe) and performing a grep search (right-hand side):

```
$ ps -ef | grep splunkd
501    4010         1    0    9:36PM
??                0:05.73 splunkd -p 8089 start
```

Now that we've understood the concept of the pipe symbol, let's see how it works in Splunk. We will start with the simplest query. Let's search the botsv1 index. To do so, log in to the search head and type the following in the search bar on the search head:

```
index = botsv1
```

As shown in *Figure 4.21*, this does not give us any results. Why? Let's look at an important factor in Splunk. Events in Splunk are timestamped. As we saw in *Chapter 3, Onboarding and Normalizing Data*, BOTS Dataset v1 covers dates in August 2016. What is the default setting on the time picker? The time picker allows you to specify what period is being searched. As *Figure 4.21* shows, the default setting is set to **Last 24 hours**:

Figure 4.21 – Results from the index=botsv1 query

We can ensure that we get results by adjusting our search in two ways:

- Adjusting the time picker to include only dates in *August 2016* (see *Figure 4.22*).

- Using the `earliest=0` condition to search across the entire timespan of the index. *Figure 4.22* shows the time picker with the dates **08/01/2016** to **08/31/2016** selected:

Figure 4.22 – Adjusting the time picker to include only August 2016

Figure 4.23 shows the use of the `earliest=0` command:

Figure 4.23 – Using the earliest keyword

The alternative to using the time picker on the search bar is to specify the time range using the **earliest** and **latest** keywords. As the name implies, the earliest keyword allows us to specify the beginning of the time range for the search. For example, we can use the following command if we want to retrieve all the data in the botsv1 index:

```
index=botsv1 earliest=0
```

The earliest keyword takes several arguments, as seen in the following syntax:

```
earliest=[+|-]<time_integer><time_unit>@<time_unit>
```

Let's look at a few scenarios.

We want to retrieve all the events in the botsv1 index within the last 4 hours:

```
index=botsv1 earliest=-4h
```

We want to retrieve all the events in the botsv1 index for the last day but only include events from the very start of the day. We can use the @ symbol to indicate that we want to snap the results to the beginning of the day. For example, the following search would give us all the events going back to the start of the fifth day:

```
index=botsv1 earliest=-5d@d
```

We can also specify custom dates. For example, we can return the events that occurred since *January 15, 2006, at 4:56 P.M.* using the following command:

```
index=botsv1 earliest="01/15/2006:16:56:00"
```

Consequently, the latest keyword does the opposite. It gives an end date for the date range. So, for example, the following query will search for all the events between *January 15, 2006, at 4:56 P.M.* and *January 27, 2006, at 11 P.M.*:

```
index=botsv1 earliest="01/15/2006:16:56:00"
latest="01/27/2006:23:00:00"
```

Note that this is the equivalent of using the **Date & Time Range** menu on the time picker.

There are many other possibilities for using the earliest and latest keywords that extend beyond the scope of this book. You should review the **Time Modifiers** page (https://splk.it/3JzdKx0) in the Splunk docs for further use.

Let's add some complexity to our simple Splunk query. Suppose we wanted to only search the data in the IIS logs. In *Chapter 3, Onboarding and Normalizing Data*, we saw that IIS logs are stored in a sourcetype called iis. We can amend our query to include only those logs, as seen in the following code block:

```
index=botsv1 earliest=0 sourcetype=iis
```

Now, suppose we are only interested in the IIS logs from a specific client ("23.22.63.114"). We can use the following query:

```
index=botsv1 earliest=0 sourcetype=iis c_ip="23.22.63.114"
```

We can also use common mathematical symbols such as greater than (>) and less than (<) to filter out data. For example, the following query retrieves all successful web events (`status>200`) in the IIS logs:

```
index=botsv1 earliest=0 sourcetype=iis c_ip="23.22.63.114" sc_
status>200
```

We can also use wildcard characters in queries to widen search results. For example, the following query will give us all the events from the `23.22.63.114` client, where the user visited the `index.php` page:

```
index=botsv1 earliest=0 sourcetype=iis c_ip="23.22.63.114" cs_
uri_stem=*index.php
```

This search would also include any php file that ends with `index.php`, including `a_index.php`, `iis_index.php`, `www.test.com/index.php`, and `www.test1.test2.com/test_index.php`.

Sometimes, we want to exclude events. For example, we want to exclude all events with a user agent of `"Python-urllib/2.7"`:

```
index=botsv1 earliest=0 sourcetype=iis NOT cs_User_
Agent="Python-urllib/2.7"
```

Alternatively, we could use the exclamation mark (`!=`) to negate this user agent in the following search query:

```
index=botsv1 earliest=0 sourcetype=iis cs_User_Agent!="Python-
urllib/2.7"
```

Several of the search queries we've covered so far use multiple filters. Multiple filters are combined with an implied AND operator. For example, Splunk interprets the previous query as follows:

```
index=botsv1 AND earliest=0 AND sourcetype=iis AND cs_User_
Agent!="Python-urllib/2.7"
```

So, what should we use if we want to write a condition that requires only one of the conditions to match? For example, suppose we want to see all logs from ip 23.22.63.114 and 52.23.25.56. We would use the OR operator, as follows:

```
index=botsv1 earliest=0 sourcetype=iis c_ip="23.22.63.114" OR
c_ip="52.23.25.56"
```

It's important to note that, just like the AND operator, the search command is implied at the beginning of every search. So, Splunk interprets the previous search as follows:

```
search index=botsv1 earliest=0 sourcetype=iis c_
ip="23.22.63.114" OR c_ip="52.23.25.56"
```

We do not need to include the search command at the beginning of a search. However, there will be instances where you have transformed the data further down in the search query and then apply the search command to the transformed data, like so:

```
index=botsv1 earliest=0 sourcetype=iis c_ip="23.22.63.114" OR
c_ip="52.23.25.56"
| <transforming commands>
| search...
```

All of the search queries we have written so far have used key/pair filters such as c_ip="23.22.63.114"; however, we can search raw Splunk events (_raw) by specifying search terms. For example, the following example finds any events in the IIS logs that are login events (containing the word login):

```
index=botsv1 earliest=0 sourcetype=iis login
```

However, you should use quotation marks if the search term contains more than one word. For example, if we wanted to find all logs in the Fortigate data where there is traffic to/from "Russian Federation", we would use the following query:

```
index=botsv1 earliest=0 sourcetype=fortigate_traffic "Russian
Federation"
```

Now that we have written some simple search queries and explored how to write basic filters, let's use the pipe symbol to add clauses to format and transform the data.

Formatting and transforming data

In this section, we will look at some commands that can be added to the basic queries that we wrote in the previous section. To use these commands, we can add a pipe symbol and follow it with the new command.

The first command we will look at is the `eval` command. The `eval` command is one of the most important formatting commands in Splunk. This command allows us to perform calculations and either change the value of fields or create new fields. The form of the `eval` command is as follows:

```
... | eval <field>=<expression>, [<field>=<expression>]
```

Note that we use the *pipe* symbol in this search. The left-hand side of the pipe symbol passes results to the `eval` statement. If the field specified in `eval` exists, then the value of the field is replaced. If not, Splunk creates a new field. Note that this new field is not persistent – that is, it only exists for the duration of the search. Using `eval` does not change the data as it resides on disk but merely changes the results of the search.

The Splunk documentation (`https://splk.it/3d7llbk`) provides a list of evaluation functions that can be used in the expression part of the statement. We will look at some of these functions in the following subsections.

Simple mathematical functions

Suppose we wanted to determine how many megabytes are in each event in the `stream:tcp` logs. We can use the `eval` function to calculate the number of **Megabytes** (**MB**) by dividing the `bytes` field by `(1024*1024)`. Remember that a kilobyte is `1024` bytes and a megabyte is `1024` kilobytes. We can use the following search to calculate the result:

```
index=botsv1 sourcetype="stream:tcp"
| eval MB = bytes/(1024*1024)
```

Look at the **INTERESTING FIELDS** area on the left-hand side of the page for the new **MB** field. *Figure 4.24* shows the **MB** field after the search has been executed:

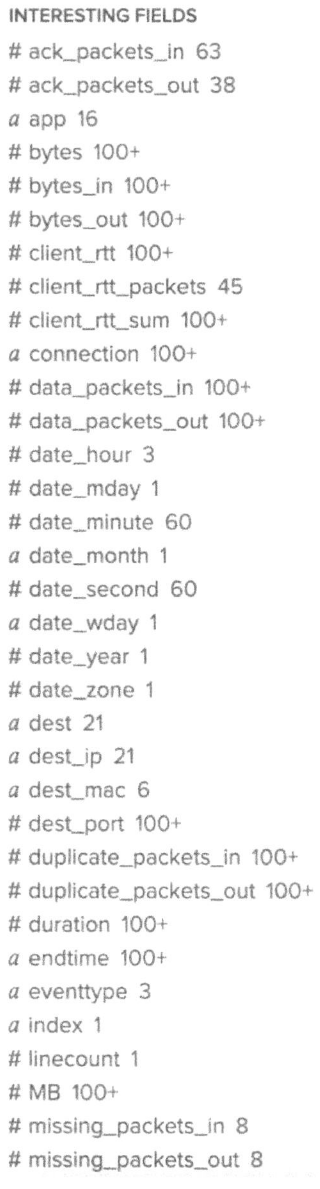

INTERESTING FIELDS

\# ack_packets_in 63

\# ack_packets_out 38

a app 16

\# bytes 100+

\# bytes_in 100+

\# bytes_out 100+

\# client_rtt 100+

\# client_rtt_packets 45

\# client_rtt_sum 100+

a connection 100+

\# data_packets_in 100+

\# data_packets_out 100+

\# date_hour 3

\# date_mday 1

\# date_minute 60

a date_month 1

\# date_second 60

a date_wday 1

\# date_year 1

\# date_zone 1

a dest 21

a dest_ip 21

a dest_mac 6

\# dest_port 100+

\# duplicate_packets_in 100+

\# duplicate_packets_out 100+

\# duration 100+

a endtime 100+

a eventtype 3

a index 1

\# linecount 1

\# MB 100+

\# missing_packets_in 8

\# missing_packets_out 8

Figure 4.24 – The new MB field in the list of interesting fields

Now, let's add some complexity to the previous example using a few Splunk functions.

The round(X, Y) function is used to perform the mathematical round function on numerical values. Let's observe how this function works by adding it to the previous example. Click on the new **MB** field we just generated. *Figure 4.25* shows the output:

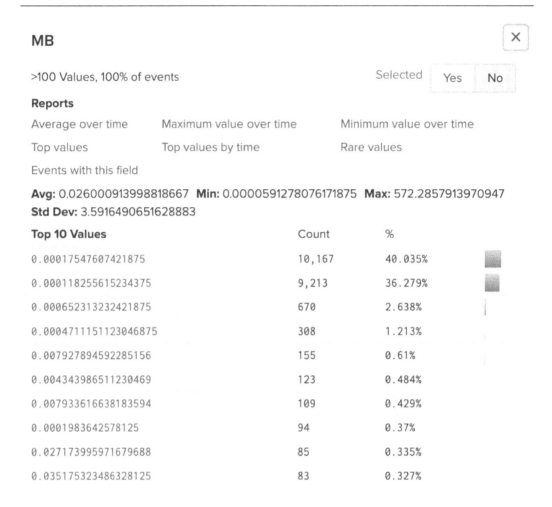

Figure 4.25 – The MB field values

Those are very long decimal numbers! Let's round the result to two digits using the following Splunk query:

```
index=botsv1 sourcetype="stream:tcp"
| eval MB = bytes/(1024*1024)
| eval MB = round(MB,2)
```

Figure 4.26 shows the results of the **MB** field after we round the values to two decimal places:

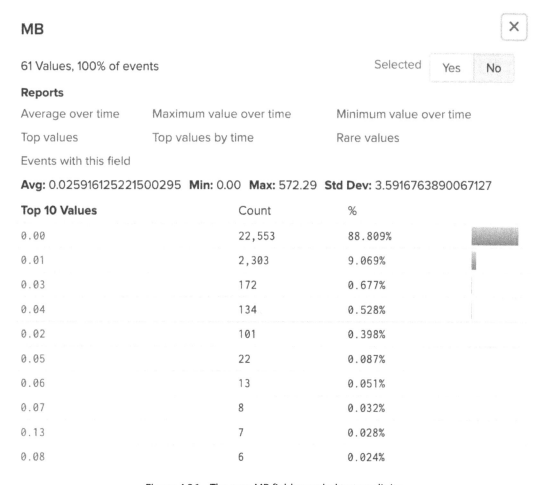

Figure 4.26 – The new MB field rounded to two digits

The `eval` function can also be used with non-numeric fields. Let's look at the next command, which can be used to change the case of a string field.

The `lower()` and `upper()` functions can be used to convert a string into uppercase and lowercase, respectively. Let's look at logon events in the Windows event logs using the following Splunk query:

```
index=botsv1 sourcetype=wineventlog EventCode=4624
```

Figure 4.27 shows the **Account_Name** field in the results:

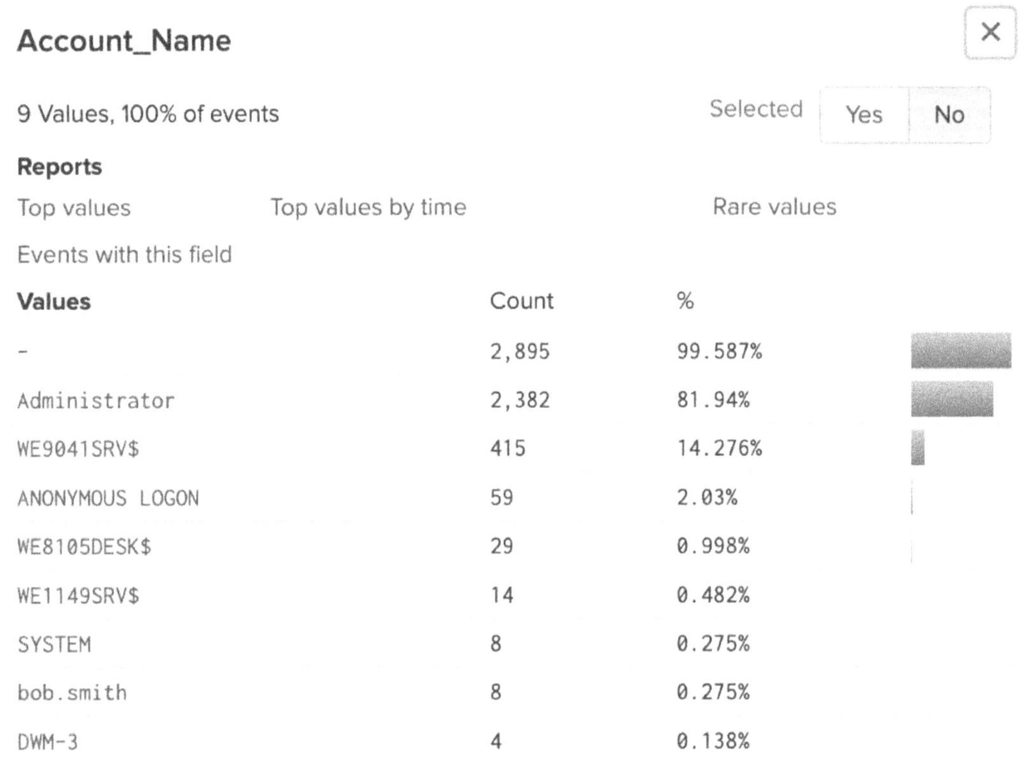

Account_Name   ✕

9 Values, 100% of events   Selected   Yes   No

Reports

Top values   Top values by time   Rare values

Events with this field

Values	Count	%	
–	2,895	99.587%	
Administrator	2,382	81.94%	
WE9041SRV$	415	14.276%	
ANONYMOUS LOGON	59	2.03%	
WE8105DESK$	29	0.998%	
WE1149SRV$	14	0.482%	
SYSTEM	8	0.275%	
bob.smith	8	0.275%	
DWM-3	4	0.138%	

Figure 4.27 – The Account_Name field for logon events in the Windows event logs

We can see that some of the **Account_Name** values are in uppercase, and some are in lowercase. This could make it difficult to make certain comparisons. Let's convert all the Account_Name values into uppercase using the following Splunk query:

```
index=botsv1 sourcetype=wineventlog EventCode=4624
| eval Account_Name = upper(Account_Name)
```

Note that in this example, we are overwriting the values in the Account_Name field. Again, this action is not persistent – that is, it does not change the way the values are stored on disk. *Figure 4.28* shows the values of **Account_Name** after we convert it into uppercase:

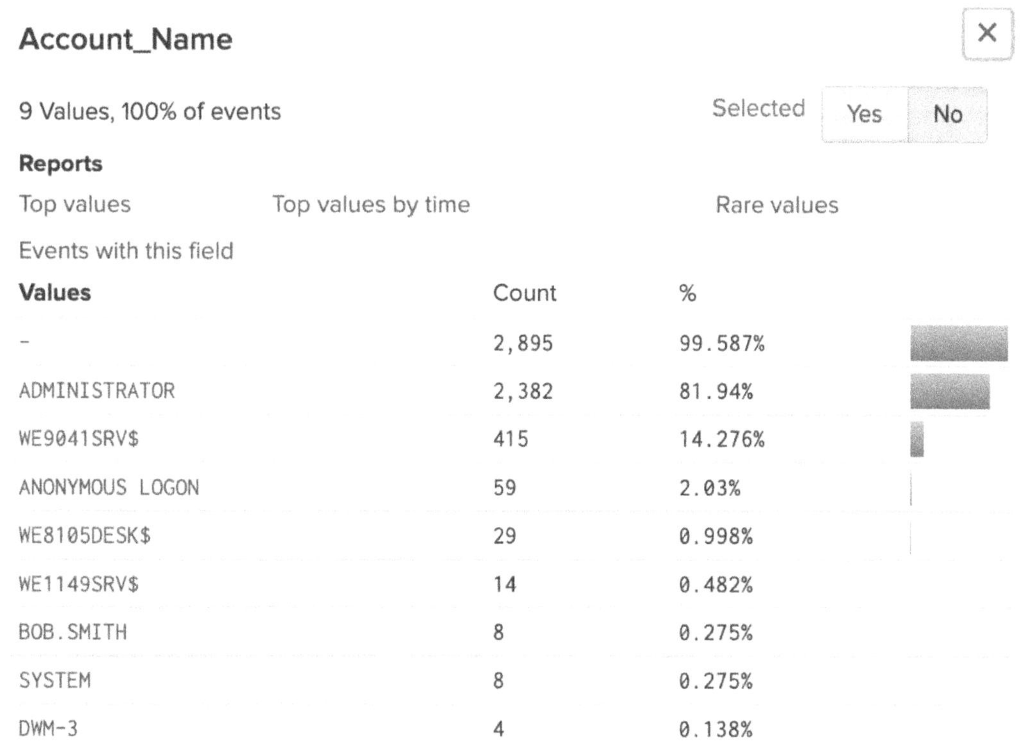

Account_Name

9 Values, 100% of events

Selected   Yes   No

Reports

Top values   Top values by time   Rare values

Events with this field

Values	Count	%	
–	2,895	99.587%	
ADMINISTRATOR	2,382	81.94%	
WE9041SRV$	415	14.276%	
ANONYMOUS LOGON	59	2.03%	
WE8105DESK$	29	0.998%	
WE1149SRV$	14	0.482%	
BOB.SMITH	8	0.275%	
SYSTEM	8	0.275%	
DWM-3	4	0.138%	

Figure 4.28 – Account_Name after being converted into uppercase

What if we wanted to know the length of a field? We can use the `len()` function, as shown in the following Splunk query, which calculates the length of the DNS queries in the `stream:dns` logs:

```
index=botsv1 sourcetype="stream:dns" "query_type{}"=A
| eval queryLen = len(query)
```

The `if` statement is a common construct in programming. It is also very useful in Splunk. We specify a condition in the first part of the `if` statement. If the condition evaluates to true, the field is set to X; otherwise, it is set to Y. Suppose we wanted to see the amount of traffic to non-US destinations. Run the following Splunk query to see all the destination countries in the `fortigate_traffic` logs:

```
index=botsv1 sourcetype=fortigate_traffic
```

Figure 4.28 shows the destination countries in the `fortigate_traffic` logs:

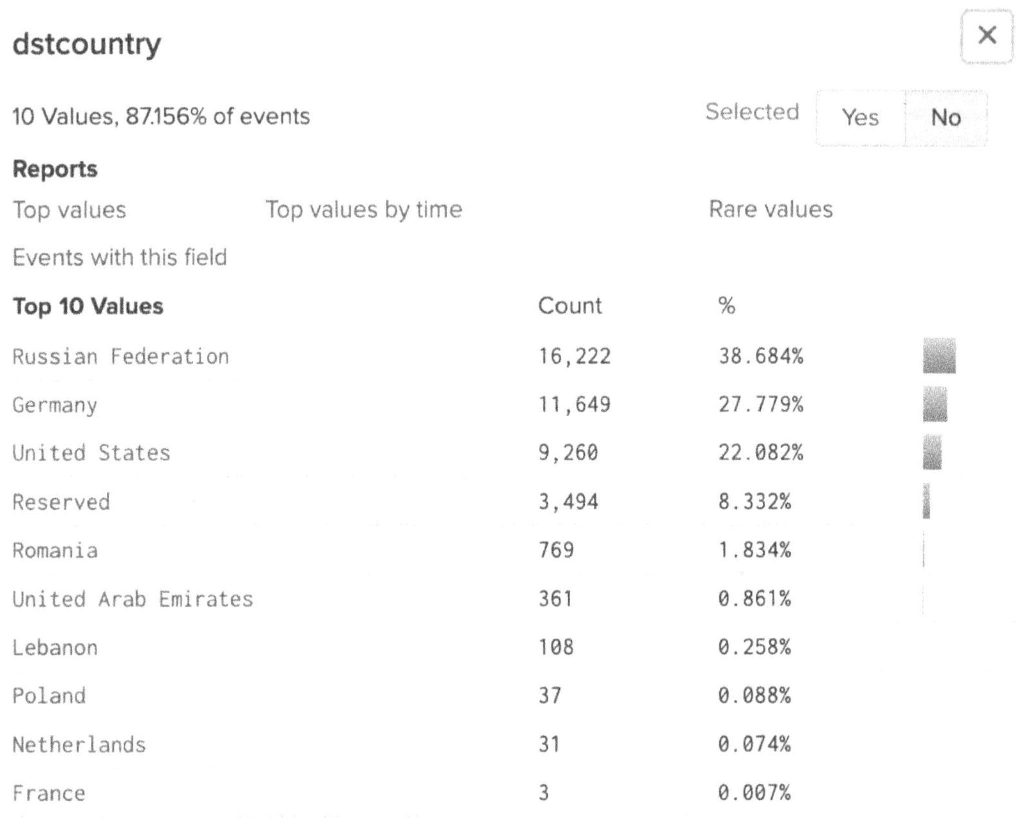

dstcountry   ✕

10 Values, 87.156% of events   Selected   Yes   No

Reports

Top values   Top values by time   Rare values

Events with this field

Top 10 Values	Count	%	
Russian Federation	16,222	38.684%	
Germany	11,649	27.779%	
United States	9,260	22.082%	
Reserved	3,494	8.332%	
Romania	769	1.834%	
United Arab Emirates	361	0.861%	
Lebanon	108	0.258%	
Poland	37	0.088%	
Netherlands	31	0.074%	
France	3	0.007%	

Figure 4.29 – The destination countries in the fortigate_traffic logs

There are several destination countries, so let's add a new clause to the query to set the label of non-US countries to "International":

```
index=botsv1 sourcetype=fortigate_traffic
| eval dstcountry = if(dstcountry="United States", "United
States", "International")
```

We use the if statement to compare the dstcountry field. If the value of the field is "United States", then we set the destination field to "United States". If not, then we set the destination field to "International". *Figure 4.30* shows the output after the if statement is executed:

dstcountry   ✕

2 Values, 100% of events   Selected   Yes   No

Reports

Top values   Top values by time   Rare values

Events with this field

Values	Count	%	
International	38,854	80.754%	
United States	9,260	19.246%	

Figure 4.30 – dstcountry after the if statement is executed

The `case` statement is another interesting construct that allows us to calculate fields based on the values of other fields. Suppose we wanted to categorize traffic events based on the number of bytes. If the number of bytes in an event is less than 500, we label it as **Small**. If the number of bytes is less than 5,000, we label it as **Medium**. If the bytes field contains a value greater than or equal to 5,000, we label it as **Large**. Note that we are including a default condition (`1=1`), which assigns the label to **Unknown**:

```
index=botsv1 sourcetype=stream:tcp
| eval byte_size = case(bytes < 500, "Small", bytes < 5000,
"Medium", bytes >= 5000, "Large", 1=1, "Unknown")
```

Figure 4.31 shows the resulting **byte_size** field:

byte_size   ✕

3 Values, 100% of events   Selected   Yes   No

Reports

Top values   Top values by time   Rare values

Events with this field

Values	Count	%	
Small	19,878	78.275%	
Large	2,862	11.27%	
Medium	2,655	10.455%	

Figure 4.31 – The byte_size field labels a traffic event as Small, Medium, or Large

Splunk timestamps are stored in epoch time. By default, displaying the datetime in a search will return the datetime in the standard format of **2016-08-24T13:27:43.000-05:00**. However, sometimes, we want to display the datetime in a special format or we want to extract only a specific component of the datetime such as the year, month, day, hour, min, or second. For example, we want to extract only the month from the date **2016-08-24T13:27:43.000-05:00**. We can use `strftime()` and `strptime()` to work with datetime fields. For example, if we wanted to display only the month and day from the current datetime, we can use the following command:

```
index=botsv1 sourcetype=suricata
| eval month_day=strftime(_time, "%m/%d")
```

This will extract only the month and day from `_time` for each event and assign it to a field called month_day in the format MM/DD. For example, the `2016-08-24T13:27:43.000-05:00` datetime will be displayed as **08/24**.

The `eval` command is a very powerful command for formatting data and creating new fields. However, there are other powerful commands that we can use in Splunk.

The `fields()` command allows us to return only certain fields from the search query. This allows us to focus only on those fields and reduces search time. For example, the following Splunk query will return only the `_time`, `c_ip`, and `s_ip` fields from the IIS logs:

```
index=botsv1 sourcetype=iis
| fields _time, c_ip, s_ip
```

Figure 4.32 shows the fields that are displayed:

INTERESTING FIELDS

a c_ip 1

a s_ip 1

Figure 4.32 – The fields command only returns the fields specified

A regular expression (**regex**) is a sequence of characters that can be used to specify a search pattern in text. The Splunk `regex` command is a powerful tool when searching through Splunk logs. This first example returns all the `wineventlog` events that do not include a computer account identified by an `Account_Name` that ends with a dollar sign (`$`). Note that this could be achieved using a wildcard character (`*`) as well:

```
index=botsv1 sourcetype=wineventlog
| regex Account_Name!="\w+\$"
```

The following example looks at the site field of the `stream:http` logs and only returns the events where the site is an `ip` address. The pattern consists of a set of four sets of integers (`\d+`) separated by a period (`\.`):

```
index=botsv1 sourcetype=stream:http
| regex site="\d+\.\d+\.\d+\.\d+"
```

As we saw in the *Field extractions* section in *Chapter 3, Onboarding and Normalizing Data*, the Splunk `rex` function uses the concept of regular expressions to extract parts of a string. For example, we extracted the domain from a URL using the following Splunk query:

```
index=botsv1 earliest=0 sourcetype=iis cs_Referer=*
| rex field=cs_Referer http://(?<referer_domain>(\w+\.\w+|\
d+\.\d+\.\d+\.\d+))\/
```

Figure 4.33 shows the newly extracted `referer_domain` field:

referer_domain

2 Values, 3.898% of events

Selected Yes No

Reports

Top values   Top values by time   Rare values

Events with this field

Values	Count	%	
imreallynotbatman.com	375	78.782%	
71.39.18.126	101	21.218%	

Figure 4.33 – The extracted referer_domain field using the rex command

In this section, we covered commands such as `eval`, `fields`, `regex`, and `rex`. The `eval` command can be used with multiple functions to perform tasks such as modifying time, performing calculations, and making decisions using `if()` and `case()` statements. These are only a few uses of the `eval` command. You are encouraged to review the Splunk documentation for further uses of the commands discussed in this section.

Summary

We focused on writing Splunk queries in this chapter. Before looking at the queries, we explored the Splunk search interface in the **Search and Reporting** app. We looked at seven different parts of the search interface, including the search bar, interesting fields, and time picker. We wrote simple filters using key/value conditions, including specifying the index and sourcetype in the `index=botsv1 sourcetype=iis` query. We also learned how we can increase the complexity of our queries using the pipe symbol. We then used this knowledge to get more out of our searches by using the pipe symbol and introducing commands such as `eval`, `fields`, `regex`, and `rex`. The `eval` command can be used with a variety of Splunk functions, including `round()` and `lower()`, which work on numerical and string values, respectively. Commands such as `rex` can be used to extract values from Splunk events using regular expressions.

We will explore more advanced reporting commands in *Chapter 5, Reporting Commands, Lookups, and Macros*.

## 5

Reporting Commands, Lookups, and Macros

We introduced SPL in *Chapter 4*, *Introduction to SPL*, by looking at the structure of basic Splunk searches. We also looked at a few commands, such as `eval` and `fields`. These commands are called *streaming* commands and are performed on each event returned from a search. However, the power of Splunk comes from the variety of available commands. In this chapter, we will look at other types of commands, including other streaming, generating, transforming, orchestrating, and dataset processing commands. This chapter is not a replacement for the Splunk documentation. We will not explore all the commands in detail; instead, we will introduce a selection of commonly used commands in the form of examples. However, by the end of this chapter, we will have covered sufficient Splunk commands to fully appreciate Splunk.

In this chapter, we will cover the following topics:

- Exploring more Splunk commands
- Enhancing logs with lookups
- Simplifying Splunk searches with macros

Exploring more Splunk commands

There are six types of commands in Splunk: distributable streaming, centralized streaming, generating, transforming, orchestrating, and dataset processing commands. In some cases, the way a command functions depends on where it is in the search. We will explore the different types of commands in the following subsections.

Streaming commands

We covered eval, fields, regex, and rex in *Chapter 4, Introduction to SPL*. These commands are streaming commands – that is, they are executed on the results of a search. There are two types of streaming commands:

- **Distributed streaming**: Runs on the indexer or the search head. We will look at the rename command in this section.

- **Centralized streaming**: Runs only on the search head. We will look at the head command in this section.

The rename command is an example of a distributed streaming command. It is used to rename fields. It is very useful for situations where the field names are long or in cases where we want a more professional-looking report. The following is an example of the rename command.

First, let's run the following search:

```
index=botsv1 sourcetype="iis"
| fields _time, c_ip, s_ip, s_port, sc_status
```

Figure 5.1 shows the results of this search. The fields displayed are as specified in the fields command:

Figure 5.1 – Results before running the rename command

Now, let's add the rename command to the search and rerun it:

```
index=botsv1 sourcetype="iis"
| fields _time, c_ip, s_ip, s_port, sc_status
| rename c_ip as src, s_ip as dest, s_port as port, sc_status
as action
```

Figure 5.2 shows the results of this search. Notice that the fields have been renamed in the **Interesting fields** list:

Figure 5.2 – Search results from running the rename command

The head command is an example of a centralized streaming command. The head command returns the first *N* number of events returned from a search. For example, the following search returns only the first 10 iis events returned by the search:

```
index = botsv1 sourcetype="iis"
| head 10
```

Remember that the head command is executed only on the search head after results have been returned from the indexers.

Now, let's look at a different kind of command that generates data.

Generating commands

As the name denotes, generating commands generate data. We will look at the inputlookup, tstats, and makeresults commands in this section. The inputlookup command, for example, generates data from a lookup. We will explore lookups in the *Enhancing logs with lookups* section. The tstats command generates data from indexed fields, which are stored in tsidx files. These fields may come from indexed data or datamodels. Commands such as inputlookup work on lookups (inputlookup) or index-time fields or accelerated datamodels (tstats), so they execute much faster than other types of commands. The makeresults command generates events in memory.

The following code allows us to generate 10 random numbers, and then determine if those numbers are even or odd:

```
| makeresults count=10
| eval random_id = random()
| eval even_or_odd=if(random_id%2==0, "Even", "Odd")
```

We used the `makeresults` command to generate 10 events. The events are all timestamped with the current time that the search executes. It's important to note that generating commands are preceded by a pipe (|) symbol. If we leave the pipe out, Splunk will simply run a search for the phrase *makeresults*. So, we must remember to include the pipe when running generating commands.

The next line generates a random number using the `random()` command. We use the `eval` command to execute this part of the search. We use the `eval` command again on the next line. This time, we are using an `if` statement to determine if the generated random number in each event is even or odd. Note the use of the modulus operator (%), which tells us whether the `random_id` field is divisible by two (even or odd). *Figure 5.3* shows the search results:

Figure 5.3 – Search results of the makeresults search

Now, let's look at a new type of command, called a transforming command.

Transforming commands

We use transforming commands to order the results of the search into a table. Let's look at the `table`, `stats`, `chart`, `timechart`, and `addtotals` commands.

table

The `table` command is probably the simplest transforming command since all we need to do is specify the fields to be displayed. Let's look at a few examples.

The following example displays the client ip (`c_ip`), server ip (`s_ip`), server port (`s_port`), and server status (`sc_status`) from the `iis` logs:

```
index=botsv1 sourcetype="iis"
| table _time, c_ip, s_ip, s_port, sc_status
```

Figure 5.4 shows the results of the search:

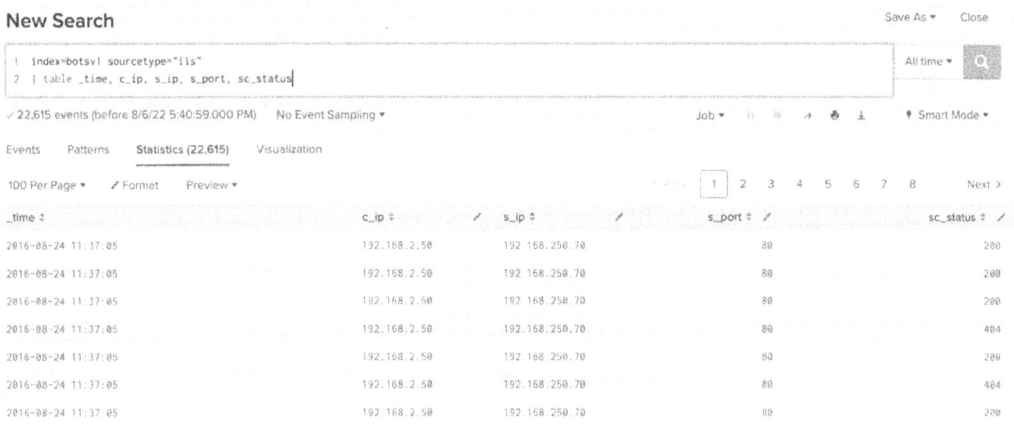

Figure 5.4 – The results of running the table command on the IIS logs

Notice that the results are displayed in the **Statistics** tab. If we wanted to see all the raw events that match, we could change the search mode to **Verbose Mode**, as we learned in *Chapter 4, Introduction to SPL*.

Let's make our next example more interesting. Suppose we discovered that port 23 (TELNET) was left exposed on one of our devices. We need to run a search to determine whether there was any traffic to port 23 on this host. We can use the following search:

```
index=botsv1 sourcetype="fortigate_traffic"
srccountry!="Reserved" dstport=23
| table _time, srcip, srccountry, dstip, dstport, action,
service
```

Here, we are using Splunk filtering to specify that we want the data from the next-generation firewall Fortigate logs. We also specified that we do not want to include any logs where `srccountry` is internal to the network (`Reserved`). Lastly, we indicated that the destination port should be *TELNET port (23)*. *Figure 5.5* shows the results of the search:

Figure 5.5 – Results of the table command showing traffic to port 23

The `table` command allows us to display a set of fields in tabular format. But what if we wanted to add aggregate fields, such as a count of several events or an average number of bytes by country? We will discuss the `stats` command in the next section.

stats

The `table` command works great when we want to get all the events that match our criteria. However, sometimes, we may want to generate aggregate data. For example, instead of returning all the TELNET traffic to our destination in the previous example, we can modify our search to only give us a count of events using the following search:

```
index=botsv1 sourcetype="fortigate_traffic"
srccountry!="Reserved" dstport=23
| stats count
```

The `stats` command aggregates all the events and gives us the count. *Figure 5.6* shows the result of this search:

Figure 5.6 – Using stats to get the number of events

The result is a single number. Again, the result shows up in the **Statistics** tab. The `stats` command works with other aggregate functions such as `distinct_count()` or `dc()`, `sum()`, `avg()`, `min()`, `max()`, and many others. The following example determines the number of distinct countries that sent traffic to the TELNET port from our previous example:

```
index=botsv1 sourcetype="fortigate_traffic"
srccountry!="Reserved" dstport=23
| stats dc(srccountry) as "Distinct Countries"
```

This search uses the `dc()` function, as well as the `as` keyword. The `as` keyword renames the result of `dc(srccountry)` to **"Distinct Countries"**. *Figure 5.7* shows the results of the search:

Figure 5.7 – Using the dc() function with the stats command

We can use multiple functions with the `stats` command. For example, we can display the count, maximum, minimum, and average number of bytes sent from `src_ip=40.80.148.42` using the following search:

```
index=botsv1 sourcetype="fortigate_traffic"
srccountry!="Reserved" src_ip=40.80.148.42
| stats count max(bytes) as max_bytes, min(bytes) as min_bytes,
avg(bytes) as avg_bytes
| eval avg_bytes= round(avg_bytes,2)
```

The search also renames the aggregate values using the `as` keyword. We are also using the `eval` command and the `round()` function to round the `avg_bytes` field to the nearest two decimal places. *Figure 5.8* shows the results of this search:

Figure 5.8 – Displaying the count, maximum, minimum, and average bytes for srcip=40.80.148.42

So far, we have aggregated field values over the entire set of filtered data. The `by` keyword is used to group the data by specified fields. For example, the following search displays the total number of `fortigate_traffic` events from each country:

```
index=botsv1 sourcetype=fortigate_traffic
| stats count by srccountry
```

Figure 5.9 shows the result of this search:

Figure 5.9 – The number of events per country when using the by keyword

We can use the by keyword to group by multiple fields. For example, we can display the number of times that bob.smith has logged on to devices using the following search:

```
index=botsv1 sourcetype=win* EventCode=4624 Account_Name="bob.
smith"
| stats count by user, host
```

Figure 5.10 shows the results of this search:

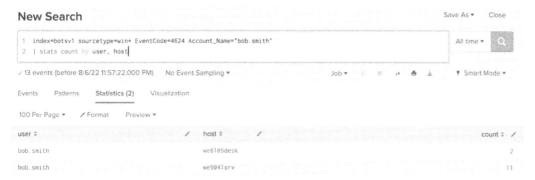

Figure 5.10 – Grouping by multiple fields

In addition to the aggregate functions we have looked at so far, the stats command can be used with the list() and values() functions, which allow you to display multivalue field results. *Table 5.1* compares the list() and values() functions:

	list()	values()
Number of values	A default limit of 100 values	No default limit
Uniqueness	Not distinct	Distinct
Order of results	Order of input events	Lexicographical order

Table 5.1 – Comparison of the list() and values() functions

The following examples illustrate how the list() and values() functions can be used. The first example displays all the users who have logged into a Windows device on the network. To retrieve these values, we can use the Event ID property for a successful login (4624) and the Windows sourcetype (wineventlog). We are also using the as keyword to rename the Account_Name field. Let's run this search using the list() function:

```
index=botsv1 sourcetype=wineventlog EventCode=4624
| stats list(Account_Name) as users
```

Figure 5.11 shows the results from this search:

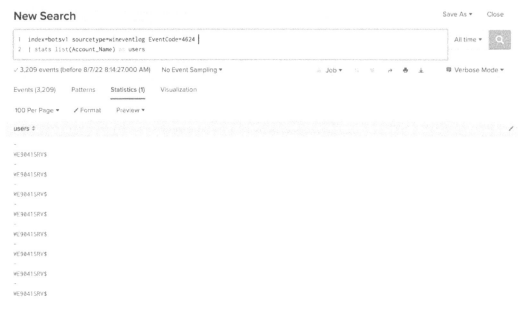

Figure 5.11 – Example of the list() function

The list () function does not return distinct values, so this search returns 100 users. Unfortunately, this would not be helpful in an investigation since it does not return all the successful logons on the network. In the following example, we are replacing the list () function with the values () function and a much better result:

```
index=botsv1 sourcetype=wineventlog EventCode=4624
| stats values(Account_Name) as users
```

Figure 5.12 shows the output of this search:

Figure 5.12 – Using the values() function to display distinct users

This result shows us all the users with successful logons. The results are distinct. As a side note, we can use a function called `mvcount()` to count how many results are in a multivalue result. Alternatively, we could use a `stats distinct_count()` function as well. The following code block shows the use of the `mvcount()` function:

```
index=botsv1 sourcetype=wineventlog EventCode=4624
| stats values(Account_Name) as users
| eval c=mvcount(users)
```

Figure 5.13 shows the result:

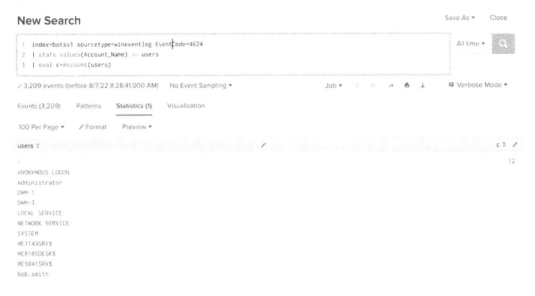

Figure 5.13 – Counting the number of users using mvcount()

The following code block rewrites the Splunk search to use the `distinct_count` command:

```
index=botsv1 sourcetype=wineventlog EventCode=4624
| stats dc(Account_Name) as distinct_users, values(Account_
Name) as users
```

Figure 5.14 shows the result:

Figure 5.14 – Counting the number of users using dc()

Additionally, we can group the successful logins by the host using the following search:

```
index=botsv1 sourcetype=wineventlog EventCode=4624
| stats values(Account_Name) as users by host
```

Figure 5.15 shows the result of this search:

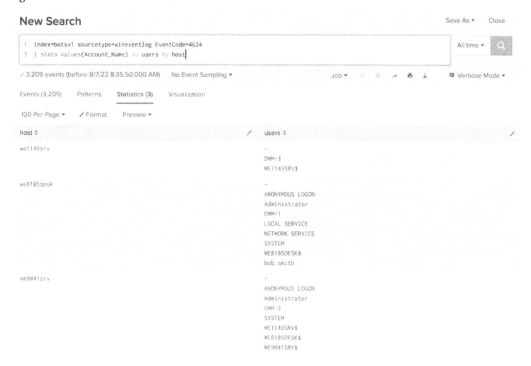

Figure 5.15 – Using the values() function and by keyword to display successful logins by host

The `stats` command can also be used with data order functions such as `first()` and `last()`. For example, suppose we suspect that a host (`71.39.18.122`) has been compromised. We want to determine which was the first `srcip` to connect to that host. We are using the `fortigate_traffic` logs and the `first()` function in the following example:

```
index=botsv1 sourcetype=fortigate_traffic dstip=71.39.18.122
|        stats first(srcip) as first_attack
```

Figure 5.16 shows the result as a single value:

Figure 5.16 – Using the first() function to show the first host to connect to 71.39.18.122

Now that we know that the first attack came from 188.243.155.61, we want to know what time the first encounter was. We can use the earliest() function for this task:

```
index=botsv1 sourcetype=fortigate_traffic dstip=71.39.18.122
src_ip=188.243.155.61
| stats earliest(_time) as first_attack_time
| convert ctime(first_attack_time)
```

The earliest() function works by time order. The stats function in our example returns epoch time. We can use the convert command to convert the time into a more readable format (*mm/dd/ YYYY HH:MM:SS*) using the ctime() function. *Figure 5.17* shows the results of this search:

Figure 5.17 – Using the earliest() function to get earliest(_time)

Here, we used the count keyword to count the number of events. However, there is also a function called count(). Let's look at an example where the stats command is used with the count() function. We will use this function to count events based on whether they meet a condition. Let's make it interesting by using a nested eval command. How does that work? We will tell Splunk to count the number of events based on the value of another field. The following example calculates the ratio of successful (`sc_status=200`) to failed (`sc_status>200`) connections and calculates the ratio of successes to failures:

```
index=botsv1 sourcetype=iis
| stats count(eval(sc_status==200)) as successes count(eval(sc_
status>200)) as failures
| eval ratio=round(successes/failures, 1)
```

Let's dissect this some more. The `count()` function counts all the events from the `iis` sourcetype. However, the nested `eval` means that we can determine if an event was successful or a failure based on the `sc_status` field. So, we would read it as follows:

```
if an iis event has a sc_status = 200:
then successes=successes + 1
else if an iis event has an sc_status > 200:
then failures = failures + 1
```

Note that we use the `as` keyword to rename the results of the `count()` function. Now, we can use the `eval` command and the `round()` function to find the ratio of successes to failures rounded to the nearest decimal.

Figure 5.18 shows that the ratio is 50%:

Figure 5.18 – Using count(eval()) to determine the ratio of successes to failures

Now that we have explored the `stats` command, we will move on to some other interesting commands. Note that these commands are specialized versions of `stats` and can be substituted for each other.

chart

The `chart` command operates with statistical commands such as the `stats` command. However, the output of the `chart` command can be used in various types of charts, such as *column*, *pie*, *line*, and *area* charts.

Our first example uses the `count` function to display the number of failures in the `iis` logs:

```
index=botsv1 sourcetype=iis
| chart count
```

This returns a single value count, as shown in *Figure 5.19*:

Figure 5.19 – Using the chart command to count events

Next, we will write a search to display all the IIS traffic by `sc_status` using the by keyword:

```
index=botsv1 sourcetype=iis
| chart count by sc_status
```

Figure 5.20 shows the results of this search:

Figure 5.20 – Using the chart command with the by keyword

Let's use two fields with the by keyword, as seen in the following example:

```
index=botsv1 sourcetype=iis
| chart count by sc_status, c_ip
```

Figure 5.21 shows the results:

Figure 5.21 – Using multiple fields with the by keyword and chart command

The result is that the data is displayed by sc_status and c_ip, where the rows are sc_status values and the columns are c_ip values. sc_status is referred to as the **<row-split>** field and c_ip is referred to as the **<column-split>** field.

The chart command can also be used with the OVER keyword. The following search gives us the same results as the previous search:

```
index=botsv1 sourcetype=iis
| chart count OVER sc_status by c_ip
```

Figure 5.22 shows the results. Compare it to the results in *Figure 5.21*:

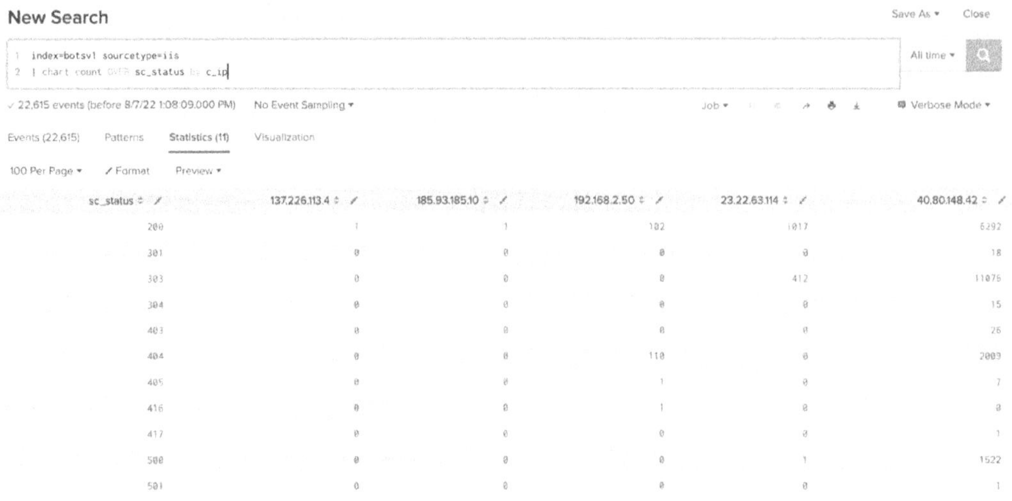

New Search

```
1  index=botsv1 sourcetype=iis
2  | chart count OVER sc_status by c_ip
```

22,615 events (before 8/7/22 1:08 09.000 PM)   No Event Sampling ▾

Events (22,615)   Patterns   Statistics (11)   Visualization

100 Per Page ▾   / Format   Preview ▾

sc_status ≎	137.226.113.4 ≎	185.93.185.10 ≎	192.168.2.50 ≎	23.22.63.114 ≎	40.80.148.42 ≎
200	1	1	102	1017	6292
301	0	0	0	0	18
303	0	0	0	412	11075
304	0	0	0	0	15
401	0	0	0	0	26
404	0	0	110	0	2003
405	0	0	1	0	7
416	0	0	1	0	0
417	0	0	0	0	1
500	0	0	0	1	1522
501	0	0	0	0	1

Figure 5.22 – Using the OVER keyword to group our results by sc_status and c_ip

Using the OVER keyword in this case is purely cosmetic and improves readability. The results are split over the sc_status field (rows) and the c_ip field (columns).

Now, let's look at a different type of chart command that we can use to create a time series chart.

timechart

The timechart command is used to create a time series chart. For example, we can plot the HTTP statuses in our suricata logs over time using the following search:

```
index=botsv1 sourcetype=suricata
| timechart count by status
```

Figure 5.23 shows the results:

Figure 5.23 – Using timechart to create a time series chart of HTTP status codes

What are the OTHER and NULL columns in the results? The timechart command will only return 10 results by default. All the leftover values are pooled into the OTHER column. The NULL column pools every event where the status field is NULL in the raw events. The timechart command has the option of setting useother and usenull to *false*. When useother is set to false, timechart returns only 10 columns. We can adjust this limit by using the limit option. For example, limit=15 returns 10 columns. When usenull=f, the NULL column is not included in the results. The following code block modifies the previous search to set the limit to 15 and removes the NULL column:

```
index=botsv1 sourcetype=suricata
| timechart count by status useother=f limit=15 usenull=f
```

Figure 5.24 shows the results of this search:

Figure 5.24 – Using the timechart command to display status codes over time

Splunk automatically breaks time into bins based on the time duration. Looking at the results, we can see that there were events on *8/10/2016*. What if we wanted to look closer at this period? We can change the default behavior by using the span option. The following example search returns the number of events in the suricata logs broken down into bins of 5-minute intervals. This would make it easier to catch spikes in traffic:

```
index=botsv1 sourcetype=suricata
| timechart count span=5m
```

Figure 5.25 shows how we can narrow down the time period using the time picker:

> Presets

> Relative

> Real-time

> Date Range

∨ Date & Time Range

Between ▾	08/10/2016	16:35:00.000	and	08/10/2016	17:30:00.000
		HH:MM:SS.SSS			HH:MM:SS.SSS

Apply

Figure 5.25 – Time period of interest

Figure 5.26 shows the results of this search:

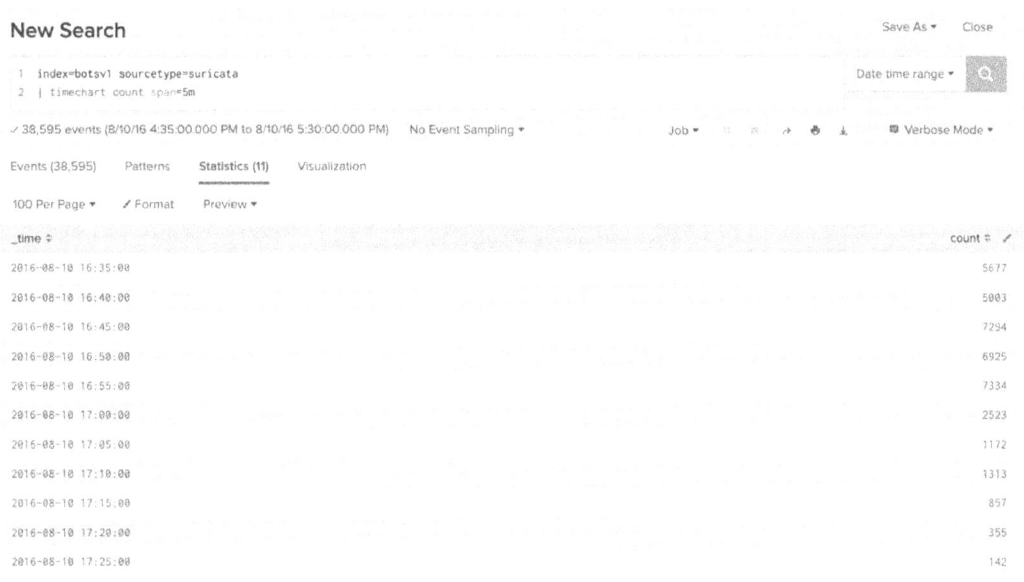

Figure 5.26 – Results of the timechart command with span=5m

Notice that the time is shown in 5-minute intervals.

addtotals

addtotals is used with transforming commands such as stats, chart, and timechart to display the totals for numeric columns and rows. The following search charts Fortigate traffic logs and groups them by dstport and srcip. We are using the addtotals command with additional options to sum the columns and rows:

```
index=botsv1 sourcetype=fortigate_traffic
| chart sum(bytes) OVER dstport by srcip useother=f
| addtotals col=t fieldname="Port Total" labelfield=dstport
label="Host Total"
| fillnull
```

Here, we used the chart command with the sum() function to get the sum of bytes. We displayed them by dstport and srcip. We only want the default 10 column results, so we specified useother=f. Next, we used the addtotals command with the following options:

- col=t: By default, the addtotals command only adds up the rows in the results. Using col=t instructs Splunk to find the sum of the columns as well as rows.

- `fieldname="Port Total"`: By default, the `addtotals` command names the column containing the totals with the `"Total"` label. Using the `fieldname` option instructs Splunk to rename that column to `"Port Total"`.

- `labelfield=dstport`: The `labelfield` tells Splunk where to put the label for the column totals.

- `label="Host Total"`: The `label` field tells Splunk what to label the row containing the column totals.

- `Fillnull`: The `fillnull` column sets any null/empty values to 0.

Figure 5.27 shows the result of this search:

dstport	118.193.22.194	118.193.22.195	118.193.22.196	192.168.250.100	192.168.250.20	192.168.250.40	192.168.250.41	192.168.250.70	23.22.63.114	40.80.148.42	Port Total
53	0	0	0	215	334187	65377	0	0	0	0	399783
80	0	0	0	154825187	0	0	0	21841	8914198	82067863	243029861
123	0	0	0	152	0	0	456	0	0	0	608
137	0	0	0	128410	0	0	0	0	0	0	126410
138	0	0	0	0	0	0	0	0	0	0	0
443	0	0	0	3716861	0	22212	0	0	0	0	3739073
1327	0	0	0	0	0	0	0	578698	0	0	578698
3791	0	0	0	0	0	0	0	1448813	0	0	1448813
6892	0	0	0	1684288	0	0	0	0	0	0	1684288
7783	0	0	0	68874	0	0	0	0	0	0	68874
8000	128	128	5123	0	0	0	0	0	0	1100	6479
8834	0	0	0	0	0	9109147	0	0	0	0	9109147
44445	0	0	0	29479	0	0	0	0	0	0	29479
54513	0	0	0	0	1162	0	0	0	0	0	1162
55556	0	0	0	19330	0	0	0	0	0	0	19330
Host Total	128	128	5123	159673790	335349	9196736	456	2049352	8914198	82068963	260243215

Figure 5.27 – Adding columns to a chart using the addtotals command

We have looked at several transforming commands. However, there are so many more. This section was meant to give you an idea of the possibilities of using transforming commands. You are encouraged to review the Splunk documentation for further commands. We will move on to the last two types of commands in the following sections.

Orchestrating commands

Orchestrating commands do not affect the final search results, but they affect some aspects of the search. For example, you can supplement fields using the `lookup` command. We will look more closely at lookups in the *Enhancing logs with lookups* section. Another example is the `localop` command, which forces subsequent commands to run locally on the search head rather than sending them to the indexers.

Now, let's look at some dataset processing commands.

Dataset processing commands

Dataset processing commands require the complete search results before they can be executed. We will look at dedup, join, and sort in the following sections.

dedup

The following search uses the dedup command to remove any duplicate hosts and actions from the wineventlogs search results:

```
index=botsv1 sourcetype=wineventlog
| table _time, action, host, user
| dedup host, action
```

Remember that the table command will return _time, action, host, and user for all the events in wineventlog sourcetype. Once the search results have been completed, the dedup function goes through them and returns only one row per host and action. *Figure 5.28* shows the results of this search. We can use the arrows next to the action field in the results to sort the action values. This shows that there is one allowed row for each host, one failure row for the host, and so on:

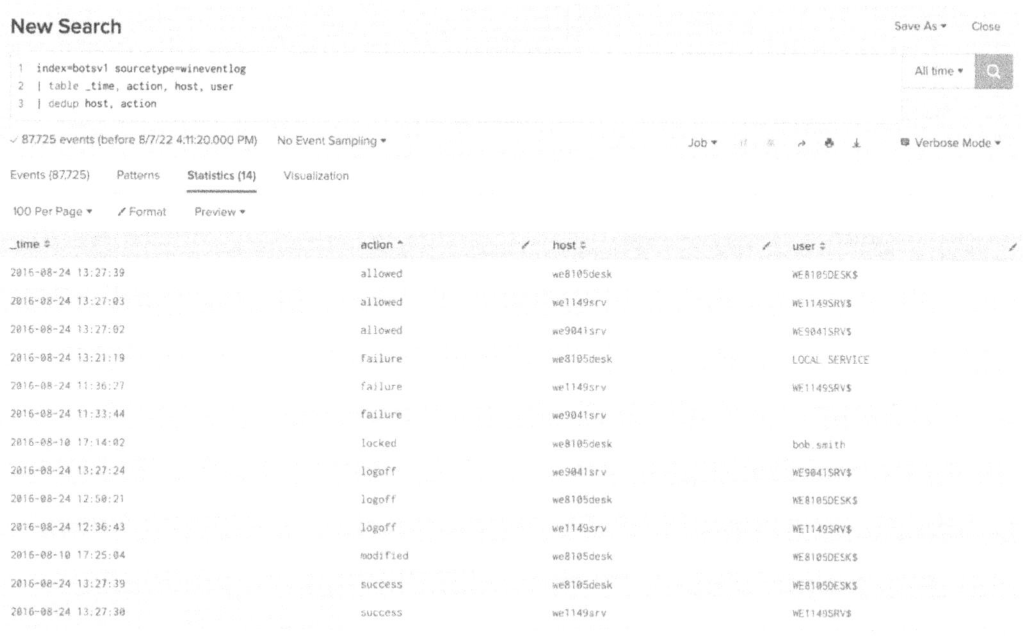

Figure 5.28 – Using dedup to remove duplicate action/host combinations

We will discuss the join command in the next section.

join

The `join` command can be used to combine the results of the main search with the results of a `subsearch`. A **subsearch** is a search that is run as part of another search. `subsearch` is enclosed in square brackets and is executed first. The outer search runs and, like a SQL join, the results from the outer join are crossed with `subsearch`. The following example searches the `stream:tcp` logs and joins them with the Fortigate traffic to retrieve the apps that the host has accessed. We are also introducing the `sort` command here, which is another transforming command. The `sort` command orders the results by the field specified. We sort `_time` in increasing order:

```
index=botsv1 sourcetype=stream:tcp
|        table _time, dest
|        join dest
                [ search index=botsv1 sourcetype=fortigate_
traffic
                |        stats values(app) as firewall_app by
dstip
                |        rename dstip as dest
]
| sort _time
```

Figure 5.29 shows the results of the `join` command:

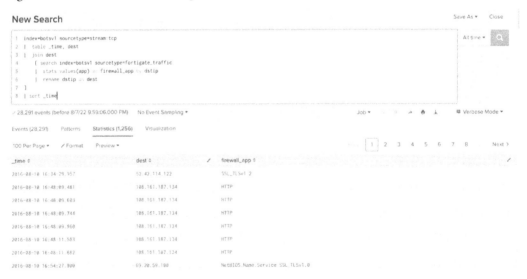

Figure 5.29 – Using the join command to get the app for each host in the stream:tcp logs

We will learn about using lookups to enhance our events in the next section.

Enhancing logs with lookups

Lookups are very useful for enhancing search results. Lookups can be used to add extra clarifying information to search results. For example, we can use a lookup to convert HTTP status codes into user-readable strings. Given a username or ID, we can use a lookup containing additional information such as the user's full name, manager, or department to add context to search results. The username or ID is piped from an earlier part of the search and used as a key to access the additional information in the lookup. In this section, we will explore the use of the `inputlookup` and `lookup` commands. The `inputlookup` command is a generating command. It is usually used with a lookup file that contains **Comma-Separated Values** (**CSV**). The Splunk **Settings** menu contains a link to all the lookups stored in Splunk. The following steps will guide you and show you the lookups available in the Splunk Addon for Microsoft Windows, which we installed in *Chapter 2, Setting Up the Splunk Environment*:

1. Navigate to **Settings** | **Lookups** on the search head (see *Figure 5.30*):

Figure 5.30 – The link to the Lookups menu is the sixth link under the KNOWLEDGE section

2. There are three options in the **Lookups** menu:

    I.   **Lookup table files**: A list of lookup files (. `csv` files).

    II. **Lookup definitions**: A list of lookup definitions. A lookup definition is an alias given to a lookup file so it can be used with the `lookup` command. We will discuss this later in this section.

III.   **Automatic lookups**: A list of automatic lookups. An automatic lookup is programmed to run in the background. For example, the Windows add-on contains automatic lookups that map Windows Event IDs to generate the signature field.

Figure 5.31 shows the different options in the **Lookups** menu:

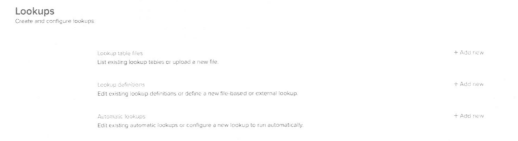

Figure 5.31 – The Lookups menu

3.   Click on the **Lookup table files** option. This shows a list of all lookup table files available on the search head (see *Figure 5.31*). We can change the app context so that we can see lookup table files in only the selected app. We can also use the filter to select only lookup tables **Created in the App** (permissions are set to **App**) or **Visible in the App** (permissions are set to **Global**). Use the filter to select **Splunk Add-on for Microsoft Windows** and select **Created in app**. Do you see a lookup called **windows_signatures_850.csv**? This lookup contains the signatures for each **EventCode** field in the **wineventlog** sourcetypes:

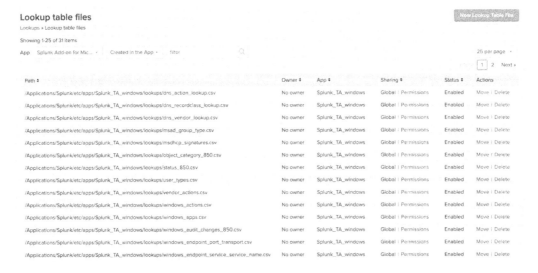

Figure 5.32 – The list of lookups created in the Splunk Add-on for Microsoft Windows

4. Navigate back to the **Search and Reporting** app and type the following in the search bar to see the list of Windows EventCodes:

```
| inputlookup windows_signatures_850.csv
```

5. We can search through a lookup by using the `search` command after a pipe (|). For example, the following searches for `EventCode 624` in the `windows_signatures_850.csv` lookup:

```
| inputlookup windows_signatures_850.csv
| search signature_id = 624
```

Figure 5.33 shows the result of this search:

Figure 5.33 – The lookup entry for signature_id=624 in windows_signatures_850.csv

6. Navigate back to the **Lookups** menu and click on the **Lookup Definitions** link. Select **Splunk Add-on for Windows** in the **App** dropdown and select **Created in the App**. Enter the word *signature* in the text field. This lists all the lookup definitions containing the word *signature*. The table contains the **Name** property of the lookup definition, **Type** (**file** or **kvstore**), **Supported fields** (the header of the lookup), **Lookup file** (the file in the **Lookup Table** menu), and the **Owner**, **App**, **Sharing**, **Status**, and **Action** columns. Do you see the lookup definition for the **windows_signatures_850.csv** lookup table? It is called **windows_signature_lookup** (see *Figure 5.34*):

Figure 5.34 – List of lookup definitions containing the word signature

7. Navigate back to the **Lookups** menu and click on **Automatic Lookups**. Select the **Splunk Add-on for Microsoft Windows** app and **Created in the App** options. Enter *signature* to search for any automatic lookup containing the word *signature*. Do you see the automatic lookup that corresponds to the lookup definition of **windows_signature_lookup**? Several automatic lookups use this lookup definition. *Figure 5.35* lists some of these automatic lookups:

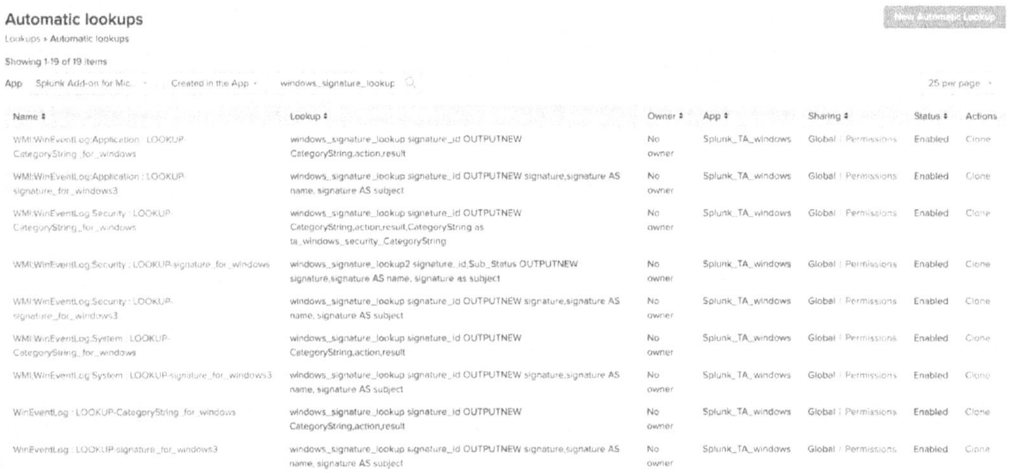

Figure 5.35 – List of automatic lookups that use windows_signature_lookup

Each of these automatic lookups is executed when a search containing the **wineventlog** sourcetype is run.

In addition to the `inputlookup` command, we can run the `lookup` command manually to add extra fields to our data. Using a text editor such as vi or notepad, we can create a `.csv` file containing the locations of each of the devices in our dataset, as shown in *Table 5.2*. We name this file **device_location.csv**:

host	department
we1149srv	Accounting
we8105desk	Sales
we9041srv	Payroll

Table 5.2 – The device_location.csv file containing the locations of each of the devices in our setup

We can use this CSV to create a lookup definition using the following steps:

1. Navigate to the **Settings** | **Lookups** | **Lookup Tables** | **Add New** page.

2. Click the **Choose File** button to upload the **device_location.csv** file to the search head.

3. Enter **device_location.csv** in the **Destination filename** text box (see *Figure 5.36*):

Add new
Lookups » Lookup table files » Add new

Destination app	search
Upload a lookup file	**Choose File** device_location.csv
	Select either a plaintext CSV file, a gzipped CSV file, or a KMZ/KML file. The maximum file size that can be uploaded through the browser is 500MB.
Destination filename *	device_location.csv
	Enter the name this lookup table file will have on the Splunk server. If you are uploading a gzipped CSV file, enter a filename ending in ".gz". If you are uploading a plaintext CSV file, we recommend a filename ending in ".csv". For a KMZ/KML file, we recommend a filename ending in ".kmz"/".kml".

Cancel   Save

Figure 5.36 – Creating a lookup table file

4. Set the permissions of the **device_location.csv** lookup to **Global**.

5. Click **Settings | Lookups | Lookup Definitions | Add New** and enter the name of the new lookup definition as **device_location_lookup** (see *Figure 5.37*):

Add new
Lookups » Lookup definitions » Add new

Destination app	search
Name *	device_location_lookup
Type	File-based
Lookup file *	device_location.csv
	Create and manage lookup table files.
	☐ Configure time-based lookup
	☐ Advanced options

Cancel   Save

Figure 5.37 – Creating the device_location_lookup definition

6. Set **Type** to **File-based** and use the dropdown to select the **device_location.csv** lookup table.

7. Click **Save**.

8. Don't forget to update the permissions for the new **device_location_lookup** definition to **Global**.

   Now, let's test out our new lookup definition.

9. Open the **Search and Reporting** app and enter the following search in the search bar:

```
index=botsv1 sourcetype="wineventlog" user=Administrator
OR user=bob.smith
| lookup device_location_lookup host OUTPUT department
| stats count by host, department, user
```

Figure 5.38 shows the results of the **search** search:

New Search

```
1  index=botsv1 sourcetype="wineventlog" user=Administrator OR user=bob.smith
2  | lookup device_location_lookup host OUTPUT department
3  | stats count by host, department, user
```

✓ 39,297 events (before 8/7/22 8:15:19.000 PM)   No Event Sampling ▾

Events (39,297)   Patterns   Statistics (5)   Visualization

100 Per Page ▾   ✓ Format   Preview ▾

host ⇕	department ⇕	user ⇕	count ⇕
we1149srv	Accounting	Administrator	301
we8105desk	Sales	Administrator	7762
we8105desk	Sales	bob.smith	565
we9041srv	Payroll	Administrator	13699
we9041srv	Payroll	bob.smith	16970

Figure 5.38 – Using the lookup command to add the department field to the search results

In this section, we used lookups to enhance our search results. In the next section, we will explore how we can create macros to simplify searches.

Simplifying Splunk searches with macros

Macros are chunks of SPL that can be inserted into a Splunk search. These chunks do not have to be entire commands. Think of these macros as placeholders for SPL. So far, we have started all our searches with the following key/value pairs referencing the index and sourcetype properties that we intend to search:

```
index=botsv1 sourcetype=<sourcetype_name>
```

Let's create a macro that we can use instead of typing these two key/value pairs every time.

Navigate to **Settings | Advanced Search | Search Macros | Add New** and enter the following values:

- **Destination app**: *search*
- **Name**: *bots_st(1)*

- **Definition**: *index=botsv1 sourcetype=st*

- **Arguments**: *st*

Then, click **Save** (*see Figure 5.39*):

Add new

Advanced search » Search macros » Add new

Destination app   search

Name *   Enter the name of the macro. If the search macro takes an argument, indicate this by appending the number of arguments to the name. For example: mymacro(2)

bots_st(1)

Definition *   Enter the string the search macro expands to when it is referenced in another search. If arguments are included, enclose them in dollar signs. For example: $arg1$

index=botsv1 sourcetype=st

☐ Use eval-based definition?

Arguments   Enter a comma-delimited string of argument names. Argument names may only contain alphanumeric, '_' and '-' characters.

st

Validation Expression   Enter an eval or boolean expression that runs over macro arguments

Validation Error Message   Enter a message to display when the validation expression returns 'false'.

Cancel   Save

Figure 5.39 – Creating a search macro called bots_st(1)

Let's test our new search macro by typing the following in the search bar:

```
`bots_st("wineventlog")` user=Administrator OR user=bob.smith
| lookup device_location_lookup host OUTPUT department
| stats count by host, department, user
```

Here, we surrounded the search macro definition with backticks (`` ` ``) and entered `sourcetype` as an argument. Now, we can use this macro for all the sourcetypes in the `botsv1` index.

Search macros are useful features of Splunk. We will use them in later chapters as we continue with our case study.

Summary

In this chapter, we covered six categories of Splunk search commands. We learned that the streaming commands such as the implicit `search` command and `rename` are executed on the results of a search. We found out that generating commands such as `makeresults`, `tstats`, and `inputlookup` generate data during a search. For example, the `tstats` command generates data from indexed fields stored in `tsidx` files. Transforming commands such as `table`, `stats`, and `chart` change the output of a search. We looked at how we can alter the functions and syntax of some of the commands to change the way the data is displayed. We also learned that orchestrating commands such as `lookup` supplement fields into the search results. Dataset processing commands such as `dedup`, `join`, and `sort` require the complete search results before they can be executed. The `join` command combines search results with the results of a `subsearch`. We also learned how we can enhance Splunk events with lookups by creating lookup tables and definitions. Finally, we looked at how macros can be used to simplify searches.

We will use some of the commands we learned about in this chapter to create tables and charts in *Chapter 6, Creating Tables and Charts Using SPL*.

6

Creating Tables and Charts Using SPL

In this chapter, we will create and format tables and other interesting charts. We will use the logs from the Bots Dataset v1 app to expound on the commands and functions introduced in *Chapter 5, Reporting Commands, Lookups, and Macros*. By the end of this chapter, we will be able to apply these commands to create informative and eye-catching visualizations.

In this chapter, we will explore the following topics:

- Creating and formatting tables
- Creating and formatting charts
- Creating advanced charts

Creating and formatting tables

Up to this point, we have learned various basic commands in Splunk. From this point on, we will use the features of Splunk that we have learned so far to analyze the data in the Bots Dataset v1 app. What are we looking for? We are looking for *indications of a compromise*. Be aware that this is not an extensive analysis of the logs. In fact, we will look at only some of the logs with the goal of understanding the data as well as applying some of the commands that we have covered. You are encouraged to further analyze the logs once you are comfortable with the material.

You are advised that the logs in the Bots Dataset v1 app consist of data from an actual, real-life malicious attack. As a result, you may come across profane language or questionable material in fields such as URLs. We have attempted to ensure that snapshots and other material in this book do not contain anything offensive.

We begin this section by looking at the **Internet Information Services** (IIS) web server logs in the
`iis` sourcetype. Let's examine the fields in this sourcetype:

1. Enter the following Splunk query in the search bar on your search head:

   ```
   index=botsv1 sourcetype=iis
   ```

   Figure 6.1 shows a sample event from this query:

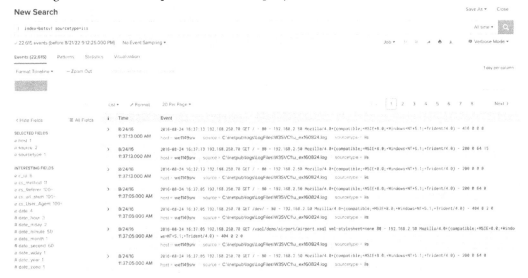

Figure 6.1 – Events in the `iis` sourcetype

2. Next, use the `table` command to display the following fields:

   - `_time`—The time the event occurred

   - `c_ip`—The client host that connects to the web server

   - `s_ip`—The server host running the IIS web server

   - `s_port`—The destination port

   - `cs_uri_stem`—The URI being requested from the server

   - `cs_Referer`—The site that referred the server to this URI

   - `sc_status`—A *200* HTTP status for the request indicates a successful request; *>200*
     means there was a problem

3. The following Splunk query displays the fields:

```
index=botsv1 sourcetype=iis
| table _time, c_ip, s_ip, s_port, cs_uri_stem, cs_
Referer, sc_status
```

Figure 6.2 shows the output of this query:

Figure 6.2 – Output of table command

We used the `table` command to explore some of the important fields in the `iis` sourcetype, including `_time`, `c_ip`, `s_ip`, `s_port`, `cs_uri_stem`, `cs_Referer`, and `sc_status`. At first glance, we see traffic between two internal hosts, `192.168.2.50` and `192.168.250.70`. Note that the IP address for class C falls within the range of `192.168.0.0` – `192.168.255.255`. This means that both hosts (`192.168.2.50` and `192.168.250.70`) are within our network. We see that the traffic is destined for server port (`s_port`) 80, which tells us that it's HTTP traffic. Let us use the arrows next to each field header in the output to order the fields. Toggling the server IP address (`s_ip`) and `s_port` shows that the results only show `s_ip= 192.168.250.70` and `s_port=80`—that is, our server IP address and destination port are always the same. Therefore, those two fields do not contribute any value to our search.

4. To remove these two fields, we simply remove them from the `table` command to give the following query:

```
index=botsv1 sourcetype=iis
| table _time, c_ip, cs_uri_stem, cs_Referer, sc_status
```

We see that there are some successful traffic events (`sc_status=200`) as well as `File Not Found` events (`sc_status=404`).

5. Let's use the formatting features on the table to highlight the unsuccessful traffic (`sc_status>200`) by setting the color of each field to **RED** and setting all successful events to **GREEN**. Click on the paintbrush icon next to the `sc_status` field to display the formatting menu (see *Figure 6.3*):

Figure 6.3 – The results showing the formatting menu

6. Click on **Color** and select **Ranges** in the dropdown. Use the **x** sign next to each range to remove them so that there are only two ranges left, as shown in *Figure 6.4*.

7. Enter the values indicated in *Figure 6.4*. Set the first range to **Green** and the second range to **Red**. Use the **x** sign on the formatting dialog to close the window:

Figure 6.4 – Setting color options for ranges

Look at the `_time` field. The events are not chronological. Toggling the arrow next to the `_time` field allows us to order the events chronologically, as shown in *Figure 6.5*. This could also be done using the `sort` command. However, we are only interested in changing the way the data is displayed, so using the formatting option suffices. However, the changes in the output using the toggle arrows next to the headers are only temporary. Those settings disappear if we refresh the page or rerun the search.

Figure 6.5 shows the results of toggling the arrow so that it is upward facing and displays the `_time` field in ascending order:

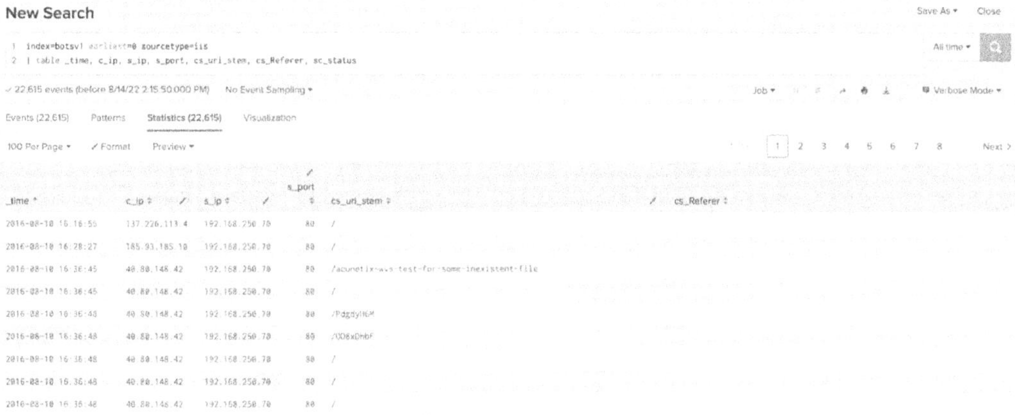

Figure 6.5 – Ordering _time using the arrow

This is interesting! Before we used the arrows to order the logs, we could only see internal class C traffic on the first page of the output. In other words, each event showed data flow between hosts with an IP address that falls in the `192.168.0.0/16` **Classless Inter-Domain Routing (CIDR)** notation. However, using the arrows to order the logs in chronological order, we see that the first three IIS events are coming from external hosts (`137.226.113.4`, `185.93.185.10`, and `40.80.148.42`)—that is, they are not class C IP addresses. What are these hosts? Is this normal traffic? A good cybersecurity analyst would next use an online tool such as viewdns.info to determine the owner of each IP address and to find out which sites are hosted on those servers. We may even use a tool such as VirusTotal to determine whether there is any known malicious activity from the IP addresses in question. In fact, a quick look at viewdns.info shows that this traffic is owned by people or organizations in Germany and Ukraine, respectively. We determine that this is not normal traffic since we should not have traffic to our web server from either of these countries.

In the next section, we use the `timechart` and `chart` commands to observe the behavior of these devices.

Creating and formatting charts

In the previous section, we discovered traffic from some questionable external hosts. We'll now dig deeper into the other log sources to discover more information about this activity.

We will use the highlighted commands in *Table 6.1*:

Chart type	Works great for	Search structure
Line chart	Displaying trends over time	`| timechart count [by comparison_category]`
Area chart	Showing changes in aggregated values over time	`| timechart count [by comparison_category]`
Column chart	Comparing fields or calculated values	`| stats count by comparison_category`
Bar chart	Comparing fields or calculated values	`| stats count by comparison_category`

Single-value chart	Displaying numeric changes in trends. Can also be used to display single values.	`| timechart count`
		
		OR
		
		`| stats count`

Pie chart	Comparing categories	`| stats count by comparison_category`
Scatter chart	Displaying the relationship between discrete values in two dimensions	`| stats x_value_ aggregation y_ value_aggregation by name_category [comparison_category]`
Bubble chart	Displaying the relationship between discrete values in three dimensions	`| stats x_value_ aggregation y_ value_aggregation size_aggregation by name_category [comparison_category]`
Choropleth map	Displaying aggregated values in a geographic region	`| stats count by featureId | geom geo_countries featureIdField=featureId`

Table 6.1 – Highlighted charting options discussed in this section

Remember that we saw concerning traffic from the host with IP address 40.80.148.42. It appears to be generating a lot of traffic to the web server. Which other sourcetypes do we have that can give us insight into this activity? Let us look at the stream:http logs. Follow these steps:

1. Enter the following search query in the search bar:

    ```
    index=botsv1 earliest=0 sourcetype="stream:http" c_
    ip=40.80.148.42
    | timechart count
    ```

2. This query uses the timechart command, which displays a count of events over time. Click on the **Visualization** tab to visualize the data.

    Figure 6.6 shows the menu for choosing Splunk visualization options:

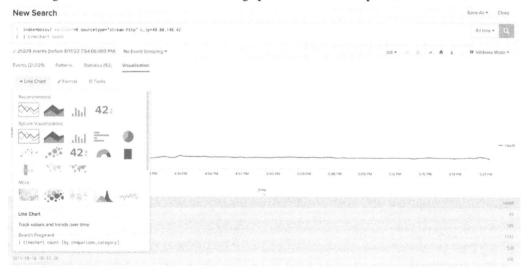

Figure 6.6 – Splunk visualization options menu

3. We cover most of the charting options displayed in the **Splunk Visualizations** section of *Figure 6.6*. The icons displayed include the following (from left to right):

    · **Line chart**

    · **Area chart**

    · **Column chart**

    · **Bar chart**

    · **Pie chart**

    · **Bubble chart**

- Scatter plot chart
- Single-value chart
- Radial gauge
- Filler gauge
- Marker gauge
- Cluster map
- Choropleth map

Figure 6.7 shows the traffic trend for host 40.80.148.42 using a line chart:

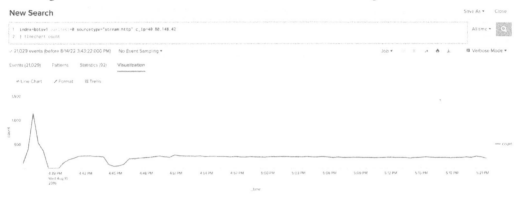

Figure 6.7 – A line chart showing a spike in activity for the 40.80.148.42 IP address

Why is *Figure 6.7* important? What does it tell us? We are looking for a change in behavior for this host. Has there been a spike in the stream:http logs from this host? Is this a host that we've seen before in the logs? We see that *Figure 6.7* shows a spike in traffic at the beginning of the period. *Figure 6.8* shows the same data in the form of an area chart:

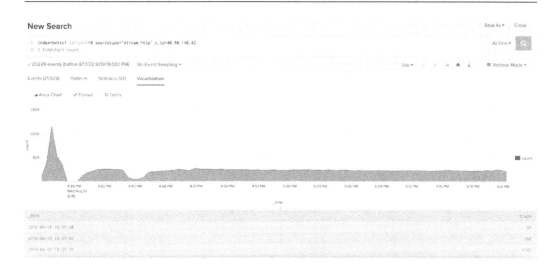

Figure 6.8 – An area chart showing a spike in activity for the 40.80.148.42 IP address

4. Let's dig further into these results. Click on the top of the spike to view the 1,143 events that correspond to the spike. This will initiate a **drilldown action**. By default, clicking on the Splunk visualization allows you to drill down into the raw data. In this case, the drilldown displays the raw events associated with this spike of 1,143 events. What kind of traffic did we see? *Figure 6.9* shows a raw event:

Figure 6.9 – Raw events corresponding to the spike at 8/10/16 4:37:59

We see multiple fields that make up a `stream:http` log in the event. Look at the `accept` field! What does this field mean? What is `acunetix/wvs`? A Google search shows that Acunetix is a *web application security scanner* (see *Figure 6.10*). That would explain the spike in traffic. Someone is scanning the site! **Reconnaissance scans** are automated attacks whose primary goal is to learn about the destination host. A successful scan will allow the attacker to discover open ports, bad passwords, and other vulnerabilities that would make it a good target for an attack:

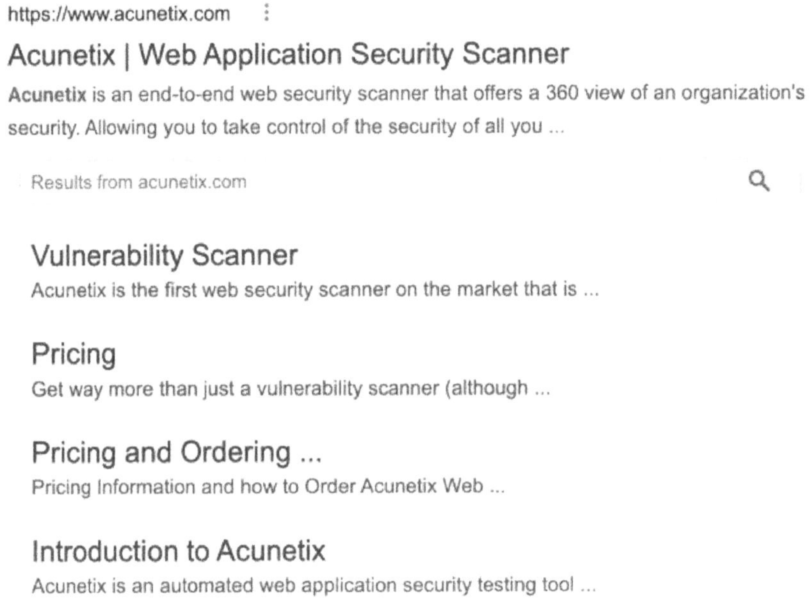

https://www.acunetix.com   ⋮

Acunetix | Web Application Security Scanner

Acunetix is an end-to-end web security scanner that offers a 360 view of an organization's security. Allowing you to take control of the security of all you ...

Results from acunetix.com   🔍

Vulnerability Scanner
Acunetix is the first web security scanner on the market that is ...

Pricing
Get way more than just a vulnerability scanner (although ...

Pricing and Ordering ...
Pricing Information and how to Order Acunetix Web ...

Introduction to Acunetix
Acunetix is an automated web application security testing tool ...

Figure 6.10 – Acunetix web application security scanner

5. What does an Acunetix scan event look like? Enter the following in the search bar to find out:

```
index=botsv1 earliest=0 sourcetype="stream:http" c_
ip=40.80.148.42 "acunetix"
```

Note that we are using a search for the `"acunetix"` string in the `stream:http` logs. This will give us any event containing the term `"acunetix"` without specifying a field name. *Figure 6.11* shows an example of one of these events:

```
server: Microsoft-IIS/8.5
server_rtt: 44229
server_rtt_packets: 1
server_rtt_sum: 44229
site: imreallynotbatman.com
src_content: areas%5b%5d=%bf'%bf%22&ordering=alpha&searchphrase=all&searchword=&task=search
src_headers: POST /joomla/index.php/component/search/ HTTP/1.1
Content-Length: 78
Content-Type: application/x-www-form-urlencoded
Referer: http://imreallynotbatman.com:80/
Cookie: ae72c62a4936b238523950a4f26f67d0=v7ikb3m59romokqmbiet3vphv3
Host: imreallynotbatman.com
Connection: Keep-alive
Accept-Encoding: gzip,deflate
User-Agent: Mozilla/5.0 (Windows NT 6.1; WOW64) AppleWebKit/537.21 (KHTML, like Gecko) Chrome/41.0.2228.0 Safari/537.21
Acunetix-Product: WVS/10.0 (Acunetix Web Vulnerability Scanner - Free Edition)
Acunetix-Scanning-agreement: Third Party Scanning PROHIBITED
Acunetix-User-agreement: http://www.acunetix.com/wvs/disc.htm
Accept: */*


src_ip: 40.80.148.42
```

Figure 6.11 – An Acunetix scan event

6. *Figure 6.11* shows that the site being scanned is imreallynotbatman.com. We use the following query to determine if this is the domain with the highest amount of traffic:

```
index=botsv1 earliest=0 sourcetype="stream:http" c_
ip=40.80.148.42
| rex field=url"H|http://(?<target_domain>.*)\.com\/\w+?"
| stats count by target_domain
| sort - count
| head 1
```

7. We use the rex command to extract the domain portion of the URL for each stream:http event from 40.80.148.42.

8. We name the field target_domain. Remember that the rex command extracts the value matched by the regex specified. In this case, we are looking for a string of characters that comes between http:// and .com/. The last part of the regex (\/\w+?) indicates that there may or may not be more characters after the domain name.

9. Next, we use the stats command to get a count of each target_domain—that is, our newly extracted field—in the stream:http logs.

10. Then, we use the sort command to sort by the count field. We sort in descending order, as indicated by the dash (-) before the count function.

11. Finally, we use a command called `head` to give us the first row of the results. This will be the `target_domain` with the highest count or the most traffic. *Figure 6.12* shows the result of this query:

Figure 6.12 – The domain with the most traffic

Note that we could have replaced the code in *steps 9-11* by using the `top` command. The `top` command finds the most command value of a field. We could replace the last three lines of our search with the following:

```
index=botsv1 earliest=0 sourcetype="stream:http" c_
ip=40.80.148.42
| rex field=url"[Hh]ttp://(?<target_domain>.*)\.com\/\
w+?"
| top 1 target_domain
```

You may wonder about the initial `[Hh]ttp` part of the regex. Although most URLs are case insensitive and we would expect `http://` in most logs, a quick perusal of the `url` field showed us that some events start with `Http://` instead. Sometimes, it is important to review the results after we run the query to ensure that our results are correct. We could also use the `(?i)` regex construct to tell `rex` to ignore the case. We could also convert the URLs to upper- or lowercase before executing the `rex` command. Feel free to explore these different methods, but be mindful of the effect your changes have on the execution of the Splunk queries. Remember—you can review the **Job Inspector** output using the **Job** dropdown to examine the execution times.

12. What else are we able to learn about this Acunetix scanning traffic? Let's look in our intrusion detection Suricata logs for traffic from IP address `40.80.148.42`. Although advanced commands help with analysis, sometimes just browsing through the traffic can help us make interesting discoveries. Browse through the different fields in the `suricata` sourcetype using the following search query:

```
index=botsv1 earliest=0 sourcetype="suricata" src_
ip=40.80.148.42
```

Figure 6.13 shows a sample of the Suricata logs. The `event_type` field lets us know that this event is an alert. Remember that you can use the + sign in these JSON logs to expand the events:

```
>    8/10/16          { [-]
     4:52:47.038 PM      alert: { [-]
                            action: allowed
                            category: Web Application Attack
                            gid: 1
                            rev: 6
                            severity: 1
                            signature: ET WEB_SERVER PHP tags in HTTP POST
                            signature_id: 2011768
                         }
                         dest_ip: 192.168.250.70
                         dest_port: 80
                         event_type: alert
                         flow_id: 2430614826
                         http: { [-]
                            hostname: imreallynotbatman.com
                            http_method: POST
                            http_refer: http://imreallynotbatman.com/joomla/administrator/index.php?option=com_extplorer&tmpl=component
                            http_user_agent: Mozilla/5.0 (Windows NT 6.1; WOW64; Trident/7.0; rv:11.0) like Gecko
                            length: 0
                            protocol: HTTP/1.1
                            url: /joomla/administrator/index.php
                         }
                         in_iface: eth1
                         proto: TCP
                         src_ip: 40.80.148.42
                         src_port: 49490
                         timestamp: 2016-08-10T15:52:47.038023-0600
                         tx_id: 7
                      }
                      Show as raw text

     host = suricata-ids.waynecorpinc.local    source = /var/log/suricata/eve.json    sourcetype = suricata
```

Figure 6.13 – Sample Suricata logs

13. Which fields interest you in these logs? Let's zoom in on the `alert_category` field. Which kinds of alerts were generated from this traffic? We use the following search query to find out:

```
index=botsv1 earliest=0 sourcetype="suricata" src_
ip=40.80.148.42
| stats count by alert.category
| sort count
```

14. Use the **Visualization** tab and click on the first link to select **Pie Chart** to display the results in the form of a pie chart. The pie chart allows us to see the different signature categories detected by Suricata. Each slice of the pie represents the proportion of events that matched the signature category. For example, Suricata detected a high volume of traffic that can be categorized as a **Web Application Attack**. *Figure 6.14* shows the resulting pie chart:

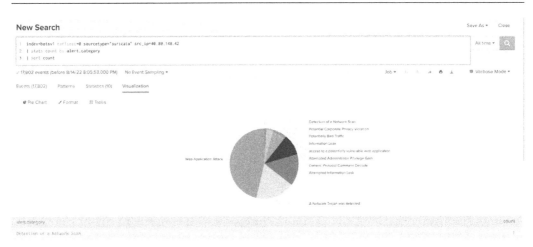

Figure 6.14 – Pie chart showing alert categories in Suricata data

15. There are several different signatures in each category. Let's use the `stats` command to display the alert signatures per category. We will use the `values()` function to list the signatures in each `alert.category` from IP address `40.80.148.42`. The following search query achieves this result:

```
index=botsv1 earliest=0 sourcetype="suricata" src_
ip=40.80.148.42
| stats count values(alert.signature) as signature by
alert.category
```

Figure 6.15 shows the result of this search. Did you notice the signature containing Acunetix traffic? Which category does that signature fall under?

Figure 6.15 – Categories and signatures in the Suricata logs

16. We can use this list to see the individual signatures. We can also count the number of attack signatures in each category by displaying the traffic in a column chart using the following search query:

```
index=botsv1 earliest=0 sourcetype="suricata" src_
ip=40.80.148.42
| chart count over alert.category by alert.signature
```

17. We use the `chart` command and split the data over `alert.category by alert.signature`. Click on the **Visualization** tab and select **Column Chart** in the first drop-down option. *Figure 6.16* shows the result of this query:

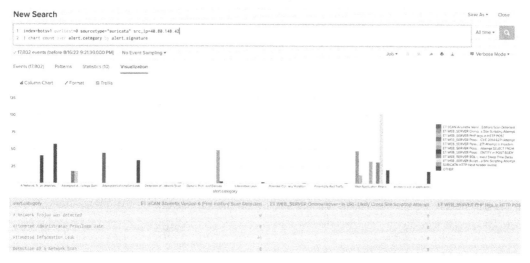

Figure 6.16 – The alert categories and signatures in the form of a column chart

One of the goals of visualizing data is to gain insight. *Figure 6.16* is not the clearest chart. It does not solve the problem of determining how many of each signature were seen in each category. In this case, we do not need to change the search query. A view of the grayed-out table below the chart shows us that the data is already aggregated in the format we want. However, the chart needs to be formatted properly.

18. Let's use the **Format** menu to improve the chart. We click on the second option (**Format**) and select the middle option in **Stack Mode**. This mode allows us to stack the signatures in a single column for each category (see *Figure 6.17*):

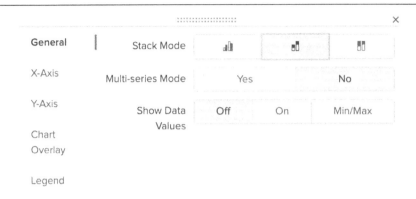

Figure 6.17 – Using the Format menu to select Stack Mode

The resulting visualization can be seen in *Figure 6.18*:

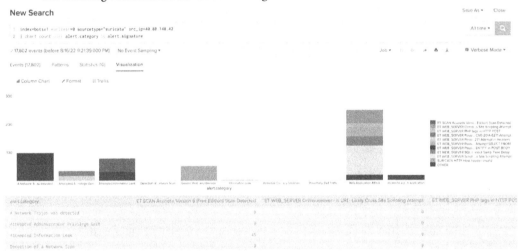

Figure 6.18 – A stacked column chart

Note how the different signatures are stacked. This makes the chart much easier to read. We can also see that ET WEB_SERVER Script Cross Site Scripting Attempt in the **Web Application Attack** category appears to be the attack that was executed the most frequently.

19. So far, we can tell that the attack may be coming from the 40.80.148.42 host. Now, let us confirm the target host that is being scanned. We can find this out using a simple query using stats. Let us look at the dest_ip field for all the traffic from our attacker host:

```
index=botsv1 earliest=0 sourcetype="suricata" src_
ip=40.80.148.42
| stats count by dest_ip
```

Figure 6.19 is a pie chart showing the two different hosts that are targeted by the scans. Based on the amount of traffic to `192.168.250.70`, we can conclude that it is the affected device:

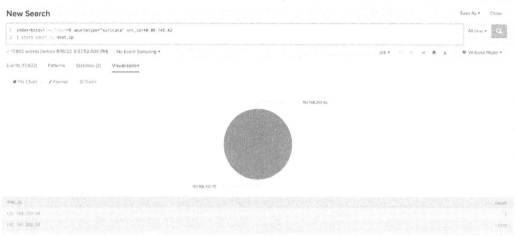

Figure 6.19 – Pie chart shows the probable target host 192.168.250.70

20. Let's use the single-value chart to show the targeted host on our network. First, we sort the results by count in descending order and remove the `dest_ip` field. Then, we select the **Single Value** chart option:

```
index=botsv1 earliest=0 sourcetype="suricata" src_
ip=40.80.148.42
| stats count by dest_ip
| sort - count
| fields dest_ip
```

Figure 6.20 shows the result displayed as a single-value chart. It is a great way of displaying values in a dashboard:

Figure 6.20 – Single-value chart shows the probable target host 192.168.250.70

21. On a side note, let's confirm that this is the host being targeted by looking at the `dest` field in the next-generation firewall (Fortigate) logs. As mentioned earlier, networks have internal (`class C`) and external IP addresses. Examine the Fortigate logs using the following query:

```
index=botsv1 src=23.22.63.114 OR src=40.80.148.42
sourcetype=fortigate_traffic
```

Figure 6.21 shows that the `dstip` field is not `192.168.250.70`, as we see in *Figure 6.20*:

Figure 6.21 – Fortigate logs

22. The Fortigate appliance in our case study shows the `dest` field as the external IP address for the network. Use the following Splunk query to show that the destination for all traffic going through the Fortigate appliance from our attacker hosts (`23.22.63.114` and `40.80.148.42`) is `71.39.18.126`:

```
index=botsv1 src=23.22.63.114 OR src=40.80.148.42
sourcetype=fortigate_traffic
| stats count by dest
```

Figure 6.22 shows the result of this query:

Figure 6.22 – External IP from Fortigate logs

23. Once traffic gets to the Fortigate appliance, it is translated to the internal host IP address of the destination. We see that this is stored in the `tranip` field. Examine the translation between the external IP address and internal IP addresses using the following query:

```
index=botsv1 src=23.22.63.114 OR src=40.80.148.42
sourcetype=fortigate_traffic
| stats count by src, dest, tranip
```

Figure 6.23 shows the output:

Figure 6.23 – Translated IP addresses in the fortigate_traffic sourcetype

The single-value option can also be used to show changes in values. Let's execute an example by showing the change in traffic between 11 a.m. and noon on 8/24/2016.

24. Use the following search query in the search bar:

```
index=botsv1 sourcetype="stream:http"
| timechart count span=5m
```

25. We want to see the change in traffic, so we will break out time into 5-minute intervals using `span=5m`. Use the **Date & Time Range** option on the time picker to select the *1-hour* period, as shown in *Figure 6.24*:

Figure 6.24 – Time picker setting for showing a change in traffic

Figure 6.25 shows the output in the **Statistics** tab. Note that the number of events drops from **8** to **7** in the last two periods. In other words, the difference between the last two periods is -1:

Figure 6.25 – Table chart shows the traffic every 5 minutes

26. Select the **Single Value** chart on the **Visualization** tab to display the result. The value shows the count in the last period (*11:59 a.m.*) as well as *an arrow* and the number **-1** indicating the drop in traffic by one event. *Figure 6.26* shows the output:

Figure 6.26 – Single-value chart shows a change in traffic every 5 minutes

27. Now that we have identified the target host and the scanner, was there any other source host? Let's use the following Splunk query to display the traffic by `src_ip`:

```
index=botsv1 earliest=0 sourcetype=stream:http dest_ip="1
92.168.250.70"
| timechart count by src_ip usenull=f
```

Figure 6.27 shows the three sources of traffic to `192.168.2.70` (`192.168.250.50`, `23.22.63.114`, and `40.80.148.42`). We use `usenull=f` to remove any NULL values.

We see a spike in traffic from 40.80.148.42 on 08/10/2016 but we also see another spike from another external host (23.22.63.114):

Figure 6.27 – Line chart shows source traffic to target host 192.168.250.70

28. Sometimes, we want to enhance time charts so that there is a distinction between lines that are closely spaced together. We can accomplish that by using the **Scale** option in the **Format** menu of the **Visualization** tab. Click on **Visualization** | **Format** | **Y-Axis** | **Scale** | **Log** (see *Figure 6.28*):

Figure 6.28 – Changing the scale using the Scale option on the Format menu

29. Compare the scale of the time charts in *Figure 6.27* and *Figure 6.29*. Notice that it is easier to read when displayed in *log* scale:

Figure 6.29 – Line chart shows source traffic to target host 192.168.250.70 (log y axis)

30. What does the traffic from `23.22.63.114` look like? We use the following Splunk query to view the traffic (HTTP methods) between `192.168.250.70` and `23.22.63.114`:

```
index=botsv1 earliest=0 sourcetype=stream:http dest_
ip="192.168.250.70" src_ip="23.22.63.114"
| stats count by http_method
```

Figure 6.30 shows the type of traffic displayed as a bar chart. There are several GET and POST requests:

Figure 6.30 – Bar chart shows HTTP methods between 192.168.250.70 and 23.22.63.114

31. Let's examine the raw events between `192.168.250.70` and `23.22.63.114` using the following query:

```
index=botsv1 earliest=0 sourcetype=stream:http dest_
ip="192.168.250.70" src_ip="23.22.63.114"
```

Figure 6.31 shows the output of the query:

Figure 6.31 – Brute-force attack on 192.168.250.70

It appears that there is some suspicious information in the `form_data` field. What does it look like to you? It looks like a login attempt. We see what appears to be the URI path, including the `username` and `passwd` fields with the values `admin` and `rock`, respectively. The login attempt is to access `http://imreallynotbatman.com/joomla/administrator/index.php`. We also see that the `http_user_agent` field shows `Python-urllib/2.7`. We think this may be a Python script trying to brute-force our server.

32. We use the following query to display the `_time` and `form_data` fields from the raw event:

```
index=botsv1 earliest=0 sourcetype=stream:http dest_
ip="192.168.250.70" src_ip="23.22.63.114" form_data=*
| table _time, form_data
|sort _time
```

There is a lot of traffic between these two hosts but not every traffic event is a login attempt. Therefore, we include `form_data=*` to display only the events where an attempt was made to log in to the `imreallynotbatman.com` site. *Figure 6.32* shows the output of this query:

Figure 6.32 – Table chart shows brute-force attack on 192.168.250.70

33. Do we have a command that we can use to extract the password from the `form_data` field? Yes, we do! We use the `rex` command to extract the portion of alphanumeric characters that follow the `passwd=` string in the `form_data` field. Then, we use the `table` command to display the data:

```
index=botsv1 earliest=0 sourcetype=stream:http dest_
ip="192.168.250.70" src_ip="23.22.63.114" form_data=*
| rex field=form_data "passwd=(?<passwd>\w+)\&?"
| table _time, form_data, passwd
```

Figure 6.33 shows the output with the extracted `passwd` field. The values in this field show an assortment of passwords:

Figure 6.33 – Table chart shows extracted passwords

The attacker is trying to gain access to the imreallynotbatman.com site using a Python script from 23.22.63.114. We confirmed that they are using a Python script by looking at the http_user_agent field. What do you think the attacker will do once the Python script has successfully brute-forced the site? The attacker proceeds to access the site using a browser.

34. Let's look at the http_user_agent field to determine when this occurs. It is likely that the attacker is not going to use the same server as the one hosting the Python script. They may not have a browser on that server. Therefore, we will expand our search to include only attempts to log in to 192.168.250.70 by any source host. In addition, we modify the previous query so that it displays the http_user_agent field:

```
index=botsv1 earliest=0 sourcetype=stream:http dest_
ip="192.168.250.70" form_data=*
| rex field=form_data "passwd=(?<passwd>\w+)\&?"
| search passwd=*
| table _time, src, form_data, passwd, http_user_agent
```

35. We first specify our usual search filters including the form_data field because we want to ensure that we are only searching the brute-force attack logs. Next, we extract the passwd field using the rex command. Now that we have the passwd field, we can search for all rows that have a password. We have used this style before when we specified form_data=*. Using the wildcard in this way basically tells Splunk to give us all rows where those fields have data. Finally, we use the table command to display the fields we are interested in. *Figure 6.34* shows the output:

Figure 6.34 – Login attempts to imreallynotbatman.com

Well, this is interesting! We see that the first row is an attempt to access the imreallynotbatman.com site using a Mozilla-type browser from 40.80.148.42 using a password of batman.

It looks like the attackers guessed the password (`batman`) and decided to use a browser to log in. We use the toggle arrows next to the `passwd` field in the output to display the passwords in ascending order. Scroll down to see that there are two rows containing the `batman` password. One row shows the instance when the Python script attempts to log in to `imreallynotbatman.com` (`http_user_agent="Python-urllib/2.7"`), and the other row shows the login using the Mozilla browser (`http_user_agent=Mozilla/5.0 (Windows NT 6.1; WOW64; Trident/7.0; rv:11.0) like Gecko`). *Figure 6.35* shows the output:

Figure 6.35 – Two login events

36. Let's generate some statistics about this part of the attack by answering the following question:

How many distinct passwords did the Python script use?

We use the `dc` function in the following query to find out:

```
index=botsv1 earliest=0 sourcetype=stream:http dest_
ip="192.168.250.70" src_ip=23.22.63.114
| rex field=form_data "passwd=(?<passwd>\w+)\&?"
| search passwd=*
| stats dc(passwd)
```

Figure 6.36 shows that there were `412` passwords:

Figure 6.36 – Number of distinct passwords

37. Let's make the result more presentable by adding a caption and color. We click on the **Visualization** tab and click **Format**. We then enter the word `passwords` in the **Caption** textbox (see *Figure 6.37*):

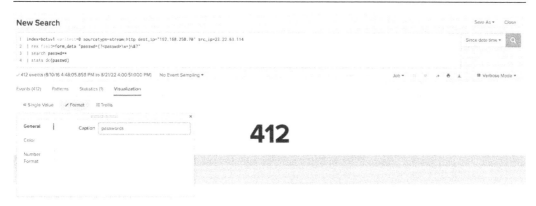

Figure 6.37 – Adding a caption to the Single Value chart

38. Next, we click on the **Color** option in the **Formatting** menu and click **Yes** for **Color**. A series of ranges appear. We can use the color ranges to programmatically alter the color of the **Single Value** result. We display the number of passwords in red by entering the values in *Figure 6.38*:

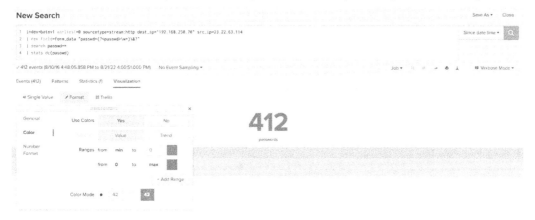

Figure 6.38 – Changing the color of the Single Value result

39. What is the *average size in bytes* of each login event? We use the avg function in the following query to find out:

```
index=botsv1 earliest=0 sourcetype=stream:http dest_
ip="192.168.250.70" src_ip=23.22.63.114
| rex field=form_data "passwd=(?<passwd>\w+)\&?"
| search passwd=*
| stats avg(bytes) as bytes
```

40. *Figure 6.39* shows that the average size in bytes was 854.1771844660194. Let's change the precision of this number. We could do this using the `eval` command in the Splunk query, but since we are just concerned about making the chart pretty, we will make the change using the **Format** menu:

Figure 6.39 – Unformatted single value

41. Display the result as a **Single Value** chart by clicking **Visualization | Single Value Chart**. Use the **Number Format** option in the **Format** menu to set the **Precision** value to two decimal places (0.00) and enter the word `bytes` in the **Unit** textbox. *Figure 6.40* shows the **Format** menu and the output:

Figure 6.40 – Changing precision and units in a Single Value chart

42. There is an increase in *DNS* traffic at about 4:57 p.m. on 8/10/2016. Which host is making those DNS requests?

43. We can use the `fortigate_traffic` sourcetype to determine the source of this traffic. We specify `dstport=53`, or we can use `service=DNS`. Then, we will use the `timechart` command to display the DNS requests for each source host. The following query accomplishes this task:

```
index=botsv1 sourcetype=fortigate_traffic dstport=53
 | timechart count by srcip
```

We click on the **Visualization** tab and select the **Line Chart** visualization. You will notice that the events all seem to fall within a short period (see *Figure 6.41*):

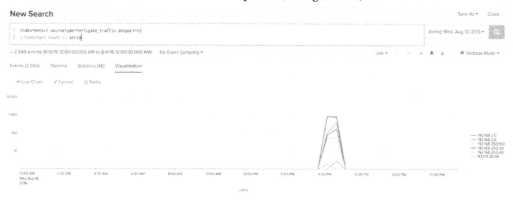

Figure 6.41 – DNS traffic before zoom

44. We can zoom in by clicking on the chart and dragging it to enlarge it. A gray box will show up on the chart, and when released, the chart will be expanded, as shown in *Figure 6.42*. Clicking on the **Reset Zoom** button resets the chart:

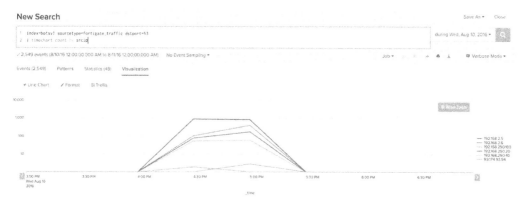

Figure 6.42 – DNS traffic after zoom

We could also zoom in on the period by selecting the **Data & Time** range using the time picker. Enter the date and time as shown in *Figure 6.43* to focus on the time:

Figure 6.43 – Time picker settings for zooming in to the time period

Figure 6.44 shows the chart after we have zoomed in using the time picker:

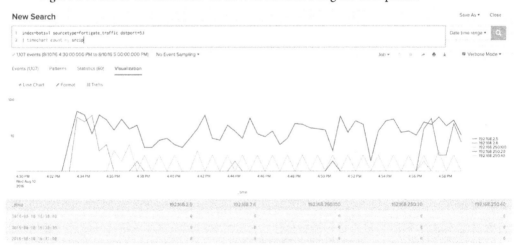

Figure 6.44 – Line chart showing DNS queries by source host

Looking carefully, we see that there is a spike around 4:57 p.m. from 192.168.250.20.

45. Use a bar graph to display the top 10 destination ports detected on 8/10/2016. We can accomplish this by using the `fortigate_traffic` sourcetype and the following query:

```
index=botsv1 sourcetype="fortigate_traffic"
| stats count by dstport
| sort - count
| head 10
```

We first use the `stats` command to count all the destination ports. Then, we use the `sort` command to order the counts in descending order. Finally, we use the `head` command to display the top `10` ports. We click on the **Visualization** tab and select **Bar Chart**. *Figure 6.45* shows the results of this query:

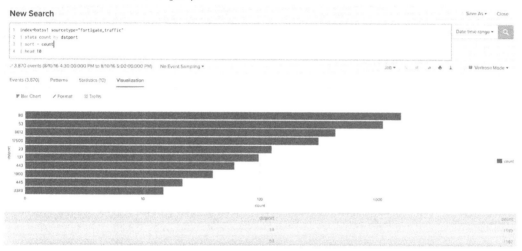

Figure 6.45 – Bar chart showing the top 10 destination ports

In this section, we explored a variety of charting options. We explored the formatting of line charts. We used column charts to stack alert signatures based on alert categories. We experimented with single-value charts and learned how they can be used to indicate changes in values over time. We also created pie charts and area charts. In the next section, we explore more advanced charts.

Creating advanced charts

The charts we have looked at so far have been relatively simple. We did not require any special commands to prepare the data. In this section, we look at three chart types that are more advanced.

Table 6.2 reminds us of the charting options we have covered so far, as well as the three charts that we will cover in this section:

Chart type	Works great for	Search structure
Line chart	Displaying trends over time	`| timechart count [by comparison_category]`
Area chart	Showing changes in aggregated values over time	`| timechart count [by comparison_category]`
Column chart	Comparing fields or calculated values	`| stats count by comparison_category`
Bar chart	Comparing fields or calculated values	`| stats count by comparison_category`

Single-value chart	Displaying numeric changes in trends. Can also be used to display single values.	`| timechart count`
		
		OR
		
		`| stats count`

Pie chart	Comparing categories	`| stats count by comparison_category`
Scatter chart	Displaying the relationship between discrete values in two dimensions	`| stats x_value_aggregation y_value_aggregation by name_category [comparison_category]`
Bubble chart	Displaying the relationship between discrete values in three dimensions	`| stats x_value_aggregation y_value_aggregation size_aggregation by name_category [comparison_category]`
Choropleth map	Displaying aggregated values in a geographic region	`| stats count by featureId` `| geom geo_countries featureIdField=featureId`

Table 6.2 – Different charts available in Splunk

Now, let's look at scatter plots.

Scatter plots

A scatter plot is a chart used to plot two numerical values. The position of the point on the *x* and *y* axes determines the value of the data point. In Splunk, a scatter plot chart requires two aggregate values such as count, sum(), or avg(). For example, the following search shows the number of events and the number of bytes for each host, which is communicated to the target host (192.168.250.70):

```
index=botsv1 "192.168.250.70" sourcetype=fortigate_traffic
| stats count sum(bytes) as bytes by src
```

To display a scatter plot in Splunk, we click on the **Visualization** tab and select **Scatter Chart**.

One of the advantages of using a scatter plot is that it makes it easy to detect outliers. For example, *Figure 6.46* shows that the data point on the extreme right is an outlier:

Figure 6.46 – Scatter plot showing count and sum(bytes)

Interestingly, this is the 23.22.63.114 source host that we have seen before. Do you remember what that host did? Yes—this is the host that executed the brute-force attack on our source. We can see that the behavior of the host indicates that it generated many events (count > 1400). On the other hand, host 40.80.148.42 sent fewer malicious events but transferred more bytes. This host was possibly the host that dropped the malicious executable after the reconnaissance phase of the attack. In fact, we can look at the data to see whether there were any file transfers between the two hosts. The following query shows that there was a file transfer signature in the fortigate_traffic logs for the two hosts in question:

```
index=botsv1 "192.168.250.70" sourcetype=fortigate_traffic
src="40.80.148.42" app="File.Upload.HTTP"
```

Figure 6.47 shows the two "File.Upload.HTTP" events from 40.80.148.42 (srcip) to 192.168.250.70 (tranip):

Figure 6.47 – File transfer signature

The following query of the `suricata` sourcetype also helps us identify an outlier. We can identify the `40.80.148.42` host as malicious based on the number of events and the number of distinct signatures that are detected by Suricata:

```
index=botsv1 earliest=0 sourcetype="suricata"
dest=imreallynotbatman.com
| stats count dc(signature) as signatures by src
```

Figure 6.48 shows the chart. Note that we removed the legend by setting **Legend** to **None** in the **Format** options:

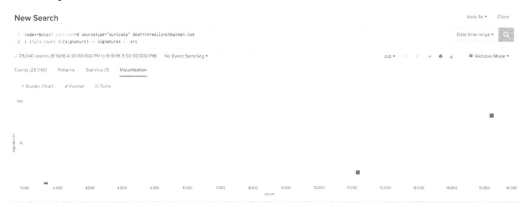

Figure 6.48 – Scatter plot chart shows the count and distinct signatures by src

We look at bubble charts in the next section.

Bubble charts

Bubble charts are like scatter plots, but the size of each point on the chart represents a measure of some aggregate in the data. For example, the following Splunk query of the `suricata` data generates the count, total bytes, and distinct count of signatures for all the external traffic in the Suricata logs:

```
index=botsv1 earliest=0 sourcetype="suricata" NOT (src=192.168*
OR src=2001:* OR src=fe80:* OR src=0*)
| stats count sum(bytes) as bytes dc(alert.signature) as sig_
count by src
```

We select **Visualization** and choose **Bubble Chart**. The resulting bubble has three dimensions:

- **Count**—Indicated by the location of each data point on the *x* axis

- **Total bytes**—Indicated by the location of each data point on the *y* axis

- **Distinct signatures**—Indicated by the size of the bubble

Figure 6.49 shows a very large bubble on the rightmost side of the chart. Can you guess which host is represented by this large bubble? If you guessed 40.80.148.42, you are correct:

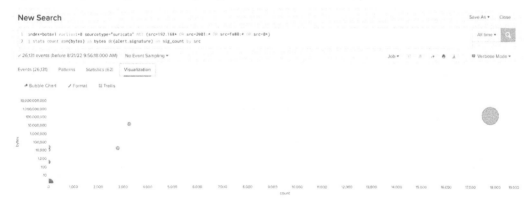

Figure 6.49 – Bubble plot chart shows the count and number of bytes by src

Now, let's look at ways that we can display data on maps.

Choropleth maps

Splunk map visualizations allow us to see where traffic originates geographically. There are two types of maps in Splunk:

- **Cluster maps**—Show aggregated values in a geographical region

- **Choropleth maps**—Useful for showing how an aggregated value ranges across a geographic region

The following query shows the source countries for the traffic in our `fortigate_traffic` sourcetype. We eliminate events where the `srccountry` type is `Reserved` (usually indicating a `class C` host) and any traffic from the `United States`. We click on the **Visualization** tab and select **Choropleth Map**:

```
index=botsv1 earliest=0 sourcetype=fortigate_traffic
srccountry!=Reserved srccountry!="United States"
| stats count by srccountry
| geom geo_countries featureIdField=srccountry
```

To generate a choropleth map, we first need to generate an aggregate of a field. In our preceding example, we are counting the number of events from each source country. This aggregate could range from counts to the distinct number of signatures to the size of bytes. The next step in the query uses the `geom` command to specify to Splunk that we want a choropleth map. We specify the `geo_countries` lookup, which is part of the lookups available in Splunk. We indicate that we will be aggregating based on the `featureIdField` specified (`srccountry`).

As with most charts, a choropleth map has multiple formatting options, such as the following:

- **Zoom on Scroll**—Determines whether using the scroll feature on the mouse triggers a zoom of the map (see *Figure 6.50*)

- **Latitude/Longitude/Zoom**—Define the initial display of the map and allow us to specify which area of the world that we want to focus on (see *Figure 6.50*):

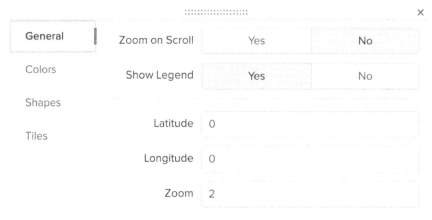

Figure 6.50 – Format options for a map chart

- **Colors**—Defines which colors and what intensity and scaling are used to represent the aggregate values (see *Figure 6.51*):

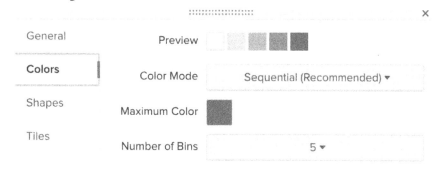

Figure 6.51 – Color options for a map chart

Figure 6.52 shows the resulting choropleth chart:

Figure 6.52 – Final choropleth map

The charts discussed in this section not only enhance the insights that we get from Splunk but also allow us to almost immediately detect outliers. Sometimes, a simple table will suffice for conveying research, but other times, a beautiful choropleth chart makes a much bigger impression.

Summary

In this chapter, we explored some of the visualizations available in Splunk. We looked at integrating some of the commands that we covered in previous chapters to create some interesting charts, including line, pie, column, bar, and single-value charts. We also gained insight into the `Bots Dataset v1` app when we generated these charts. Finally, we used the same dataset to generate some more advanced charts, including scatter plots, bubble charts, and maps.

We will expand on these examples in *Chapter 7, Creating Dynamic Dashboards*.

7
Creating Dynamic Dashboards

Now that we know how to create tables and charts, let's explore incorporating these visualizations into dashboards. Dashboards are a great way of communicating information with others. Splunk dashboards can be created with *filters*, *tokens*, and *drilldowns* to make them more dynamic. We can also embed *reports* and *JavaScript code*. Splunk dashboards are composed of one or more panels that can be grouped to tell a story. Classic Splunk dashboards were created using *Simple XML*. Therefore, a classic dashboard in Splunk is an XML file composed of commonly used XML tags such as `<form>`, `<title>`, and `<input>`, as well as Splunk-specific tags such as `<table>`, `<chart>`, and `<search>`. Splunk introduced Splunk Dashboard Studio in version 8.2x. Splunk Dashboard Studio is a set of tools that can be used to build aesthetically pleasing dynamic dashboards. First, we will create a dashboard using Simple XML and then we will create a dashboard using Splunk Dashboard Studio. Let's get started!

In this chapter, we will explore the following topics:

- Adding tables and charts to dashboards
- Adding inputs, tokens, and drilldowns
- Exploring the dashboard source
- Adding reports and drilldowns to dashboards
- Experimenting with the new Dashboard Studio

Adding tables and charts to dashboards

We will start with a basic dashboard panel containing a table we created in *Chapter 6, Creating Tables and Charts Using SPL*. As a review, let's complete the following steps:

1. Run the following query in the search bar:

    ```
    index=botsv1 earliest=0 sourcetype=iis
    | table _time, c_ip, s_ip, s_port, cs_uri_stem, cs_
    Referer, sc_status
    ```

    This query displays IIS logs in the form of a table. *Figure 7.1* shows the result of running this query:

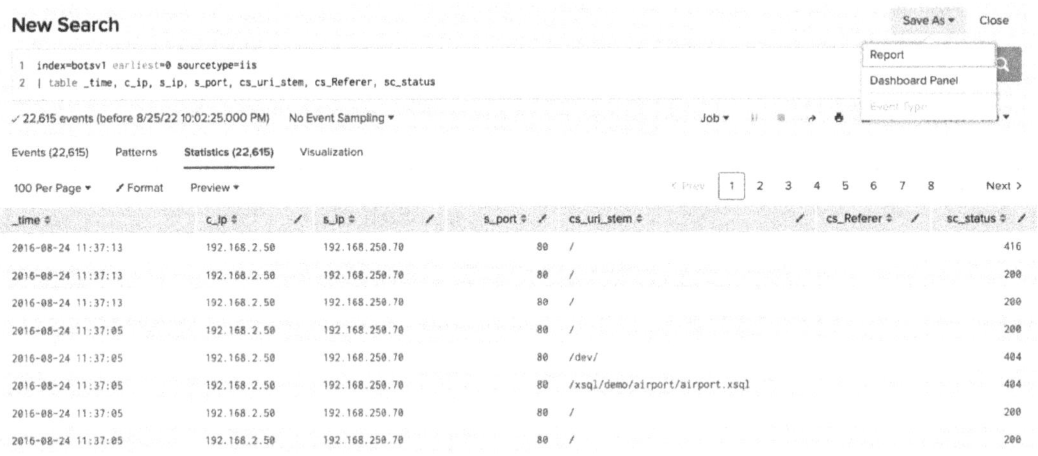

Figure 7.1 – Saving a search as a Dashboard Panel

Notice the **Save As** dropdown in the top-right corner of the search bar. This dropdown allows you the save the results of the query as a *single report* or as a *dashboard panel*. A Splunk *report* is the saved results of a single search. A Splunk *dashboard* can comprise several different objects, including reports, housed in one or more panels.

2. Let's click on the **Dashboard Panel** option to save the search results as a panel.

3. Enter the following information into the dialog box, as shown in *Figure 7.2*:

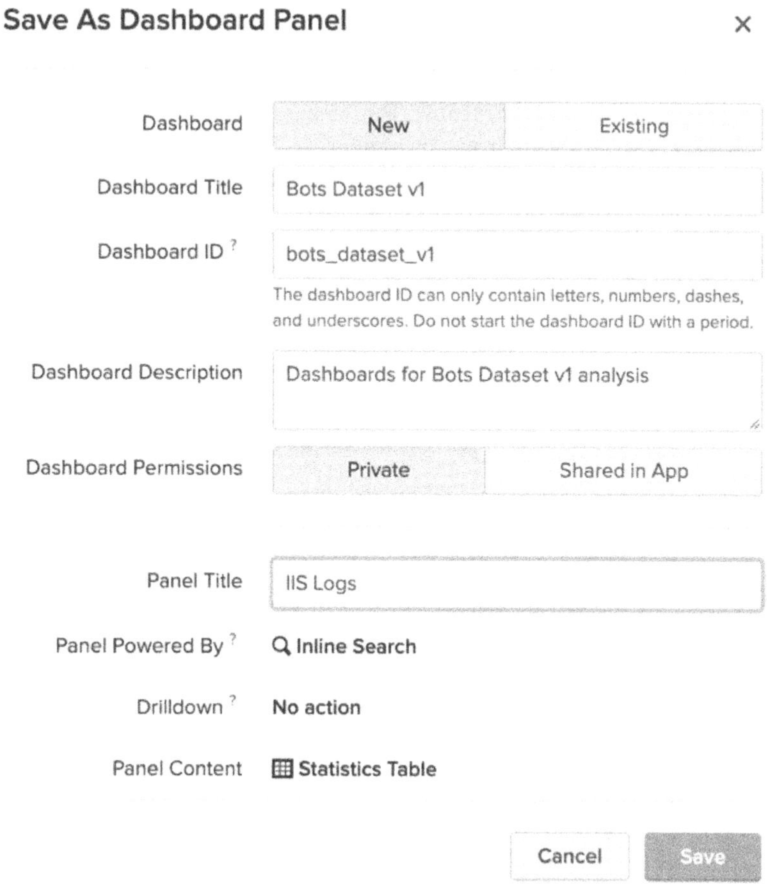

Save As Dashboard Panel   ✕

Dashboard	New	Existing

Dashboard Title   Bots Dataset v1

Dashboard ID ?   bots_dataset_v1

The dashboard ID can only contain letters, numbers, dashes, and underscores. Do not start the dashboard ID with a period.

Dashboard Description   Dashboards for Bots Dataset v1 analysis

Dashboard Permissions	Private	Shared in App

Panel Title   IIS Logs

Panel Powered By ?   🔍 Inline Search

Drilldown ?   No action

Panel Content   ▦ Statistics Table

Cancel   Save

Figure 7.2 – Creating a dashboard containing a table

The following information can be seen in the preceding screenshot:

- **Dashboard: New**
- **Dashboard Title**: Bots Dataset v1
- **Dashboard Description: Dashboards for** Bots Dataset v1 **analysis**
- **Dashboard Permissions: Shared in App**
- **Panel Title: IIS Logs**
- **Paneled Powered By: Inline Search**
- **Drilldown: No action**
- **Panel Content: Statistics Table**

These choices indicate that we would like to create a new dashboard called `Bots Dataset v1`. This is a **Shared in App**, which means that it will be shared with other users of the *Bots* app. Then, we must enter panel-specific information. We assign the *IIS Logs* title to the panel and indicate that it will be an *inline search*. This means that the search will run and populate the table whenever the dashboard loads. In addition, we specify that we will display the results in the form of a Splunk table. Remember that a dashboard (such as our new `Bots Dataset v1` dashboard) can contain multiple panels.

4. Clicking **Save** will result in a confirmation window indicating that the panel has been saved to the dashboard (see *Figure 7.3*):

Your Dashboard Panel Has Been Created   ✕

The panel has been created and added to bots_dataset_v1. You may now view the dashboard.

View Dashboard

Figure 7.3 – Confirmation message

5. Then, click **View Dashboard** to see our new dashboard, as shown in *Figure 7.4*):

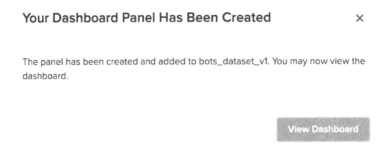

Bots Dataset v1   Edit   Export ▾   ...
Dashboards for Bots Dataset v1 analysis

IIS Logs

_time ⇅	c_ip ⇅	s_ip ⇅	s_port ⇅	cs_uri_stem ⇅	cs_Referer ⇅	sc_status ⇅
2016-08-24 11:37:05	192.168.2.50	192.168.250.70	80	/		200
2016-08-24 11:37:05	192.168.2.50	192.168.250.70	80	/		200
2016-08-24 11:37:05	192.168.2.50	192.168.250.70	80	/		200
2016-08-24 11:37:05	192.168.2.50	192.168.250.70	80	/cwhp/CSMSDesktop/about.jsp		404
2016-08-24 11:37:05	192.168.2.50	192.168.250.70	80	/		200
2016-08-24 11:37:05	192.168.2.50	192.168.250.70	80	/vsmc.html		404
2016-08-24 11:37:05	192.168.2.50	192.168.250.70	80	/		200
2016-08-24 11:37:05	192.168.2.50	192.168.250.70	80	/		200
2016-08-24 11:37:05	192.168.2.50	192.168.250.70	80	/+CSCOE+/logon.html		404
2016-08-24 11:37:05	192.168.2.50	192.168.250.70	80	/		200
2016-08-24 11:37:05	192.168.2.50	192.168.250.70	80	/		200
2016-08-24 11:37:05	192.168.2.50	192.168.250.70	80	/		200
2016-08-24 11:37:05	192.168.2.50	192.168.250.70	80	/dfcweb/lib/cupm/nls/applicationproperties.js		404
2016-08-24 11:37:05	192.168.2.50	192.168.250.70	80	/		200
2016-08-24 11:37:05	192.168.2.50	192.168.250.70	80	/axis2/services/CUPMService/ping		404
2016-08-24 11:37:05	192.168.2.50	192.168.250.70	80	/		200

Figure 7.4 – Bots Dataset v1 dashboard

The new `Bots Dataset v1` dashboard contains one panel. We can see that this dashboard has the title and description that we assigned. The new panel also has a title.

6. Next, we must click on the **Edit** button at the top right to display the **Edit** options. *Figure 7.5* shows the options available:

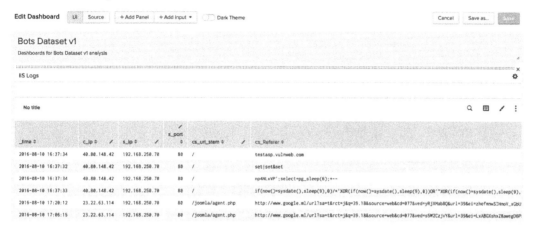

Figure 7.5 – Edit Dashboard options

The **Edit Dashboard** options are on the top left of the dashboard screen. We can edit the dashboard using a visual UI or we can look at the source. We can add a new panel by clicking the **Add Panel** button.

We've created a new panel. The options at the top of the dashboard apply to the entire dashboard. Now, let's focus on the panel to see what options are available.

Editing a dashboard panel

We can perform tasks such as editing the inline search in the panel, switching to a different visualization, or formatting the results of the query. Let's start by looking at the Splunk query:

1. Click on the magnifying glass icon to view the search. We get the option to do the following:

   * Change the search string

   * Choose whether a time picker controls the time range

   * Set the default time range

   * Set whether the dashboard panel will refresh automatically

   * Determine whether there is a progress indicator when the dashboard panel refreshes

   * Convert the dashboard into a report

   Figure 7.6 shows these options:

Figure 7.6 – Modifying the inline search

The next icon allows us to select the Splunk visualization we will use to represent the results. For example, the icon for the results we just generated using the statistics table is a table.

2. Clicking on the brush icon gives us a set of formatting options to format how the results are shown in the dashboard panel (see *Figure 7.7*):

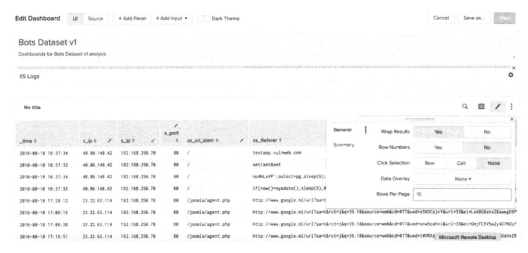

Figure 7.7 – Formatting menu for dashboard panels

3. Next, we will add a panel to the dashboard displaying HTTP traffic from `src=40.80.148.42` in the form of a time chart. We created this time chart in *Chapter 6*, *Creating Tables and Charts Using SPL*. As a reminder, here is the Splunk query:

```
index=botsv1 earliest=0 sourcetype="stream:http" c_
ip=40.80.148.42
| timechart count
```

4. Again, we must click on the **Save As** dropdown to save the resulting time chart as a **Dashboard Panel**. This time, we will not create a new dashboard. Instead, we will click **Existing** and use the dropdown to select the `Bots Dataset v1` dashboard. *Figure 7.8* shows the **Save As** options:

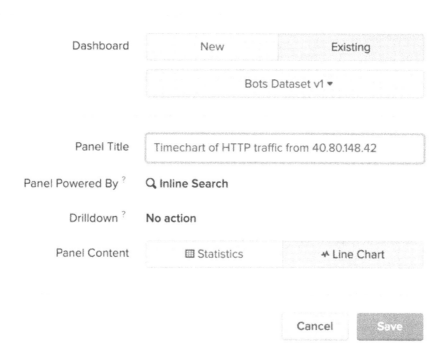

Figure 7.8 – Saving a time chart panel to the Bots Dataset v1 dashboard

Figure 7.9 shows the resulting dashboard with the latest time chart:

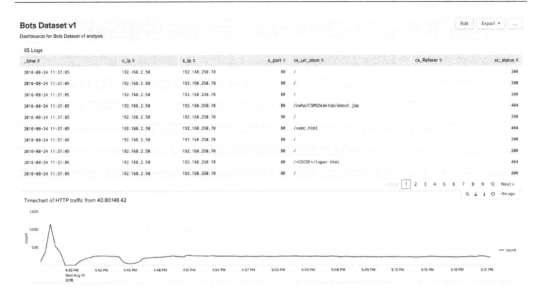

Figure 7.9 – Dashboard with two panels

5. Repeat this process to create a new panel by adding the results of the following query to the new dashboard:

```
index=botsv1 earliest=0 sourcetype="stream:http" c_
ip=40.80.148.42
| rex field=url  "H|http://(?<target_domain>.*)\.com\/\
w+?"
| stats count by target_domain
| sort - count
| head 1
```

Be sure to change the visualization to a single value and add a caption to the chart, as shown in *Figure 7.10*:

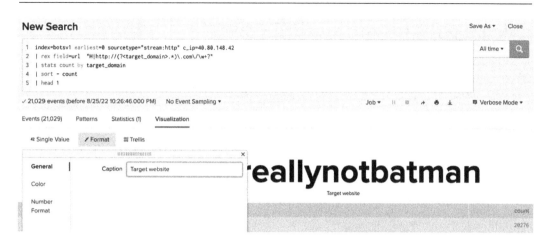

Figure 7.10 – Adding a single value panel to the dashboard

6.   We must save the new panel to the existing `Bots Dataset v1` dashboard (see *Figure 7.11*):

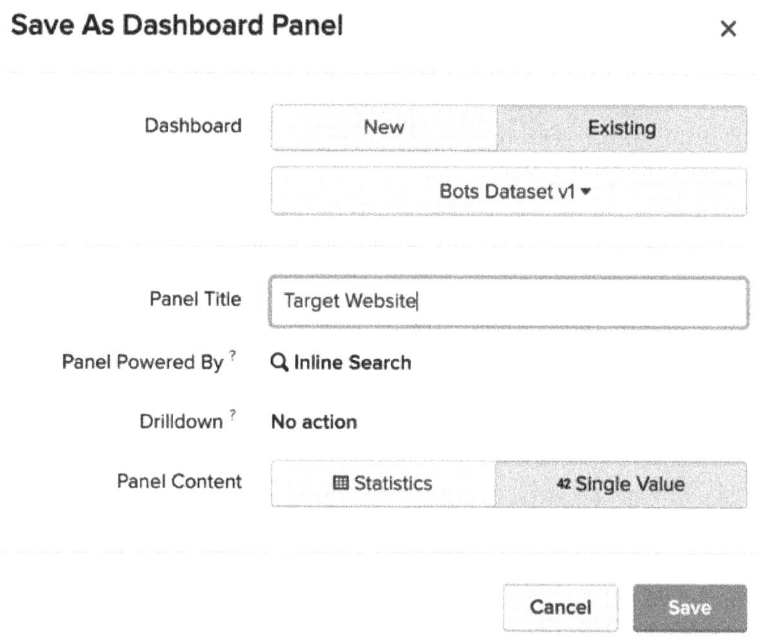

Save As Dashboard Panel   ✕

Dashboard	New	Existing

Bots Dataset v1 ▾

Panel Title   Target Website|

Panel Powered By ?   🔍 Inline Search

Drilldown ?   No action

Panel Content   ⊞ Statistics   42 Single Value

Cancel   Save

Figure 7.11 – Saving the single value chart to the dashboard

With that, we have added charts to our new dashboard. In the next section, we will add inputs, tokens, and drilldowns to the dashboard.

Adding inputs, tokens, and drilldowns

One of the advantages of Splunk is the ability to search through data. So far, we have created static dashboards. In this section, we will add inputs that will allow us to create filters for the data. We can add several different inputs to the dashboard, including the following:

- Text
- Radio buttons
- Dropdowns
- Checkboxes
- Multiselect dropdowns
- Link lists
- Time pickers
- Submit buttons

Follow these steps to create a new **Text** filter:

1. Clicking on the **Add Input** dropdown at the top of the dashboard while in **Edit** mode gives you a list of all the available options (see *Figure 7.12*):

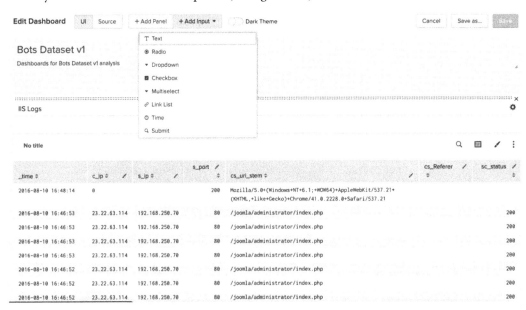

Figure 7.12 – Available input options

Let's start with a new text box field for the **IIS Logs** dashboard panel.

2. Click on the **Add Input** dropdown and select **Text**. A new input field called **field1** will be added to the dashboard, as shown in *Figure 7.13*:

Figure 7.13 – Adding a new text box input to the dashboard

Note that, initially, **field1** is not on the IIS Logs dashboard panel (it is sitting on the gray area above the dotted lines).

3. Drag, drop the new text box, and reposition it so that it is on the **IIS Logs** dashboard panel (see *Figure 7.14*):

Figure 7.14 – Repositioning inputs on the dashboard

4. Let's rename the field and set a default value by clicking the pencil next to the **x** icon attached to the field. A new box will open to allow us to make changes. First, we must enter the following values:

- **Label**: *cs_uri_stem*

- **Token**: *cs_uri_stem_field*

- **Default**: *

5. Next, click on the green **Apply** button, as seen in *Figure 7.15*:

Figure 7.15 – Renaming and setting default values for field1

Label is the value that will be displayed next to or above the input field. In this case, it will replace the default **field1** label. **Token** is the name of the placeholder variable that we add to the search. The **Default** value will be used if no other value is entered in the text box. A wildcard of * means that all the values of **cs_uri_stem** will be returned.

We assigned a token of **cs_uri_stem_field** to the text box we just created. We need to add this to our search.

6. Click on the magnifying glass in the top right of the **IIS Logs** dashboard panel to view the search query.

7. We must modify the search query so that it includes the **cs_uri_stem_field** token by replacing the old search string with the new search string.

Here's the old search string:

```
index=botsv1 earliest=0 sourcetype=iis
| table _time, c_ip, s_ip, s_port, cs_uri_stem, cs_
Referer, sc_status
```

Here's the new search string:

```
index=botsv1 earliest=0 sourcetype=iis cs_uri_stem=$cs_
uri_stem_field$
| table _time, c_ip, s_ip, s_port, cs_uri_stem, cs_
Referer, sc_status
```

The token is enclosed in two dollar signs ($). Now, when the search runs, it will return any row where the cs_uri_stem field matches the value entered in the cs_uri_stem input text box. *Figure 7.16* shows the new search query:

Figure 7.16 – Using a token in a dashboard search

Figure 7.17 shows the results when the word *administrator* is entered in the search box:

Figure 7.17 – Testing the new token

8. We must repeat this same process to create another input and token to allow us to search for **cs_Referer**. We will call this **Text** input **cs_Referer_field** and add the **$cs_Referer_field$** token to the search (see *Figure 7.18*):

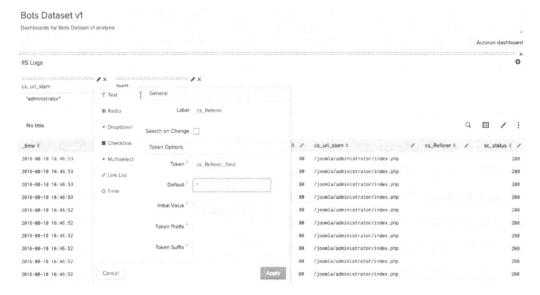

Figure 7.18 – Adding a new cs_Referer input and token

With that, we have created a text input. Now, let's create a different type of input.

Creating dropdown inputs

This time, we will create a **dropdown** to hold the **sc_status** input. Usually, a dropdown is used when there are a fixed number of options. We will use a search to generate the **sc_status** values that populate the dashboard. The search will generate a list of all the different codes that are contained in the dataset:

1. To begin, click on **Add Input** and select **Dropdown**. Enter the following values in the correct places:

    - **Label**: *sc_status*

    - **Token**: *sc_status_field*

    The options for setting up a dropdown have three sections:

- **Token options** allow us to set the *label*, *token* name, *default*, *initial* value, and *token prefix*. A **token prefix** allows us to set a value that is automatically appended to the beginning of the input. *Figure 7.19* shows the values of the **sc_status** field:

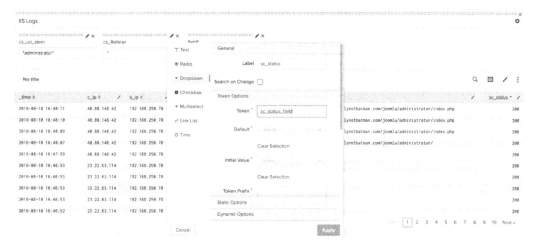

Figure 7.19 – Token options

- **Static options** allow us to enter a known or limited set of *key/value pairs* for the dropdown. For example, suppose we are aware that there are only four possible ports in the dataset, as shown in *Table 7.1*:

Port Description	Port
HTTP	80
HTTPS	443
FTP	22
TELNET	23

Table 7.1 – Sample options for a port field

We can populate our drop-down input as shown in *Figure 7.20*:

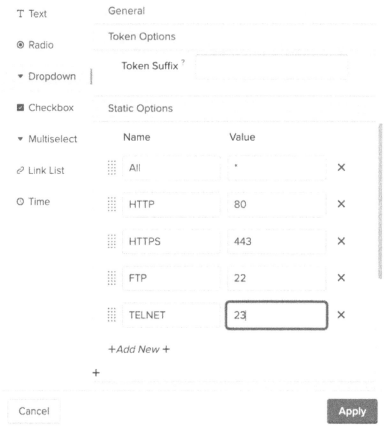

Figure 7.20 – Entering static options for a dropdown

These port descriptions are listed as labels in the dropdown that the user sees, but the value of the token will be the port number (see *Figure 7.21*):

Figure 7.21 – The resulting dropdown

- **Dynamic options** allow us to use a Splunk search query to populate the dropdown. Enter the following search string in the **Search String** box:

```
index=botsv1 earliest=0 sourcetype=iis
| stats count by sc_status
```

Figure 7.22 shows the search string:

Figure 7.22 – Populating a dropdown using a search query string

2. We must set **Field for Label** and **Value** to `sc_status`. This is different from the previous example, where the port description differed from the port number.

    What if we want to return results for every possible value of `sc_status` in the dataset? We need to include a catch-all option, as shown in *Figure 7.23*:

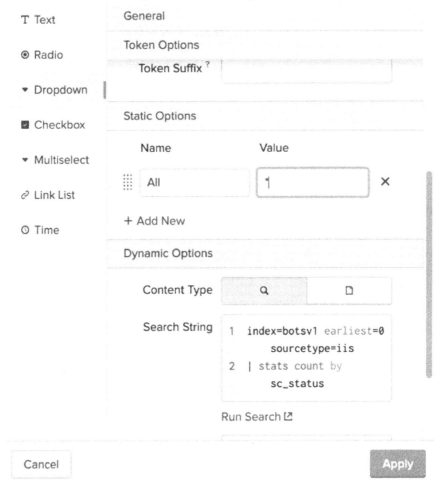

Figure 7.23 – Adding the All option

We must set the **Name** field to **All** and the **Value** field to *.

3. Add the token to the search, as shown in *Figure 2.24*:

Edit Search   ✕

Title

Search String

```
1    index=botsv1 earliest=0 sourcetype=iis cs_uri_stem=$cs_uri_stem_field$
        cs_Referer=$cs_Referer_field$
2    | table _time, c_ip, s_ip, s_port, cs_uri_stem, cs_Referer, sc_status
```

Run Search ↗

Time Range | Use time picker ▾ |

                      | All time ▸ |

Auto Refresh Delay ? | No auto refresh ▾ |

Refresh Indicator | Progress bar ▾ |

Cancel   Convert to Report   **Apply**

Figure 7.24 – Adding the token for the sc_status dropdown

Figure 7.25 shows an example of our dashboard with the following inputs:

- **cs_uri_stem**: **administrator**
- **cs_Referer**: ***
- **sc_status**: *404*:

Figure 7.25 – Using the new dashboard

Let's add a *time picker* to the dashboard.

Adding a time picker

We saw the **time picker** in the **Search and Reporting** app. We can add a time picker by clicking the **Add Input** button and selecting the **Time picker** input. *Figure 7.26* shows the dashboard with the new time picker on the **IIS Logs** panel:

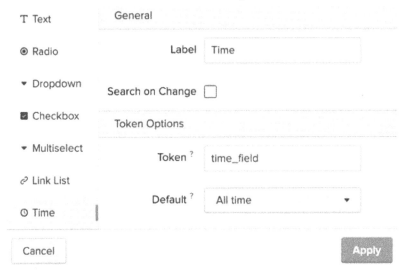

Figure 2.26 – Dashboard with new time picker

Figure 7.27 shows the token and default value of the time picker:

Figure 2.27 – Adding the token and default values for the time picker

Finally, we must rename the table headers to make our dashboard more presentable using the `rename` command:

```
index=botsv1 earliest=0 sourcetype=iis cs_uri_stem=$cs_
uri_stem_field$ cs_Referer=$cs_Referer_field$ sc_
status=$sc_status_field$
| table _time, c_ip, s_ip, s_port, cs_uri_stem, cs_
Referer, sc_status
```

```
|  rename c_ip as "Client IP", s_ip as "Server IP",
s_port as "Destination Port", cs_uri_stem as URI, cs_
Referer as Referer, sc_status as Status
```

Figure 7.28 shows the query in the **Search String** box:

Edit Search   ✕

Title		
Search String	`1   index=botsv1 earliest=0 sourcetype=iis cs_uri_stem=$cs_uri_stem_field$` `        cs_Referer=$cs_Referer_field$ sc_status=$sc_status_field$` `2	table _time, c_ip, s_ip, s_port, cs_uri_stem, cs_Referer, sc_status` `3	rename c_ip as "Client IP", s_ip as "Server IP", s_port as "Destination` ` Port", cs_uri_stem as URI, cs_Referer as Referer, sc_status as Status`	
	Run Search ⧉	
Time Range	Use time picker ▾	
	All time ▸	
Auto Refresh Delay [7]	No auto refresh ▾	
Refresh Indicator	Progress bar ▾	

Cancel   Convert to Report   **Apply**

Figure 7.28 – Renaming the table headers

The **IIS Logs** dashboard panel with filters is shown in *Figure 7.29*:

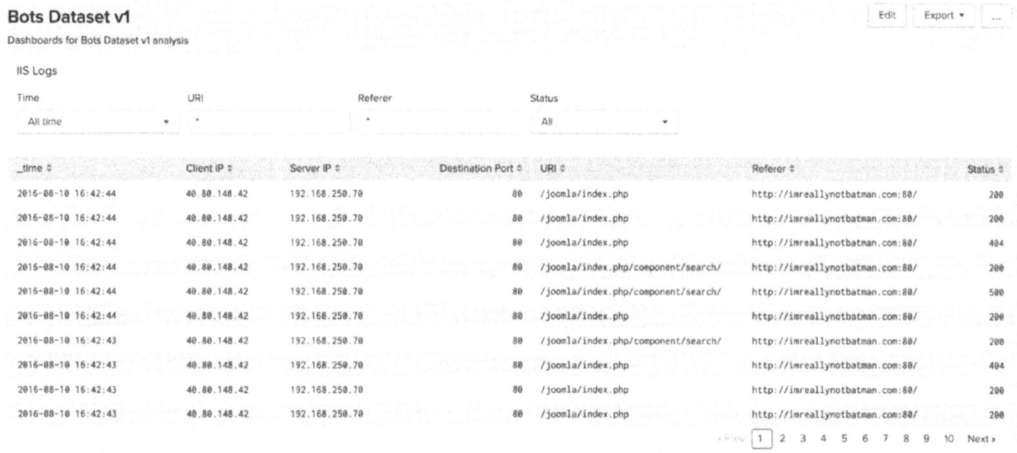

Bots Dataset v1   Edit   Export ▾   ...
Dashboards for Bots Dataset v1 analysis

IIS Logs

Time	URI	Referer	Status
All time ▾	*	*	All ▾

_time ⇕	Client IP ⇕	Server IP ⇕	Destination Port ⇕	URI ⇕	Referer ⇕	Status ⇕
2016-08-10 16:42:44	40.80.148.42	192.168.250.70	80	/joomla/index.php	http://imreallynotbatman.com:80/	200
2016-08-10 16:42:44	40.80.148.42	192.168.250.70	80	/joomla/index.php	http://imreallynotbatman.com:80/	200
2016-08-10 16:42:44	40.80.148.42	192.168.250.70	80	/joomla/index.php	http://imreallynotbatman.com:80/	404
2016-08-10 16:42:44	40.80.148.42	192.168.250.70	80	/joomla/index.php/component/search/	http://imreallynotbatman.com:80/	200
2016-08-10 16:42:44	40.80.148.42	192.168.250.70	80	/joomla/index.php/component/search/	http://imreallynotbatman.com:80/	500
2016-08-10 16:42:44	40.80.148.42	192.168.250.70	80	/joomla/index.php	http://imreallynotbatman.com:80/	200
2016-08-10 16:42:43	40.80.148.42	192.168.250.70	80	/joomla/index.php/component/search/	http://imreallynotbatman.com:80/	200
2016-08-10 16:42:43	40.80.148.42	192.168.250.70	80	/joomla/index.php	http://imreallynotbatman.com:80/	404
2016-08-10 16:42:43	40.80.148.42	192.168.250.70	80	/joomla/index.php	http://imreallynotbatman.com:80/	200
2016-08-10 16:42:43	40.80.148.42	192.168.250.70	80	/joomla/index.php	http://imreallynotbatman.com:80/	200

« Prev [1] 2 3 4 5 6 7 8 9 10 Next »

Figure 7.29 – The complete IIS Logs dashboard panel with filters

Now that we've added inputs, let's go behind the scenes and look at the dashboard source.

Exploring the dashboard source

So far, we have created our dashboard using *visual tools*. Now, let's explore the simple XML for the dashboard that we created in the *Adding inputs, tokens, and drilldowns* section. To view the simple XML source, we must click on the **Source** tab. For simplicity, we have collapsed the XML by clicking on the arrows next to the line numbers so that only the main tags are visible, as shown in *Figure 7.30*:

Figure 7.30 – Collapsed XML for the Splunk dashboard

We can see that the source of the simple XML dashboard is enclosed in an outer pair of `<form>` tags:

```
<form>
```

The *title* and *description* that we assigned to the dashboard are enclosed within the `<label>` and `<description>` tags, respectively. Each of our three panels is enclosed in a pair of `<row>` tags. Let's look at the first panel with the filters. All the inputs (text boxes, dropdown, and time picker) are enclosed in the `<fieldset>` tags:

```
<fieldset>
```

Each panel is enclosed in a set of `<panel>` tags. The title of each panel is enclosed in `<title>` tags. Each input is defined using `<input>` tags:

```
<input>
```

The *time picker* is defined using `<input type="time">`. Within the `<input>` tags, there are a pair of `<label>` tags and a set of `<default>` tags that define the label description and default time values, respectively. The *text box* is defined by using the `<input type="text"` tags. The *dropdown* input is enclosed in `<input type="dropdown">` tags. The name of the token is defined as an attribute of the `<input>` tags:

```
<search> and <query>
```

Splunk search queries in Simple XML are enclosed in `<search>` and `<query>` tags. A `<search>` tag consists of an embedded `<query>` tag. The `<search>` tag also encloses the default search period in `<earliest>` and `<latest>` tags. We can see this in the Splunk query that populates the drop-down input in *Figure 7.31*:

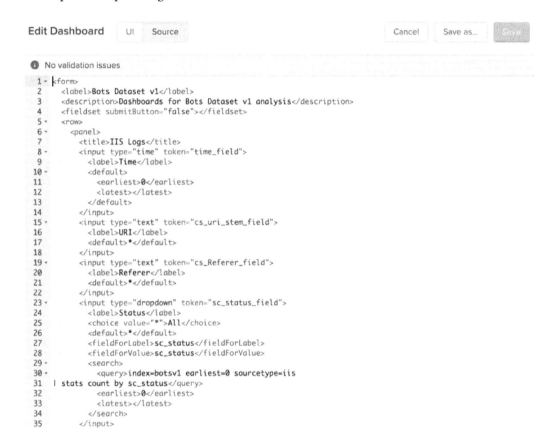

Figure 7.31 – The Simple XML for the inputs section of the dashboard

We can also see the `<search>` tag in the Splunk query that populates the results table in *Figure 7.32*:

```
36    <table>
37      <search>
38        <query>index=botsv1 earliest=0 sourcetype=iis cs_uri_stem=$cs_uri_stem_field$ cs_Referer=$cs_Referer_field$ sc_status=$sc_status_field$
39    | table _time, c_ip, s_ip, s_port, cs_uri_stem, cs_Referer, sc_status
40    | rename c_ip as "Client IP", s_ip as "Server IP", s_port as "Destination Port", cs_uri_stem as URI, cs_Referer as Referer, sc_status as Status</query>
41        <earliest>0</earliest>
42        <latest></latest>
43        <sampleRatio>1</sampleRatio>
44      </search>
45      <option name="count">10</option>
46      <option name="dataOverlayMode">none</option>
47      <option name="drilldown">none</option>
48      <option name="percentagesRow">false</option>
49      <option name="refresh.display">progressbar</option>
50      <option name="rowNumbers">false</option>
51      <option name="totalsRow">false</option>
52      <option name="wrap">true</option>
53    </table>
54   </panel>
55  </row>
56  <row>◻</row>
100 <row>◻</row>
133 </form>
```

Figure 7.32 – The Simple XML for the results table section of the dashboard

The ability to create filters gives us so much flexibility in our Splunk dashboards. You are encouraged to continue exploring new panels and filters until you are comfortable with them. We will look at adding reports and drilldowns to dashboards in the next section.

Adding reports and drilldowns to dashboards

The dashboard panels we have created so far are powered by inline searches. We can also create panels where the search results are generated by reports. Let's start by generating a report using one of the charts we created in *Chapter 6, Creating Tables and Charts Using SPL*. Enter the following query in the search bar:

```
index=botsv1 sourcetype=wineventlog EventCode=4624
| stats values(Account_Name) as users by host
```

This query generates the Account_Name property of all the users who successfully logged in to Windows grouped via the host device. *Figure 7.33* shows the results:

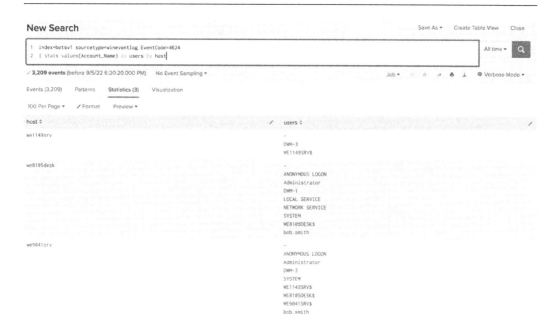

Figure 7.33 – Successful Windows logins

Let's save these new results as a new report by clicking the **Save As** dropdown and selecting **Report** (see *Figure 7.34*):

Figure 7.34 – Saving as a report

Enter the following in the **Save As Report** dialog box and leave the remaining options as their default values:

- **Title**: *Successful Windows Logins*
- **Description**: *Successful windows logins for* Bots Dataset v1

Let's look at these details in *Figure 7.35*:

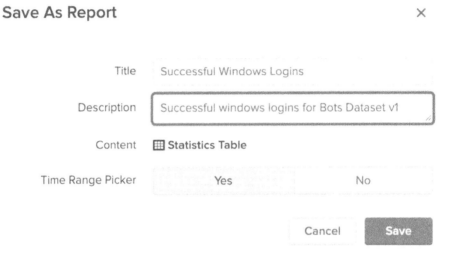

Figure 7.35 – Naming the report

We will see a confirmation message indicating that our report is complete (see *Figure 7.36*):

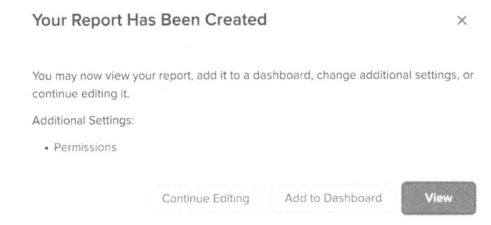

Figure 7.36 – Report created

We have the option to continue editing the report, add the report to a dashboard, or view the new report. Clicking the green **View** button takes us to the report, as seen in *Figure 7.37*:

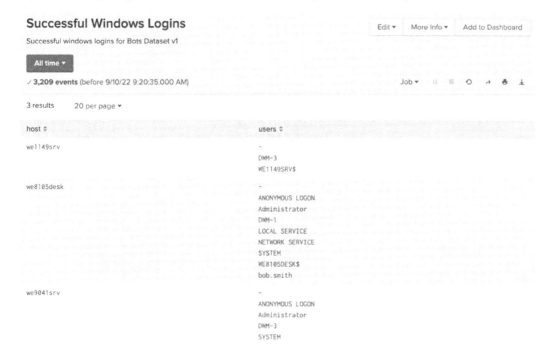

Figure 7.37 – The new report

Let's add the new **Successful Windows Logins** report as a panel to the Bots Dataset v1 dashboard by clicking **Add to Dashboard**, entering the following information, and clicking the green **Save** button:

- **Dashboard**: **Existing** (Bots Dataset v1)
- **Panel Title**: **Successful Windows Logins**
- **Panel Powered By**: **Report**

These details are shown in the following screenshot:

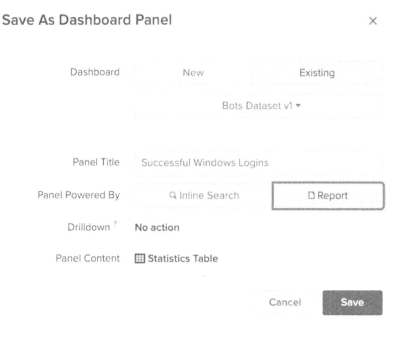

Figure 7.38 – Saving a report as a dashboard panel

The new dashboard panel is located at the bottom of the dashboard.

Splunk uses the term **drilldown** to represent an action that occurs when we click on a component in a dashboard. These actions allow us to investigate the results shown in the table or chart. An example drilldown allows us to view the raw data used to generate the results on the dashboard. In another case, we may use the drilldown to link to another dashboard, report, or Splunk component. The following options are available:

- No action
- Link to search
- Link to dashboard
- Link to report
- Link to custom URL
- Manage tokens on this dashboard (enable in-page drilldown actions)

Let's add a drilldown to the Bots Dataset v1 dashboard by clicking the **Edit** button at the top right of the dashboard. Scroll down to the **Successful Windows Logins** panel and click on the three vertical dots in the top-right corner. Select **Edit Drilldown** from the dropdown. Leave everything as-is and click **Apply**. *Figure 7.39* shows the **Drilldown Editor** area:

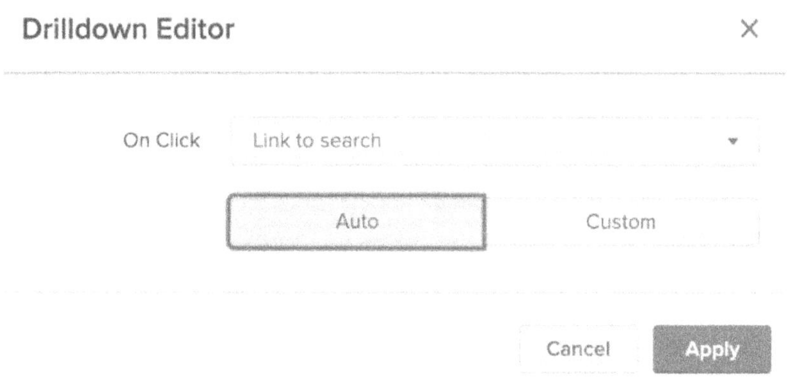

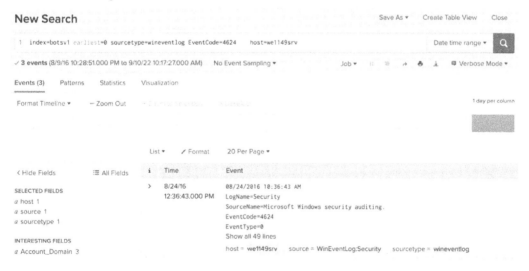

Figure 7.39 – Drilldown Editor with default options

Figure 7.40 shows what happens when we click on the **well49srv** host on the **Windows Successful Logins** panel. Note that we can see the raw events for all successful logins for host=well49srv. This is the default option:

Figure 7.40 – Drilldown for the Windows Successful Logins panel

Let's create a more interesting drilldown on the **IIS Logs** panel of the `Bots Dataset v1` dashboard. Click on the three vertical dots at the top right of the panel to open the **Drilldown Editor** area. This time, select **Manage tokens** on this dashboard. Remember the **Timechart of HTTP traffic from 40.80.148.42** panel in the `Bots Dataset v1` dashboard? We hardcoded an IP address of `40.80.148.42`. What if we wanted to see the HTTP traffic for any client IP address in the IIS logs? Let's create a drilldown on the **IIS Logs** table that will set a form **token** that we can use in the timechart:

1. First, create the drilldown by clicking the three vertical dots at the top right of the **IIS Logs** panel and selecting **Edit Drilldown**. The **Drilldown Editor** area has a simple interface.

2. Select **Manage tokens on this dashboard** from the **On Click** dropdown.

3. Then, select **Set** and enter `c_ip_field` and `$row.Client IP$` in the text boxes, as shown in *Figure 7.41*:

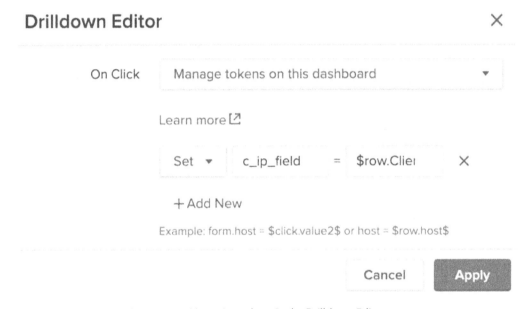

Figure 7.41 – Managing tokens in the Drilldown Editor area

This setting populates a new token called `c_ip_field` and sets it to the value of the `"Client IP"` value in the clicked row.

4. Next, we must edit the search in the **Timechart of HTTP traffic from** panel to the following query:

```
index=botsv1 earliest=0 sourcetype="stream:http" c_ip=$c_
ip_field$
| timechart count
```

Figure 7.42 shows the new timechart query:

Edit Search ☒

Title	
Search String	1 `index=botsv1 earliest=0 sourcetype="stream:http" c_ip=$c_ip_field$` 2 `| timechart count`
	Run Search ↗
Time Range	Use time picker ▾
	All time ▸
Auto Refresh Delay ?	No auto refresh ▾
Refresh Indicator	Progress bar ▾

Cancel   Convert to Report   **Apply**

Figure 7.42 – Editing the timechart query so that it includes the new filter

This will set a filter in the timechart panel.

5. Now, when we click on a row in the **IIS Logs** panel, Splunk will save the **Client IP** property in the **c_ip_field** token. This triggers a refresh of the timechart panel so that it shows the timechart for that **Client IP**.

6. Let's make things even more interesting by changing the title of the panel so that it displays the **Client IP** property. Replace the current title with **Timechart of HTTP traffic from c_ip_field**, as shown in *Figure 7.43*:

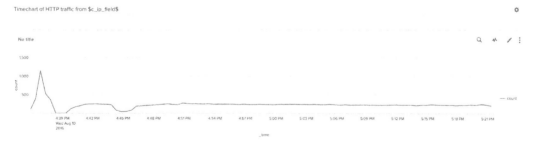

Figure 7.43 – New timechart panel with a token

Figure 7.44 shows what happens when we click on a row where the **Client IP** property is **40.80.148.42**. Note that the token change is reflected in the panel title:

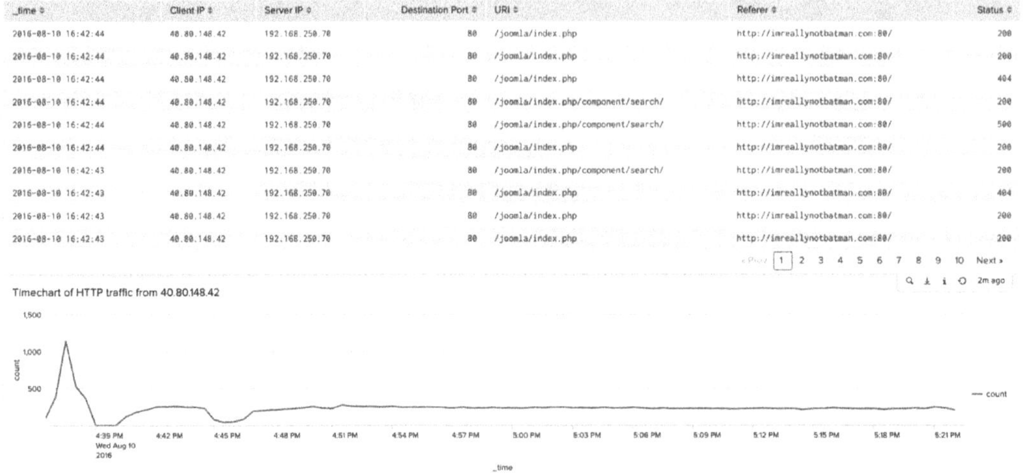

_time ⇕	Client IP ⇕	Server IP ⇕	Destination Port ⇕	URI ⇕	Referer ⇕	Status ⇕
2016-08-10 16:42:44	40.80.148.42	192.168.250.70	80	/joomla/index.php	http://imreallynotbatman.com:80/	200
2016-08-10 16:42:44	40.80.148.42	192.168.250.70	80	/joomla/index.php	http://imreallynotbatman.com:80/	200
2016-08-10 16:42:44	40.80.148.42	192.168.250.70	80	/joomla/index.php	http://imreallynotbatman.com:80/	404
2016-08-10 16:42:44	40.80.148.42	192.168.250.70	80	/joomla/index.php/component/search/	http://imreallynotbatman.com:80/	200
2016-08-10 16:42:44	40.80.148.42	192.168.250.70	80	/joomla/index.php/component/search/	http://imreallynotbatman.com:80/	500
2016-08-10 16:42:44	40.80.148.42	192.168.250.70	80	/joomla/index.php	http://imreallynotbatman.com:80/	200
2016-08-10 16:42:43	40.80.148.42	192.168.250.70	80	/joomla/index.php/component/search/	http://imreallynotbatman.com:80/	200
2016-08-10 16:42:43	40.80.148.42	192.168.250.70	80	/joomla/index.php	http://imreallynotbatman.com:80/	404
2016-08-10 16:42:43	40.80.148.42	192.168.250.70	80	/joomla/index.php	http://imreallynotbatman.com:80/	200
2016-08-10 16:42:43	40.80.148.42	192.168.250.70	80	/joomla/index.php	http://imreallynotbatman.com:80/	200

‹ Prev 1 2 3 4 5 6 7 8 9 10 Next ›

Timechart of HTTP traffic from 40.80.148.42

Figure 7.44 – Finished drilldown example

We've successfully created a Simple XML dashboard with multiple panels, inputs, drilldowns, and tokens. However, an exploration of Splunk dashboards would be incomplete without looking at the new **Splunk Dashboard Studio**, which offers different widgets for creating dashboards.

Experimenting with the new Dashboard Studio

Splunk Dashboard Studio was introduced in version *8.2x*. It offers various widgets targeted at making dashboard creation easier. We will work through a simple example in this section. In our past examples, we created dashboards by using the **Save As** option after running a search. This time, we will use the new Dashboard Studio instead:

1. First, open the **Search and Reporting** app and click **Dashboards** on the navigation bar.

2. Click the green **Create New Dashboard** button. We will see that there are two options for building a dashboard:

   • **Classic dashboards**: The traditional method that we reviewed in the first few sections of this chapter

   • **Dashboard studio**: A new builder that creates visually-rich, customizable dashboards

Enter the following values:

- **Dashboard title**: *Botsv1*
- **Description**: *Creating a dashboard using Dashboard Studio*
- **Permissions**: *Shared in App*
- **How do you want to build your dashboard**: *Dashboard Studio*
- **Select layout mode**: *Grid*
- The **Absolute** layout offers more flexibility, but the **Grid** layout is a quicker approach as Splunk automatically organizes each panel for us

These details can be seen in the following screenshot:

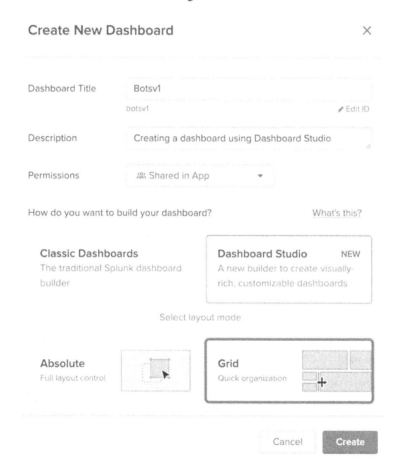

Figure 7.45 – Creating a new dashboard using Dashboard Studio

Figure 7.46 shows the blank dashboard:

Figure 7.46 – Blank Botsv1 dashboard

Let's look at the different parts of the interface:

- **Top menu on the left**:

  - **Undo/redo buttons**: Allow us to undo and redo changes to the dashboard

  - **Visualization dropdown**: Allows us to choose from a wide range of visualizations to add to the dashboard

  - **Inputs**: Allows us to choose from a set of input types, including dropdowns, text boxes, and time pickers

  - **Markdown text**: Allows us to add free text to the dashboard

  - **Configuration**: Opens the menu on the right-hand side of the screen, which allows us to make changes to different components on the dashboard

  - **Data overview**: Allows us to add data sources to the dashboard by creating searches

  - **Source mode**: Allows us to view the dashboard source

- **Buttons on the top right**:

  - **Light/dark mode**: Allows us to switch between light and dark mode

  - **View**: Allows us to preview the dashboard

  - **Save**: Saves changes to the dashboard

Let's create a simple dashboard using Dashboard Studio:

1. First, create a new table by selecting **Table** from the visualization dropdown. This will open the configuration panel on the right.

2. Create a new data source by clicking **Create Search** and entering the following information in the boxes:

- **Data Source Name**: *IIS Logs*

- **Search with SPL**:

```
index=botsv1 earliest=0 sourcetype=iis cs_Referer=*
| table _time, c_ip, s_ip, s_port, cs_uri_stem, cs_
Referer, sc_status
|  rename c_ip as "Client IP", s_ip as "Server IP",
s_port as "Destination Port", cs_uri_stem as URI, cs_
Referer as Referer, sc_status as Status
```

- **Time Range**: *Default*

Figure 7..47 shows the **Create Search** screen:

Figure 7.47 – Creating a new data source

The configuration panel will then present us with visualization options. Here, we can perform tasks such as changing the visualization type, title, description, and other formatting options.

3. Let's make a few updates to the dashboard panel by entering the following information:

    - **Title**: *IIS Logs*

    - **Description**: *IIS Logs for* `Bots Dataset v1`

4. The configuration panel also gives us the option to format columns. We can format the **Status** column by doing the following:

    A. Click on the **Add column to format** dropdown.

    B. Select the **Status** column.

    C. This adds the **Status** column to a list directly above the dropdown. Click on the pencil icon.

    D. Click on the **Text** tab in the **Dynamic Coloring** section. This opens a menu that we can use to change the color of the **Status** values.

    E. Enter the values shown in *Figure 7.48* to change the colors of the **Status** column, depending on the value:

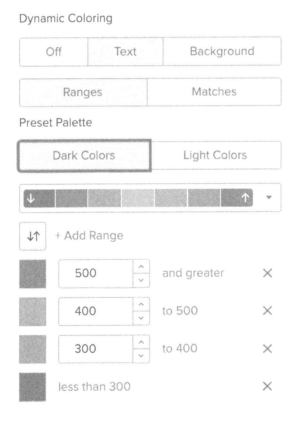

Figure 7.48 – Formatting the Status column

F.   *Figure 7.49* shows the resulting dashboard panel in **View** mode (click the **View** button at the top right):

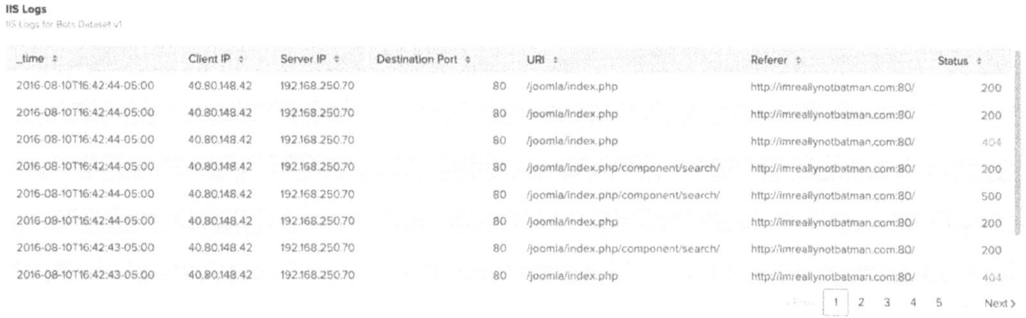

IIS Logs
IIS Logs for Bots Dataset v1

_time ⬍	Client IP ⬍	Server IP ⬍	Destination Port ⬍	URI ⬍	Referer ⬍	Status ⬍
2016-08-10T16:42:44-05:00	40.80.148.42	192.168.250.70	80	/joomla/index.php	http://imreallynotbatman.com:80/	200
2016-08-10T16:42:44-05:00	40.80.148.42	192.168.250.70	80	/joomla/index.php	http://imreallynotbatman.com:80/	200
2016-08-10T16:42:44-05:00	40.80.148.42	192.168.250.70	80	/joomla/index.php	http://imreallynotbatman.com:80/	404
2016-08-10T16:42:44-05:00	40.80.148.42	192.168.250.70	80	/joomla/index.php/component/search/	http://imreallynotbatman.com:80/	200
2016-08-10T16:42:44-05:00	40.80.148.42	192.168.250.70	80	/joomla/index.php/component/search/	http://imreallynotbatman.com:80/	500
2016-08-10T16:42:44-05:00	40.80.148.42	192.168.250.70	80	/joomla/index.php	http://imreallynotbatman.com:80/	200
2016-08-10T16:42:43-05:00	40.80.148.42	192.168.250.70	80	/joomla/index.php/component/search/	http://imreallynotbatman.com:80/	200
2016-08-10T16:42:43-05:00	40.80.148.42	192.168.250.70	80	/joomla/index.php	http://imreallynotbatman.com:80/	404

1   2   3   4   5   Next >

Figure 7.49 – The IIS Logs with a formatted Status column

5.   Scrolling to the bottom of the **Configuration** panel, we can see the option to create a drilldown. Let's create a drilldown that we will use in the next example.

6.   Click on the word **Drilldown**, select **Set Tokens | Set Another Token**, and enter the following values:

- **Token Name:** *c_ip_field*

- **Token Value:** *row.Client IP.value*

- **Default Value:** *

7.   Next, we must create a timechart. First, click on the **Add Chart** dropdown and select a **Line** chart. This will open a **New Data Source** window on the right where we can create our new timechart by entering the following values:

- **Data Source Name:** *Timechart of IIS Traffic*

- **Search with SPL:**

```
index=botsv1 earliest=0 sourcetype="stream:http" c_ip=$c_
ip_field$
| timechart count
```

- Also, enter the following visualization options after clicking the green **Apply & Close** button:

  - **Title:** *Timechart of IIS Traffic for* `$c_ip_field$`

  - **Description:** *Timechart of IIS Traffic for the Client IP clicked in the IIS Logs table previously*

Now, when we click on the **IIS Logs** table, the value of the `Client IP` field for that row will be stored in `c_ip_field`. This is reflected in the title of the **Timechart of IIS Traffic for c_ip_field** panel and the chart itself.

Figure 7.50 shows the completed dashboard:

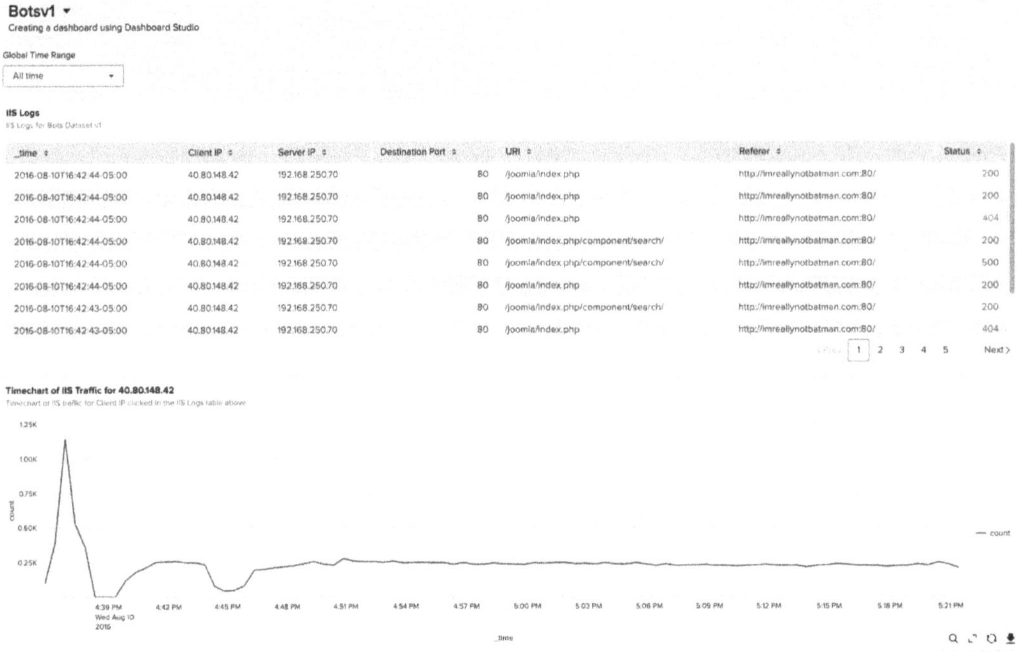

Figure 7.50 – Completed dashboard using Dashboard Studio

This section showed us how Dashboard Studio allows us to create dashboards using widgets that were not available in Simple XML. Many other features are available in Dashboard Studio, but they are beyond the scope of this book. You are encouraged to explore Dashboard Studio by adding inputs, panels, and charts of different types to appreciate the full capabilities of the tool.

Summary

In this chapter, we created dashboards and reports using Simple XML. The capabilities that Splunk offers make dashboard creation a fun and creative task. We enjoyed adding different kinds of inputs such as text boxes and dropdowns that we can use to filter data in the dashboard queries. We learned how to use tokens to pass the values from the inputs to the query. Then, we learned how to make our dashboards dynamic by introducing drilldowns. We also explored the dashboard source and observed the different parts of the XML. Finally, we used the various widgets in Splunk Dashboard Studio, which provides widgets to create a dashboard with inputs. We learned that these widgets allow users with limited Splunk experience to create dashboards.

In the next chapter, we will move away from the visualization frontend of Splunk to explore the way Splunk stores data.

Part 3:
Advanced Topics
in Splunk

This part takes a deeper dive into Splunk to explore concepts such as licensing, indexing, clusters, data models, multisite deployments, and container management.

This part comprises the following chapters:

- *Chapter 8, Licensing, Indexing, and Buckets*
- *Chapter 9, Clustering and Advanced Administration*
- *Chapter 10, Data Models, Acceleration, and Other Ways to Improve Performance*
- *Chapter 11, Multisite Splunk Deployments and Federated Search*
- *Chapter 12, Container Management*

8

Licensing, Indexing, and Buckets

The previous chapters showed us how to get data into Splunk and how to use Splunk query language to gain insight into the data and create visualizations that can be used to solve problems. In this chapter, we begin the exploration of how Splunk stores data. Splunk stores data in data structures called **buckets**. A collection of buckets is called an **index**. The process of storing incoming data into buckets is called **indexing**. Data passes through a series of **queues** and **pipelines**. The result is individual events that are stored physically on disk. Splunk organizes buckets and indexes on a filesystem in the form of raw data and index files. Splunk keeps track of the volume of incoming data using **license models**. We will look at various free and paid license models in Splunk.

In this chapter, we will explore the following topics:

- Understanding Splunk indexing and buckets
- Exploring Splunk queues
- Discussing Splunk licensing models

Understanding Splunk indexing and buckets

The strength of Splunk comes from the way data is indexed. Logically, a Splunk index is a repository of data that is stored in a uniform manner to make searching efficient. Physically, an index is a set of subdirectories called buckets. The term *indexing* in Splunk refers to the process whereby data coming from multiple sources into Splunk is organized into Splunk indexes. In this section, we will explore the mechanisms used to store data in indexes and buckets.

Raw data is forwarded from the source into Splunk. This data is converted into Splunk **events**, which are organized into indexes. An index is an immutable repository of data – that is, once data is added to an index, it cannot be edited. This goes back to the concept of the immutability of **big data** that we discussed in *Chapter 1, Introduction to Splunk and its Core Components*. There is no way to delete individual events from an index, but Splunk allows the following:

- **Deleting an entire index**
- **Deleting based on policy**, such as the age and size of an index

An index can contain multiple buckets and can get very large. Buckets within each index are arranged by the age of the incoming data. Buckets fall into five main states:

- **Hot** – buckets containing newly written data.
- **Warm** – buckets containing data that has rolled from hot buckets.
- **Cold** – buckets containing data that has rolled from warm buckets. They are usually located in a different location on disk.
- **Frozen** – buckets containing data that has rolled from cold buckets. By default, Splunk deletes data that rolls from cold buckets. However, Splunk also provides the option to store this data in frozen buckets on disk.
- **Thawed** – buckets containing data that has been restored from frozen buckets. This is one of the steps that is not automatic. This requires user intervention.

Table 8.1 shows the differences between these bucket states:

Flow of data	Bucket state	Searchable	Number of buckets open at one time	Actively written to	Relocated
	Hot	Yes	Low	Yes	N/A
	Warm	Yes	High	No	No, but the bucket is renamed
	Cold	Yes	High	No	Can be configured to store cold buckets in cheaper storage
	Frozen	No	Varies	No	Archived to cheaper storage
	Thawed	Yes	Varies	No	Data needs to be re-indexed after the thawing process

Table 8.1 – Splunk bucket states

Splunk has provided configuration options that allow us to specify how long data remains in each state. Some of these settings include the following:

- `maxDataSize` – the maximum size that a hot bucket can get before it is rolled into a hot bucket

- `maxHotBuckets` – the number of hot buckets allowable before the oldest bucket gets rolled into a warm bucket

- `homePath.maxDataSizeMB` – the maximum size of hot and warm buckets before buckets get rolled into a cold bucket

- `maxWarmDBCount` – the maximum number of warm buckets allowed before buckets get rolled into a cold bucket

- `frozenTimePeriodInSecs` – the maximum age of the oldest cold bucket before it rolls into a frozen state

- `maxTotalDataSizeMB` – the total size of an index before the oldest bucket rolls into a frozen state

- `coldPath.maxDataSizeMB` – the total size of cold buckets before the oldest bucket rolls into a frozen state

Figure 8.1 shows how data flows through Splunk buckets:

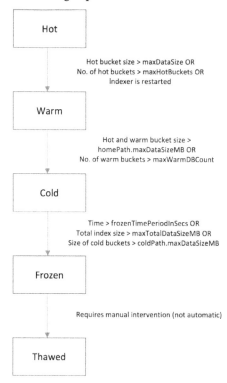

Figure 8.1 – Flow of data through bucket states

How do we configure indexes? Indexes are configured in the `indexes.conf` file. `indexes.conf` has *global* configurations and *index-specific* configurations. Global configurations are not specific to a stanza. They are applied to all indexes. *Figure 8.2* shows a sample of the default global configurations in `indexes.conf`:

```
#
# This file configures Splunk's indexes and their properties.
#

##############################################################################
# "global" params (not specific to individual indexes)
##############################################################################
sync = 0
indexThreads = auto
memPoolMB = auto
defaultDatabase = main
enableRealtimeSearch = true
suppressBannerList =
maxRunningProcessGroups = 8
maxRunningProcessGroupsLowPriority = 1
bucketRebuildMemoryHint = auto
serviceOnlyAsNeeded = true
serviceSubtaskTimingPeriod = 30
serviceInactiveIndexesPeriod = 60
maxBucketSizeCacheEntries = 0
processTrackerServiceInterval = 1
hotBucketTimeRefreshInterval = 10
rtRouterThreads = 0
rtRouterQueueSize = 10000
selfStorageThreads = 2
fileSystemExecutorWorkers = 5
hotBucketStreaming.extraBucketBuildingCmdlineArgs =
```

Figure 8.2 – Global configurations in indexes.conf

There are also index-specific defaults. *Figure 8.3* shows a sample of default configurations that are specific to indexes:

```
#######################################################################
# index specific defaults
#######################################################################
maxDataSize = auto
maxWarmDBCount = 300
frozenTimePeriodInSecs = 188697600
rotatePeriodInSecs = 60
coldToFrozenScript =
coldToFrozenDir =
compressRawdata = true
maxTotalDataSizeMB = 500000
maxGlobalRawDataSizeMB = 0
maxGlobalDataSizeMB = 0
maxMemMB = 5
maxConcurrentOptimizes = 6
maxHotSpanSecs = 7776000
maxHotIdleSecs = 0
maxHotBuckets = auto
metric.maxHotBuckets = auto
minHotIdleSecsBeforeForceRoll = auto
quarantinePastSecs = 77760000
quarantineFutureSecs = 2592000
rawChunkSizeBytes = 131072
minRawFileSyncSecs = disable
assureUTF8 = false
serviceMetaPeriod = 25
partialServiceMetaPeriod = 0
throttleCheckPeriod = 15
syncMeta = true
maxMetaEntries = 1000000
maxBloomBackfillBucketAge = 30d
enableOnlineBucketRepair = true
enableDataIntegrityControl = false
```

Figure 8.3 – Index-specific defaults

Figure 8.3 shows the default values for each of these settings. For example, maxDateSize is set to auto, which means that Splunk will manage the value of this setting. The default of maxWarmDBCount is 300 buckets, frozenTimePeriodInSecs is 188697600 seconds, and maxTotalDataSizeMB is 500000MB.

The last section of indexes.conf contains index definitions, which are individual stanzas that define indexes. If specified, a setting in this section will overwrite the configurations specified in the default index-specific section. *Figure 8.4* is a snapshot of this section containing the [main], [_internal], and [_audit] indexes:

```
###############################################################################
# index definitions
###############################################################################

[main]
homePath    = $SPLUNK_DB/defaultdb/db
coldPath    = $SPLUNK_DB/defaultdb/colddb
thawedPath  = $SPLUNK_DB/defaultdb/thaweddb
tstatsHomePath = volume:_splunk_summaries/defaultdb/datamodel_summary
maxMemMB = 20
maxConcurrentOptimizes = 6
maxHotIdleSecs = 86400
maxHotBuckets = 10
maxDataSize = auto_high_volume

[_internal]
homePath    = $SPLUNK_DB/_internaldb/db
coldPath    = $SPLUNK_DB/_internaldb/colddb
thawedPath  = $SPLUNK_DB/_internaldb/thaweddb
tstatsHomePath = volume:_splunk_summaries/_internaldb/datamodel_summary
maxDataSize = 1000
maxHotSpanSecs = 432000
frozenTimePeriodInSecs = 2592000

[_audit]
homePath    = $SPLUNK_DB/audit/db
coldPath    = $SPLUNK_DB/audit/colddb
thawedPath  = $SPLUNK_DB/audit/thaweddb
tstatsHomePath = volume:_splunk_summaries/audit/datamodel_summary
```

Figure 8.4 – The default [main], [_internal], and [_audit] stanzas

The default location of indexes is var/lib. This can be configured so that indexes are stored on a separate mounted partition with faster and more efficient storage if necessary.

The [main] stanza creates an index called main. The main index is the default index where data is stored when no index is specified at ingestion. The Path settings such as homePath and coldPath define the location on the filesystem where Splunk will store those buckets. For example, the hot buckets will be stored in the location defined by homePath ($SPLUNK_DB/defaultdb/db), the cold buckets will be stored in the location defined by coldPath ($SPLUNK_DB/defaultdb/colddb), and the thawed data will be stored in the location defined by thawedPath ($SPLUNK_DB/defaultdb/thaweddb). Remember that hot and warm buckets are stored in the same location, which is defined by homePath. All other indexes, including [_internal], [_audit], and custom indexes, are stored in a directory that include the name of the index. For example, homePath for the [_internal] index is ($SPLUNK_DB/_internaldb/db), and cold buckets for an index called [botsv1] will be stored in its coldPath at ($SPLUNK_DB/botsv1/db).

Figure 8.5 shows the structure of directories and subdirectories on the filesystem for the main index (the output was generated by executing the ls -lR defaultdb command):

```
drwx------   2                         64 Oct   6 17:27 colddb
drwx------   2                         64 Jan 16  2020 datamodel_summary
drwx------   7                        224 Oct   6 17:27 db
drwx------   2                         64 Jan 16  2020 thaweddb

defaultdb/colddb:
total 0

defaultdb/datamodel_summary:
total 0

defaultdb/db:
total 8
-rw-------   1                         10 Jan 16  2020 CreationTime
drwx--x---   2                         64 Jan 16  2020 GlobalMetaData
drwx--x---  13                        416 Jul 13  2021 db_1626119455_1626119337_0
drwx--x---  13                        416 May  3 18:08 db_1651526190_1651526190_1
```

Figure 8.5 – Directories and subdirectories in defaultdb

The lower portion of *Figure 8.5* displays metadata (the `CreationTime` file and `GlobalMetaData` directory). It also includes two buckets (`db_1626119455_1626119337_0` and `db_1651526190_1651526190_1`). Those are two buckets containing hot and warm data. The two numbers (`1651526190` and `1651526190`) in the name of the bucket specify the start and end epoch timestamps of the data in the bucket.

Figure 8.6 shows the contents of the `db_1626119455_1626119337_0` bucket:

```
defaultdb/db/db_1626119455_1626119337_0:
total 56
-rw-------   1                       2456 Jul 12  2021 1626119455-1626119337-5048096932844701314.tsidx
-rw-------   1                        100 Jul 12  2021 Hosts.data
-rw-------   1                        112 Jul 12  2021 SourceTypes.data
-rw-------   1                        143 Jul 12  2021 Sources.data
-rw-------   1                        300 Jul 12  2021 Strings.data
-rw-------   1                        124 Jul 13  2021 bloomfilter
-rw-------   1                         75 Jul 13  2021 bucket_info.csv
-rw-------   1                          0 Jul 13  2021 optimize.result
drwx------   5                        160 Jul 13  2021 rawdata
```

Figure 8.6 – Contents of the bucket

There are a few important files in *Figure 8.6*:

- `Hosts.data` – a list of all the hosts represented in the bucket.

- `Sourcetypes.data` – a list of all the sourcetypes represented in the bucket.

- `Sources.data` – a list of the sources represented in the bucket.

- `Strings.data` – a list of fields that are extracted from the data at index time.

- `1626119455-1626119337-5048096932844701314.tsidx` – the index file for the bucket. This is a binary file and cannot be viewed in an editor. It is used internally by Splunk to find data in each bucket efficiently.

- `Bloomfilter` – a data structure that helps Splunk determine whether certain keywords are found in the bucket.

- `bucket_info.csv` – a comma-delimited file that specifies, among other values, the earliest index time and latest index time of data in the bucket.

Finally, there is a `rawdata` directory in the bucket. *Figure 8.7* shows the files in the `rawdata` directory:

```
defaultdb/db/db_1626119455_1626119337_0/rawdata:
total 24
-rw-------  1                          489 Jul 13  2021 journal.gz
-rw-------  1                            8 Jul 13  2021 slicemin.dat
-rw-------  1                           23 Jul 13  2021 slicesv2.dat
```

Figure 8.7 – The rawdata directory

The `rawdata` directory contains the following files:

- `journal.gz` – the compressed file containing the event data. The events are stored in constructs called **slices**.

- `slicesv2.dat` – a file used to map `tsidx` data to slices in the compressed data (`journal.gz`).

In this section, we learned about how Splunk stores data in buckets and indexes. We will now look at the **data pipeline** that converts incoming data into Splunk events.

Exploring Splunk queues

The Splunk data pipeline is a series of processes that converts incoming data into Splunk events. These processes include breaking data into events, defining the timestamp, and extracting fields. We will use a set of keywords throughout this section, including **pipeline**, **processor**, and **queue**. A pipeline is a *Splunk thread*. There can be multiple pipelines running at the same time. There may be multiple processors/processes within a pipeline. The queue is the data structure that stores data between pipelines. Data coming into Splunk is queued before it can be processed. If a process takes longer than usual, the queues fill up. In this section, we will discuss the different segments of the Splunk data pipeline. *Figure 8.8* shows the relationship between queues, processors, and pipelines:

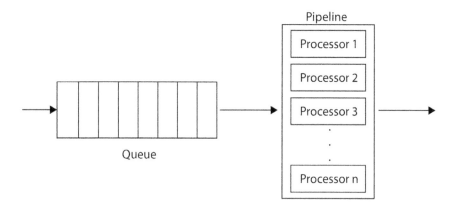

Figure 8.8 – Queues, pipelines, and processors

The Splunk data pipeline consists of four main segments:

- **Parsing**
- **Merging**
- **Typing**
- **Indexing**

Table 8.2 shows the different queues and the pipelines that they precede:

Queue	Pipeline
tcpin_cooked_pqueue	Inputs data into the indexer
parsingQueue	Parsing
aggQueue	Merging
typingQueue	Typing
indexQueue	Indexing
tcpout_queue	Sends data out via syslog
nullQueue	Sends data to dev-null

Table 8.2 – Queues precede pipelines

You will note that the two last entries in *Table 8.2* show **tcpout_queue** and **nullQueue**. tcpout_queue is used to store events that are being sent out of Splunk to another destination, such as a syslog server. nullQueue is used to delete data before it can be indexed (stored on disk). The default action for nullQueue is to send the output to dev-null.

The following processes occur when data first arrives in Splunk:

1. Raw data arrives from the source.

2. Data is queued in `tcpin_cooked_pqueue`.

3. Data is broken into `64K blocks`.

4. Splunk annotates each block with metadata. The data is annotated based on the full block of data. At this point, Splunk is not aware of the concept of individual Splunk events. Each of the following keys is applied to the entire 64K blocks of data:

    A. **Host** – the source host

    B. **Source** – the source as specified by the forwarder

    C. **Sourcetype** – the sourcetype specified by the forwarder

    D. **Index** (optional)

    E. **Character encoding** (optional)

Figure 8.9 illustrates the processes that occur when data first arrives on the indexer:

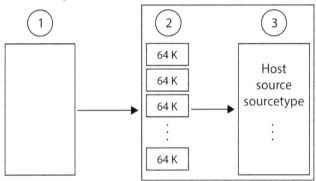

Figure 8.9 – The input phase processes

Data from this segment waits in `parsingQueue` for the next step in the process. We will discuss the parsing pipeline in the next section.

Parsing

This is the pipeline where Splunk starts looking at data more closely. Splunk refers to this stage as **event processing**. This stage of event processing involves a variety of processes, ranging from line breaking to field extraction. *Table 8.3* shows the main processes:

Process	Description	Extra Information
`utf`	UTF encoding	These four processes together are sometimes called the parsing pipeline in older Splunk documentation. The latest documentation uses the parsing phase to refer to these processes as well as the aggregator (also referred to as the `Merging` stage), `regexreplacement`, `metricschema`, and annotator (collectively referred to as the `Typing` stage).
`linebreaker`	Line breaking	
`metrics`	Metrics processing	
`header`	Header processing	
`aggregator`	Line merging Timestamp extracting	The process of `line merging` and `timestamp extraction` is also referred to as the merging stage. Events are queued in `aggQueue` before they are processed in this pipeline.
`regexreplacement`	Regex	These three processes are collectively referred to as the typing pipeline. Events are queued in `typingQueue` before they are processed in this pipeline.
`metricschema`	More metric processing	
`annotator`	Extracting punctuation	

Table 8.3 – Event processing on the indexer

We will discuss some of these processes in the next subsections.

linebreaker (line breaking)

The `linebreaker` process breaks each 64K block into individual events. It is at this point that `event breakers` settings are applied. Splunk determines how to break the blocks into events by looking at the `LINE_BREAKER` setting. The default of this setting is a sequence of newlines and carriage returns (`([\r\n]+)`). Modification of this setting is done on the forwarder in the regex format. The forwarder sends this to the indexer.

aggregator (Line merging and timestamping)

This step involves line merging based on the `SHOULD_LINEMERGE` setting. This setting is used to merge separated lines in an event. By default, `SHOULD_LINEMERGE` is set to `true` – that is, lines are merged by default. In most cases, changing this setting is not necessary. However, if this setting is set to false, then the parsing segment splits all the data into lines and then applies the `LINE_BREAKER` setting. This is very inefficient and should be avoided if the incoming data contains many multiline events. Both the `LINE_BREAKER` and `SHOULD_LINEMERGE` settings can be modified in the `props.conf` file on the forwarder.

The `aggregator` process also extracts the timestamp. This step is accomplished based on a series of precedence rules:

1. Splunk searches the event for a series of characters that match the TIME_FORMAT specified in the `props.conf` file.

2. If no explicit TIME_FORMAT is specified, then Splunk tries to determine the timestamp based on the sourcetype of the event. Remember that the sourcetype is assigned in the `input` phase. TIME_FORMAT can be assigned on a sourcetype level.

3. Determines whether Splunk needs to figure out the year of events with no year. Splunk determines the year through several methods, including looking at the year of the previous event or the current time. Once it determines the year of the previous event, Splunk does a series of checks, such as checking for year-end dates and leap years.

4. Splunk checks `file name` or `source name` for a date.

5. If the source of the data is a file, Splunk looks at `last modified date` and the time of the file.

6. Splunk uses the date identification setting in `datetime.xml`.

7. Splunk sets the date to `current system time`.

Most data coming into Splunk from a predefined sourcetype such as firewall logs or windows events have obvious timestamps. Therefore, Splunk does not usually have to go through *steps 1–7*. However, sometimes new data from application logs can prove problematic. For example, some application developers may send logs where each event contains multiple timestamps. In this case, we can use settings such as TIME_PREFIX and MAX_TIMESTAMP_LOOKAHEAD. The former identifies the series of characters (represented in a regular expression) that precedes the timestamp. MAX_TIMESTAMP_LOOKAHEAD specifies how far into the event to look for the timestamp. This setting is usually used along with the TIME_PREFIX setting. Complex regular expressions can increase the load on the indexers. Also, we would need to re-index the data if the timestamp were incorrect in the indexed data. Therefore, it is important to review new data sources before ingesting large volumes of production data. We could inform the data source owner, such as an application developer, to supply us with a sample of the data that we can analyze in a test index. We can determine the correct settings for TIME_PREFIX and MAX_TIMESTAMP_LOOKAHEAD and then begin ingesting the large volume of data.

In addition to performing line merging and timestamp extraction, Splunk also applies the metadata assigned to each block of each individual event. In addition, we will also assign some other basic default fields to each event. Some of these fields are shown in *Table 8.4*:

Field	Description
host	The IP or hostname of the source host.
source	The source of the data. This could be a filename, script, port, or modular input.

Field	Description
sourcetype	The sourcetype, which is a logical concept that groups similar data. The sourcetype is very important because settings can be applied on the sourcetype level to an entire set of data. For example, we can define a field extraction to a sourcetype called iis, which lets us know how to extract the src field from all iis events.
_time	The timestamp extracted in 2) b.
_raw	The _raw field contains the raw data of each event. Each event contains the extracted fields as well as the raw data.
_indextime	The Unix time the event was indexed. This is a hidden field.
_cd	The address (index bucket and index bucket offset) of the event in the index in epoch time. This is a hidden field.
_bkt	The bucket where the event is stored.
Index	The name of the index.
linecount	The number of lines in the event. This field is useful when troubleshooting issues with large events.
punct	The punctuation pattern of the event. This field will be extracted by a process called annotator.
splunk_server	The name of the Splunk server where the event is stored.
date_* fields	Extracted components of the timestamp (_time), such as date_hour, date_mday, and date_minute. Also includes date_zone, which is the local timezone of the event expressed in Unix time.

Table 8.4 – Default fields assigned at index time

We move on to the next step in the process.

RegexReplacement (Regex)

This step applies regular expressions from props.conf and transforms.conf to each event. This is the step where field extraction occurs. We covered field extractions in *Chapter 3, Onboarding and Normalizing Data*. It is best practice to extract fields at search time – that is, on the search head. However, it is also possible to extract fields at index time – for example, if you have a search query that almost always returns the same result but takes a long time to extract on the search head. This can result in a high load on the search head every time the search is run. Instead, we would create an index time extraction that extracts the field on the indexer. Therefore, this will be a one-time extraction and does not need to be executed every time a search runs.

If a heavy forwarder is being used, this `parsing` step is performed on the heavy forwarder before it arrives on the indexer.

These are just a few of the processes that occur in the parsing phase. Once events are processed in the parsing phase, they enter `indexQueue` where they await processing in the indexing pipeline. Next, let us explore the concept of indexing.

Indexing

As we saw in the *Understanding Splunk indexing and buckets* section, `indexing` is the process where Splunk stores both raw data and index files to disk. By the time data gets to the `indexerPipe` pipeline, it has been broken into events, timestamps have been extracted, and field extractions have occurred. At this stage, Splunk indexes the events. However, this is also the stage that some of the events may be forwarded to other destinations. There are a few processes that can do that:

- `tcp-output-generic-processor` – sends data out to `tcpout_queue` where it will be destined for another host. The receiving host will be listening on port TCP. The `indexerPipe` pipeline on a heavy forwarder sends all its events to a Splunk indexer. Sometimes, an indexer may forward data outside of Splunk to a receiving host. The receiving host and port setting is set in the `outputs.conf` file of the sending host. In cases where only some of the events are sent to a receiving host, we specify which data should be sent in the `props.conf` and `transforms.conf` settings.

- `syslog-output-generic-processor` – sends data out via a syslog (`UDP 514`) port. This is like `tcp-output-generic-processor`, and the receiving host and port are configured in `outputs.conf` and conditions for routing are set in `props.conf` and `outputs.conf`.

- `indexandforward` – indexes the data before sending it off to another indexer. There may be a need to index and then forward all the data. This is configured by setting the `indexAndForward` setting in `outputs.conf` on the indexer. You may also want to index only some of the data before forwarding it, or you may choose to forward any data that you do not want to index locally. This is called **selective indexing**. Selective indexing is enabled by modifying `inputs.conf` and `outputs.conf`.

- `indexer` – as discussed in the *Understanding Splunk indexing and buckets* section, this is the process of storing data on disk. First, the `indexer` processor calculates the license volume before writing the data to disk.

- `nullQueue` – sends data by default to `dev-null`.

There are also queues and pipelines on Splunk universal forwarders. The processors in these pipelines do preliminary processing before forwarding data to the indexer. One such pipeline is the parsing pipeline. Data enters `parsingQueue` on the universal forwarder after passing through one or more processes/pipelines, such as `structuredparsing` (processes structured data such as comma-delimited value files) and `TailReader` (monitors the end of files). `parsingQueue` leads into the parsing pipeline, which sets configurations such as `INDEXED_EXTRACTIONS` (specifies the type of file and what kind of extraction should be used to read data) and the `thruput` processor that monitors the flow of data out of the universal forwarder.

There are so many processes on the Splunk components that help us get our data into a format that makes it easy to search. We reviewed several of these processes and explored Splunk queues and pipelines. *Figure 8.10* summarizes the processes that we have covered:

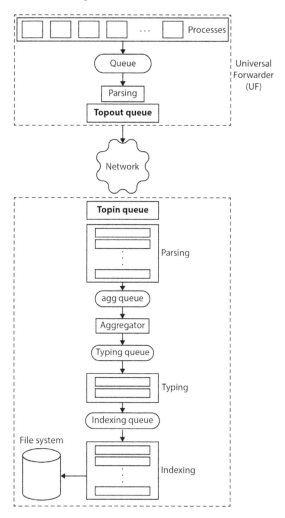

Figure 8.10 – Splunk queues and pipelines

We will move on to discussing the Splunk licensing models in the next section.

Discussing Splunk licensing models

We have got this far in the book without thinking about licenses. This is because the basic Splunk functionality can be appreciated using the free version of Splunk. **Splunk Free** is the implicit license that allows us to index 500 MB of data, run Splunk search queries, and create dashboards and reports. Splunk Free does not expire but only allows access to a limited number of Splunk Enterprise features. For example, Splunk Free does not allow for features such as `clustering` and will halt searching if there are license violations (three license warnings in a rolling 30-day window). Note that the AWS instances we created in *Chapter 2, Setting Up the Splunk Environment*, were not Splunk Free. The **Splunk Enterprise AWS** instances that we used are shipped with fully featured trial licenses, which are valid for 60 days. The license defaults to Splunk Free after the trial period.

Some of the other limitations of Splunk Free include the following:

- Although Splunk Free allows us to create dashboards and reports, they do not allow us to create alerts. If we install Splunk with a **Splunk Enterprise trial license** and that license expires and defaults to Splunk Free, we will lose any alerts that were created using the trial license.

- Access to Splunk Web does not have a login prompt, which creates possible security vulnerabilities if sensitive data is stored in Splunk during POCs. This is especially important if we are working with a Splunk Enterprise trial license that expires and defaults to **Splunk Free**.

- It is not possible to create new roles and users, as discussed in *Chapter 7, Creating Dynamic Dashboards*. Again, if a Splunk Enterprise trial license expires and defaults to Splunk Free, any roles and/or users created while on the trial license will be unavailable. In addition, any knowledge objects that these users created will be unavailable if they were not shared globally.

- As mentioned earlier, indexer and search head clustering are not available in Splunk Free since its installations are standalone deployments. It is not possible to use the deployment management tools discussed in *Chapter 2, Setting Up the Splunk Environment*. But how does licensing work? Splunk keeps a measure of the *volume of data* that is indexed as it arrives on the indexers. The method used to measure data depends on the type of data that arrives on the indexer:

    - **Event data** – Splunk measures the raw data that arrives on the indexing pipeline. Note that data replication in an indexer cluster does not count against the deployment's Splunk license quota.

    - **Metrics data** – Splunk measures metrics event data, such as the preceding event data. However, each metric event is capped at 150 bytes.

    - `_internal` and `_introspection` data – Splunk does not include these events in the license volume.

- **Summary indexing** – Splunk does not include these events in the license volume.

We have already discussed the Splunk Free and the Splunk Enterprise trial licenses. *Table 8.5*, adapted from the *Splunk Admin Manual (Types of Splunk Enterprise licenses)*, shows the different types of Splunk Enterprise licenses:

License conditions	Enterprise: < 100 GB daily index	Enterprise: > 100 GB daily index	Enterprise: infrastructure (vCPU)
Blocks a search while in violation	Yes	No	No
Displays a message when in warning or violation	Yes	Yes	No
Can be stacked with other licenses	Yes	Yes	No
Allows all features of Splunk	Yes	Yes	Yes

Table 8.5 – Types of Splunk Enterprise licenses

In addition, Splunk offers **Dev/Test** licenses that cannot be used in production environments. The differences between a Splunk Free license and a Splunk Dev/Test license include the following:

- A Dev/Test license expires after 6 months but can be renewed on request
- A Dev/Test license allows us to index 50 GB daily compared to the Splunk Free cap of 500 MB
- Searching will pause if a certain number of warnings/violations are triggered on a Dev/Test license

Splunk also offers a **Splunk Developer** license that developers can use to create Splunk apps and add-ons. This license gives more flexibility than the Splunk Dev/Test license but has less functionality than the full Splunk Enterprise license. *Table 8.6*, also adapted from the *Splunk Admin Manual (Types of Splunk Enterprise licenses)* page, compares the two licenses:

License conditions	Dev/Test	Developer
Blocks a search while in violation	Varies	Yes
Displays a message when in warning or violation	Yes	Yes
Can be stacked with other licenses	No	No
Allows all features of Splunk	No	Yes

Table 8.6 – Difference between Dev/Test and Developer licenses

Finally, the following list includes a few more specialized Splunk licenses that are available:

- **Forwarder licensing** is used for forwarders. This license is installed by default on Splunk universal forwarders. This license allows for unlimited forwarding of data. However, this license will not offer all the features required for a heavy forwarder. Heavy forwarders are usually configured with a full Splunk Enterprise license.

- **Beta licenses** allow for specific Splunk Enterprise features scheduled for release.

- **Splunk Premium App licenses**, such as the license needed for **Splunk Enterprise Security** and the Splunk **IT Service Intelligence (ITSI)** license, are licenses purchased in addition to the basic Splunk Enterprise license previously discussed. These licenses are acquired through a Splunk sales representative.

Every Splunk server that indexes data requires a Splunk Enterprise license. In addition, Splunk servers that perform management functionality also require a Splunk Enterprise license. These servers include the following:

- **Deployment server**

- **Indexer cluster manager node** – all indexer cluster nodes need to share the same license configuration

- **Search head cluster deployer**, and all search head cluster members need to have access to a Splunk Enterprise license

- **Monitoring console**

A few terms used when discussing Splunk licensing include the following:

- **License manager** – a Splunk server used to manage Splunk licenses. This can be coupled with other management components such as the deployment server, cluster manager, and monitoring console. The Splunk servers that connect to a license manager are called **license peers**.

- **License group** – a set of license stacks including the **Enterprise/Sales Trial group**, **Enterprise Trial group**, **Free group**, and **Forwarder group**. Only one group can be active at any time.

- **License stack** – one or more licenses. For example, a deployment may have a Splunk Enterprise license of 150 GB and another license of 500 GB. Those two licenses can work together as one in a stack. However, it is not possible to stack Enterprise Trial, Free, Dev/Test, and Forwarder licenses.

- **License pool** – a pool allows us to create logical partitions among Splunk components. For example, we can create a pool for different types of indexers (`test` and `production`) and assign different volumes to each type. This way, the test indexers do not consume too much of our licensed volume during testing.

Now that we understand the different licenses that are available, let us learn how to configure licenses in Splunk.

Configuring licenses

If we are dealing with a simple standalone instance, we only need to install a license on the standalone instance. Licenses are purchased and downloaded on the Splunk website (`splunk.com`). A Splunk license is basically a text file. To install the licenses, follow these steps:

1. Navigate to **Settings | Licensing** and click on **Add license**.
2. Click the **Choose file** button and browse the filesystem for the license file, or copy and paste the contents of a license file in the field provided.
3. Click the **Install** button to install the new license.
4. Restart **Splunk Enterprise**.

Now, let's discuss the configuration of the license manager. The **license manager** must be the same or a later version of its license peers. The license manager can exist on an existing management server, such as a monitoring console, deployment server, indexer cluster manager, or search head cluster deployer. Once we choose which Splunk server will serve as the license manager, we will next install the license, as we did in the standalone instance using *steps 1–4* previously. In addition, we will configure each of the license peers – that is, the nodes which will connect to the license manager in a distributed environment. We use the following steps to configure a license peer:

1. Navigate to **Settings | Licensing** on the license peer and click on the **Change to Peer** button.
2. Select **Designate a different Splunk instance as the license server** using the radio button.
3. Enter the IP address or hostname and management port (the default is 8089) into the field provided and click the **Save** button.
4. Restart **Splunk Enterprise**.
5. Optionally, we can create pools on the license manager.

We can also use the command line to configure license peers by running the following command on the license peer:

```
splunk edit licenser-localpeer -manager_uri 'https://license_
manager_host:port'
```

The Splunk license manager interface found at **Settings | Licensing** allows us to perform other tasks, such as creating, editing, or deleting license pools, adding and deleting licenses, and viewing license alerts and violations. In addition, we can review the license report, which displays charts showing the license usage for the current day as well as for the previous 30 days.

Licensing is an important component of Splunk Enterprise. It is driven by the volume of data that is indexed in Splunk.

Summary

This chapter was an exploration of how Splunk stores data. Since Splunk is a paid application, we started by looking at how licensing works in Splunk. We learned about the different licensing models, such as the Splunk Free and Splunk Enterprise licenses. We looked at the different kinds of events that count against the Splunk license and defined terms such as Splunk license groups, stacks, and pools. We ended that discussion by learning how to configure licenses using Splunk Web and the Splunk CLI. Indexes and buckets are the constructs used to store data in Splunk. We learned that indexes are a repository of data and contain multiple buckets. We learned about the different types of buckets (warm, cold, frozen, and thawed). We discovered that we could make changes to the way Splunk stores data by making changes to settings in `indexes.conf`, such as `maxDataSize` and `frozenTimePeriodInSecs`. We saw how each of these settings determines when data rolls from one bucket to the next. We explored the filesystem of a Splunk host and saw the different types of files that make up buckets and indexes. Finally, we studied queues and pipelines in Splunk. Data waits in queues until it can be processed in pipelines.

We will look at indexer and search head clusters in the next chapter. The dive into the indexer cluster will allow us to use some of the knowledge that we gained about indexes in this chapter.

9

Clustering and Advanced Administration

A **cluster** is a set of servers that are pooled together to work as one. Traditionally, the concept of a cluster is known to increase availability, fault tolerance, and efficiency. If one server fails, then the cluster reconfigures itself to ensure that the application is still available to users. For this to work, there must be a method of ensuring that data is shared between the individual cluster members or that there is some form of management or record keeping. There also needs to be a process in place to facilitate data recovery so that data fidelity can be maintained. We can configure search head and indexer clusters in Splunk to achieve all these advantages. In this chapter, we will discuss how search head and indexer clusters work and the components that make up each type of cluster. We will also look at a high-level overview of cluster configuration commands used to administer search head and indexer clusters. Finally, we'll look at the concept of access control as it applies to users and roles.

In this chapter, we will explore the following topics:

- Introducing Splunk clusters
- Understanding search head clusters
- Understanding indexer clusters

Introducing Splunk clusters

A Splunk cluster is a collection of Splunk Enterprise servers working together to ensure that data is available to users. Splunk search head and indexer clusters offer the following:

- **Protection against data loss** (indexer clusters)
- **Data availability** (search head and indexer clusters)
- **Fault tolerance** (search head and indexer clusters)

Search head clusters ensure that the efficiency of a Splunk search is not affected as users and search volume increase. *Indexer clusters* store Splunk data in a form that ensures that indexes are replicated across members of the cluster.

In the next two sections, we will look at search head and indexer clusters. We'll explore the role they play in ensuring *data loss protection*, *data availability*, and *fault tolerance* in Splunk deployments. There is also the concept of multisite clustering, where clusters are configured to exist across multiple geographical sites. However, this concept is beyond the scope of this chapter.

Understanding search head clusters

A Splunk search head cluster is a set of three or more Splunk search heads working together as one to improve search capacity and increase availability against single server failures. The exact number of search heads in the search head cluster is determined by the number of concurrent users, the number of searches run on the search heads, and the level of availability required. With a traditional unclustered search head arrangement, a failure of one search head results in the loss of search artifacts or search results, configurations, apps/add-ons, and search jobs. Configuring search heads into a search head cluster can improve availability and scalability as the number of users and searches increases.

Figure 9.1 illustrates a simple three-node search head cluster:

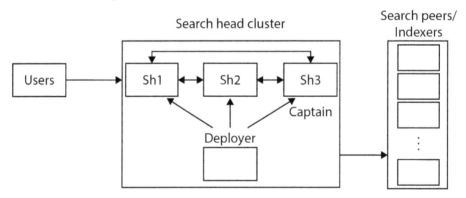

Figure 9.1 – A search head cluster

There are three main components of a search head cluster:

- The search head cluster members include the search heads and a **captain**. The elected captain is a role that one of the search heads plays. The role may switch between the different cluster members, depending on the circumstance. It is the search head that, besides its usual search head responsibilities of running search jobs, is also responsible for *coordinating job scheduling*, *search artifact*, and *configuration replication* among the cluster members, as well as *search knowledge bundle distribution*, to search peers (indexers). There is only one captain at any given time. However, the captain role is *dynamic* – that is, it can change from one cluster member to another over time. Some instances that will trigger a change in the captain include a failed captain node, network changes, or connection issues between other cluster members. The search head cluster must have the participation of the majority of the cluster members. The captain will resign if it detects that there is an issue, and the majority of members are not participating. The search heads will continue to operate ad hoc searches until a new captain can be elected. An ad hoc search is a search that is executed by a user in the search bar. Most of the searches we ran in *Chapter 4, Introduction to SPL*, were ad hoc searches.

A **saved** or **scheduled** search is a search that is saved on the search head and scheduled to run at specific times. The captain is the *scheduler* in a search head cluster. Therefore, clustered search heads are unable to execute *scheduled searches* if the captain is down. During this time, the cluster is down – that is, each cluster member is participating as a standalone search head. Once a new captain is elected, the cluster members need to resync. For example, one cluster member may have new saved searches or dashboards, or another search head may have edited another knowledge object. Each cluster member informs the captain of its changes. The captain coordinates the replication of these changes across the cluster. Sometimes, this doesn't work as planned. If this happens, we will need to do a manual resync of the cluster. Unfortunately, this means that one or more of the cluster members will lose any changes that they acquired during the cluster downtime.

Search artifacts resulting from scheduled saved searches are stored on the originating search head and replicated across the search head cluster. The captain node controls the replication of search artifacts – that is, it knows where every copy is stored. It keeps the registry of artifacts updated and informs the cluster members of any changes (referred to as the **delta**). These artifacts improve search efficiency since a non-originating cluster member can proxy search results by requesting another search head via the captain. The originating search head that initially ran the search and stored the results will respond with the search artifacts. The captain will instruct the receiving cluster member to store the search artifacts.

- The **Deployer** is the node responsible for distributing apps and configurations to the search cluster members. The deployer is not a cluster member. However, it can be bundled on the same physical or virtual server as the deployment server, cluster manager, or license manager nodes. The deployer pushes configurations to the search head cluster members, such as the method used by the deployment server to distribute configurations to the deployment clients.

- **Search peers** are the indexers that the search cluster members send search requests to.

Some search head clusters also include a load balancer between the user level and the search head cluster. This allows for an equal distribution of searches when the search load or user count is high.

Now, let's look at a high-level overview of how a search head cluster is deployed.

Configuring a search head cluster

We will assume that we have freshly installed Splunk on three search heads and that our search peers (indexers) have been configured in an indexer cluster. It's important to use fresh Splunk Enterprise installations because adding a search head with existing knowledge objects and configurations to a search head cluster overwrites its existing configurations and knowledge objects:

1. First, we will determine our replication factor – that is, the number of copies of search artifacts we want to maintain in the search head cluster. Then, we will set up a search head cluster of three search heads.

2. Next, we must decide whether our deployer will be run on a new server or an existing server, such as an existing deployment server or indexer cluster manager. The deployer will distribute apps and any new configurations to the cluster members. We do not need to do anything to enable the deploy functionality as it is enabled by default in Splunk Enterprise instances.

3. Once we have selected and/or installed the deployer node, we must configure its security key and assign a cluster label. These settings are written in the `server.conf` file, as follows:

    ```
    [shclustering]
    pass4SymmKey = shclustersecuritykey
    shcluster_label = shclusterlabel
    ```

    We will need to restart the deployer after making these changes in the `server.conf` file.

4. We must initialize the cluster members by logging on to each cluster member and running the following CLI command:

    ```
    splunk init shcluster-config -auth <username>:<password>
    -mgmt_uri <URI>:<management_port> -replication_port
    <replication_port> -replication_factor <n> -conf_deploy_
    fetch_url <deployer URL>:<management_port> -secret <
    shclustersecuritykey > -shcluster_label < shclusterlabel
    >
    splunk restart
    ```

    The parameters of the `splunk init shcluster-config` command are as follows:

    *   `auth`: Specifies the Splunk admin and passwords that you created while installing the cluster member.

    *   `mgmt_uri`: Specifies the URL of the deployer.

    *   `replication_port`: The management port that's used to listen for search artifacts from other cluster members. We mustn't use the management port (*8089*) or the replication port used on the indexers (*9997*).

- `replication_factor`: The number of copies of search artifacts that should be stored in the cluster (the default is 3).

- `Secret`: The secret key we configured in *step 2*.

- `shcluster_label`: The label we configured in *step 2*.

5. We can start the cluster captain by running the following command on the selected instance:

    ```
    splunk bootstrap shcluster-captain -servers_list
    "<URI>:<management_port>,<URI>:<management_port>,..."
    -auth <username>:<password>
    ```

    The parameters of the `splunk bootstrap shcluster-captain` command include:

- `servers_list`: A list of the cluster members configured in *step 3*

- `auth`: The username and password for the cluster captain

6. Connect the search head cluster to the indexer cluster. We will discuss this step in the next section, *Understanding indexer clusters*.

Now that we've looked at search head clusters, let's look at indexer clusters. The concept is similar but since the goal of indexer clusters is to ensure the availability of data as well as searches, we will explore the concept a bit more than we did search head clusters.

Understanding indexer clusters

A Splunk indexer cluster is a group of two or more indexers that work together to ensure that data is available to the users even in the event of node failures. In this section, we will explore how Splunk indexer clusters work. We will look at the components of a Splunk indexer cluster, review how indexing and searching work in an indexer cluster, and explore the concept of search and replication factors.

To understand the importance of a cluster, let's explore what happens when we have standalone indexers. Let's consider a simple scenario, as depicted in *Figure 9.2*:

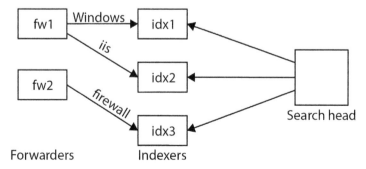

Figure 9.2 – Example of unclustered Splunk indexers

There are two forwarders (*fw1* and *fw2*) and three indexers (*idx1*, *idx2*, and *idx3*) in this scenario. Forwarder *fw1* forwards Windows event logs and IIS logs to indexers *idx1* and *idx2*, respectively. Forwarder *fw2* forwards firewall logs to indexer *idx3*. There is no sharing of information or load balancing between the indexers. When a user searches for Windows event logs, the search head (*sh*) will search all three indexers since they are configured as search peers. However, the Windows event logs will only be available on indexer *idx1*. Now, suppose there is a drive failure on indexer *idx1*, as depicted in *Figure 9.3*:

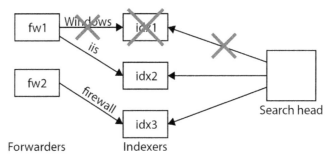

Figure 9.3 – Failed drive on idx1

Forwarder *fw1* continues to send data to indexer *idx1* but the drive has failed. Users searching on search head *sh* will get errors because indexer *idx1* is unavailable. Most importantly, since all the Windows event logs were only stored on indexer *idx1*, no Windows event logs are available. We can conclude that all the Windows event logs will be lost if this is a catastrophic failure where the drive cannot be recovered.

The introduction of indexer clustering in Splunk helped remedy this situation. A Splunk cluster helps increase the availability of the data. A well-configured Splunk indexer cluster not only allows for load balancing of logs into the Splunk indexers but also allows for replication of the logs across indexers. Before we explore how this is accomplished, let's look at the main components of an indexer cluster by reconfiguring the nodes in *Figure 9.2* into a cluster, as depicted in *Figure 9.4*:

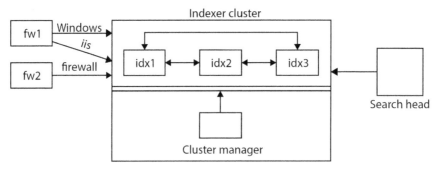

Figure 9.4 – An indexer cluster

An indexer cluster consists of three types of nodes:

1. **Cluster peers**: There must be two or more cluster peers in an indexer cluster to fully take advantage of clustering features. The exact number of cluster peers is determined by the search and replication factors (to be discussed in the next section, *Search and replication factors*) and the amount of indexed data. The cluster peers are configured as indexers to receive data. However, rather than work as standalone units, the indexers work together as a team to ensure availability and search efficiency. The following is a list of data flows that occur within an indexer cluster (note that we mention the default Splunk ports, but these ports can be customized during setup):

   A. External data received on port *9997* from forwarders to be indexed. The buckets containing this data are called primary buckets. The raw data is stored with index files, which increases search efficiency.

   B. Data received on port *8080* from other cluster peers to be replicated. The cluster peer stores these replicated buckets without index files.

   C. Data sent on port *8080* to other cluster peers to be replicated. The cluster peer stores its primary buckets and then sends copies to peers to be stored.

   D. Internal logs such as _audit and _internal to be indexed on the indexer itself. Indexers, like all Splunk servers, generate internal logs. These logs are also indexed.

   E. Search bundles containing search queries and supporting files that cluster peers use to execute searches.

   F. Search results on port *8089* in response to searches from one or more search heads.

Figure 9.5 illustrates how data flows through a clustered indexer:

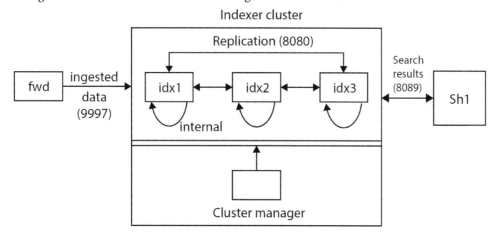

Figure 9.5 – Data flow through clustered indexers

2. **Search heads**: The search heads in a cluster are responsible for conducting searches across the indexers. A good stable indexer cluster will return all possible search results. The search head sends search bundles to the indexer peers, which return indexed data. Search results are not returned from replicated buckets. However, if there is an issue with one or more of the indexers in the indexer cluster, an error will be displayed under the search bar, indicating the possibility that the search is incomplete.

3. **Cluster manager node**: This is the node in the cluster that is responsible for coordinating the communication and flow of data between cluster peers. We can think of the cluster manager as a guide that informs each peer which of its peers it should be communicating with. The cluster manager is also the first responder whenever indexers are unavailable due to intentional shutdowns or unexpected failures. When this happens, the manager node coordinates the redistribution of buckets across indexers or pauses the flow of data to the affected indexers. The manager node is also responsible for configuration management for the indexers and is the node that the search head reaches out to in order to determine the addresses of the indexers. A common misconception is that data flows through the cluster manager node to get to the indexers. Rather, you should think of the cluster manager as a server whose main goal is to ensure that the indexer cluster is stable without interacting with the actual data flow. The cluster manager communicates with the search peers over port 8089.

Now that we understand the main components of the indexer cluster, let's investigate how a **search factor** and a **replication factor** help the cluster manager coordinate across cluster peers.

Replication factor

The **replication factor** specifies the number of copies of each data bucket that must be available to maintain fault tolerance. In *Figure 9.3*, we talked about the possibility of losing an unclustered node. Unless there is an external backup of the data, a loss of a node will be detrimental to the Splunk deployment. The concept of the replication factor allows the cluster manager to coordinate the storage of multiple copies of each bucket on the cluster peers. The main searchable copy of a bucket is called the **primary** bucket. The replication factor can be set to 2 or higher. The choice of replication factor is determined by the estimated amount of data to be stored and the amount of storage available. The default replication factor is 3.

The **search factor** is a count of the number of copies of searchable data – that is, the number of copies of indexed data stored on the search peers. Searchable data is stored with index files that are necessary for searching. For example, a search factor of 2 means that there must be at least two copies of searchable data available on the indexers for a successful search. Therefore, searchable data occupies more space on the indexers. However, the non-searchable buckets are stored in a form that makes it easy for the indexer to create a searchable copy if necessary. Since searchable data occupies more space than non-searchable data, the search factor can be equal to, but not larger than, the replication factor. The default search factor is 2.

Let's look at an example featuring an indexer cluster with four nodes, a search factor of 2, and a replication factor of 3. This means that every bucket that is ingested in the Splunk indexer cluster must have at least three copies on three separate nodes and at least two copies must be searchable. *Figure 9.6* shows the indexer cluster with four nodes, a search factor of 2, and a replication factor of 3:

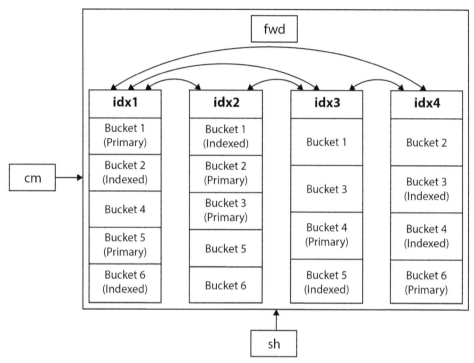

Figure 9.6 – A cluster with four indexers and six buckets

Each cell in the table represents a separate copy of a bucket. *Indexer 1* has the primary copy of *Buckets 1* and *5* and copies of *Buckets 2, 4,* and *6*. *Indexer 2* has the primary copy of *Buckets 2* and *3* and copies of *Buckets 1, 5,* and *6*. *Indexer 3* has one primary bucket (*4*) and copies of *Buckets 1, 3,* and *5*. *Indexer 4* has the primary copy of *Bucket 6* and copies of *Buckets 2, 3, 4,* and *6*. The primary buckets and the buckets marked as *(Indexed)* are *searchable*.

Let's look at five different scenarios involving our example indexer cluster:

1. The forwarder sends new data to the cluster.

2. The search head sends a search request for data stored in *Bucket 5*.

3. We discover a vulnerability, and we need to patch the cluster peers, starting with *Indexer 1*. This requires us to put the indexer offline temporarily.

4. The hard drives on *Indexer 2* and *Indexer 3* fail.

5. The cluster manager fails.

For this example, we will play the role of the cluster manager when assigning buckets to the different indexers in our sample indexer cluster. The assignments are picked at random. Our only goal is to ensure the indexer cluster maintains search and replication factors, if possible, based on the number of indexed and replicated buckets. In addition, we assume that new data is stored in a new bucket rather than added to an existing bucket.

Scenario 1 – the forwarder sends new data to the cluster

Let's suppose that the new logs arrive on *Indexer 3*. The following events will occur:

1. *Indexer 3* indexes the new data by storing the `rawdata/journal.gz` file in a local bucket, along with `.tsidx` files. *Indexer 3* communicates this information to the cluster manager.

2. The cluster manager selects peer(s) for the copies of the new bucket. For example, the cluster manager instructs *Indexer 3* to stream copies of the raw data to *Indexers 2* and *4* to maintain the replication factor of 3. The cluster manager is responsible for informing *Indexers 2, 3,* and *4* of their roles regarding the new bucket.

3. Let's suppose that the cluster manager selects *Indexer 2* to store the searchable copy. When *Indexer 2* receives the replicated raw data, it writes the `rawdata/journal.gz` file and makes its own `.tsidx` files during indexing.

4. *Indexer 4* writes its copy of the `rawdata/journal.gz` file but does not create any `.tsidx` files. The copy on *Indexer 4* is not searchable.

Figure 9.7 illustrates this scenario:

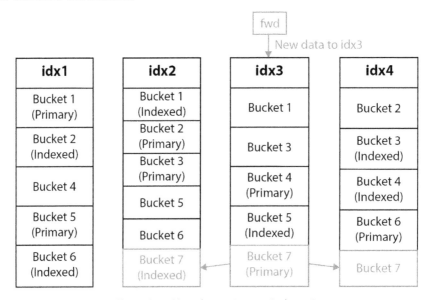

Figure 9.7 – New data arrives on Indexer 3

Let's see what happens when the search head sends a search request.

Scenario 2 – the search head sends a search request for data stored in bucket 5

The cluster manager keeps the search head informed of its search peers (*Indexers 1-4*). In addition, the cluster manager will inform the search head of the **generation ID**. The generation ID tells the search head which indexers belong to the current **generation**. These are the indexer peers that have primary buckets in the indexer cluster. When a search is executed on the search head, the search head initiates the search request to all the search peers in the current generation. The primary copy of bucket 5 in our simple example is stored on *Indexer 1*. Therefore, *Indexer 1* returns the data requested to the search head. Remember that each indexer peer knows which buckets they have indexed and/or stored. The cluster manager knows what buckets are stored on every indexer peer. It also knows the status (*Primary/Indexed/Unindexed Copy*) of each bucket.

Figure 9.8 shows the state of the indexer cluster after the search is executed:

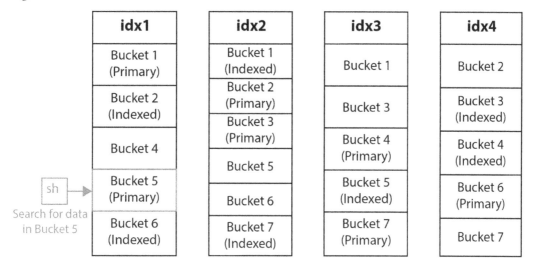

Figure 9.8 – Indexer cluster after a search for bucket 5

We look at what happens when an indexer is offline temporarily in the next scenario.

Scenario 3 – Indexer 1 is offline temporarily

In this scenario, we have discovered a vulnerability, and we need to patch the cluster peers, starting with *Indexer 1*. We will need to put *Indexer 1* offline temporarily. Before we talk about taking an indexer offline temporarily, let's look at two important states of the indexer cluster:

- **Valid**: A cluster that meets its search factor – that is, all the primary copies of the data are searchable

- **Complete**: A cluster that meets its replication and search factor – that is, the indexer cluster has the number of copies specified by the search and replication factors

The cluster manager always wants the indexer cluster to remain in the **Complete** state. A complete cluster is also valid. Splunk allows you to take a clustered indexer offline temporarily while still processing data and without disrupting searches. Splunk admins can use the splunk offline command to inform the indexer cluster manager that they would like to shut down a peer temporarily or permanently. This command allows Splunk to gracefully shut down the peer without too much disruption to the cluster. This command is referred to as the *fast offline* command if used without any parameters. The fast offline command initiates *bucket-fixing* processes after a specified period. However, when used with the --enforce-counts parameter, the offline command initiates bucket-fixing processes immediately to ensure that the cluster returns to a valid state. This involves replicating buckets from the remaining indexers and/or changing the state of remaining indexed buckets to primary buckets. Once the bucket fixing is complete, the splunk offline -enforce-counts command permanently removes an indexer from the cluster.

Figure 9.9 shows the state of the cluster after the fast offline command is run on *Indexer 1*:

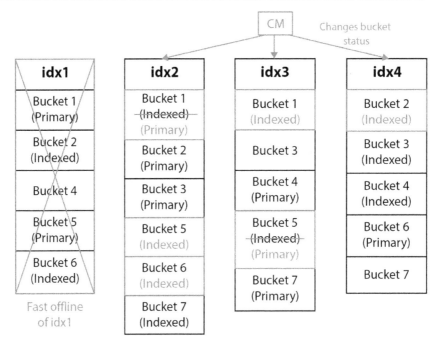

Figure 9.9 – Indexer cluster after a fast offline

Depending on how long *Indexer 1* remains offline, the following events occur:

1. The cluster manager changes the status of *Bucket 1* on *Indexer 2* to *Primary*.

2. The cluster manager informs *Indexer 3* to index its copy of *Bucket 1*. In some cases, the cluster manager will instruct a search peer to grab a copy of the .tsidx files from another peer as this is less expensive than generating its own. However, in this case, we will assume that *Indexer 3* indexes its copy of *Bucket 1*.

3.   The cluster manager informs *Indexer 4* to index its copy of *Bucket 2*.

4.   The cluster manager informs *Indexer 2* to index its copy of *Bucket 5*.

5.   The cluster manager changes the status of *Bucket 5* on *Indexer 3* to *Primary*.

6.   The cluster manager informs *Indexer 2* to index its copy of *Bucket 6*.

At this point, the indexer cluster is valid but *no longer complete*. This is because the search factor has been met (there are two searchable copies of each bucket) but the replication factor is no longer being met (there are only two copies of *Buckets 1*, *2*, *4*, *5*, and *6*).

You must perform the following steps to return the cluster to its complete state:

1.   The cluster manager informs *Indexer 3* to replicate its copy of *Bucket 4* to *Indexer 2*.

2.   The cluster manager informs *Indexer 2* to replicate its copy of *Bucket 2* to *Indexer 3*.

3.   The cluster manager informs *Indexer 4* to replicate its copy of *Bucket 6* to *Indexer 3*.

4.   The cluster manager informs *Indexer 2* to replicate its copy of *Bucket 1* to *Indexer 4*. The cluster manager informs *Indexer 3* to replicate its copy of *Bucket 5* to *Indexer 4*.

Figure 9.10 illustrates these additional five steps:

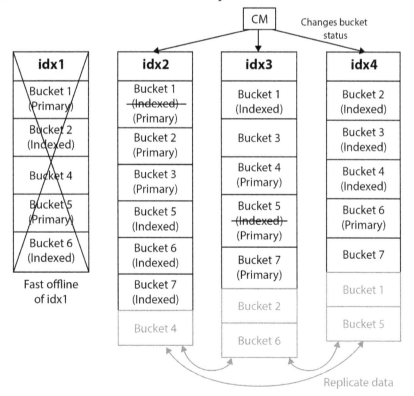

Figure 9.10 – Returning the cluster to its complete state

Scenario 4 shows what happens when more than one indexer fails.

Scenario 4 – the hard drives on Indexers 2 and 3 fail

In the previous example, we looked at a scenario where a host is intentionally shut down for maintenance. During this process, the indexer cluster was valid but not complete. In this scenario, we will consider the situation where multiple nodes are lost due to failed hard drives. We assume that *Indexer 1* has not failed but *Bucket 7* has already been added when the two indexers fail. *Indexer 2* has six buckets – indexed copies of *Buckets 1* and *7*, primary copies of *Buckets 2* and *3*, and unindexed copies of *Buckets 5* and *6*. As we saw in the previous scenario, the loss of one node places the indexer cluster in a *valid* but *incomplete* state. The cluster manager attempts to maintain the search factor number of each of these buckets by coordinating the following events:

1. We lose the indexed copy of *Bucket 1* on *Indexer 2* and lose an unindexed copy on *Indexer 3*. Therefore, only the *Primary* copy is left on *Indexer 1*. The cluster manager will request that *Indexer 1* replicates a copy to *Indexer 4*. *Indexer 4* will also index this new copy to maintain the search factor of 2.

2. We lose the primary copy of *Bucket 2* on *Indexer 2*, so the cluster manager will need to change the status of this bucket on *Indexer 1* to *Primary*. The cluster manager also instructs *Indexer 4* to index its copy of *Bucket 2*.

3. We lose the primary copy of *Bucket 3* on *Indexer 2* and an unindexed copy on *Indexer 3*. The cluster manager changes the status of the indexed copy of *Bucket 3* on *Indexer 4* to *Primary*. The cluster manager will also request that *Bucket 3* is replicated and indexed on *Indexer 1*.

4. We lose the primary copy of *Bucket 4* on *Indexer 3*, so the cluster manager changes the status of the copy on *Indexer 4* from *Indexed* to *Primary*. It also informs *Indexer 1* that it should index its copy of *Bucket 4*.

5. We lose indexed and unindexed copies of *Bucket 5* during the failure, so the cluster manager informs *Indexer 1* to replicate *Bucket 5* on *Indexer 4*.

6. There is still a *Primary* and *Indexed* copy of *Bucket 6*, so no change is needed.

7. We lose an indexed copy of *Bucket 7* on *Indexer 2* and an unindexed copy on *Indexer 3*. The cluster manager requests that *Indexer 4* index its copy of *Bucket 7* and change its status to *Primary*. The cluster manager also tells *Indexer 4* to replicate its copy to *Indexer 1*, which indexes the data to maintain the search factor of 2.

Figure 9.11 shows what happens after *Indexer 2* and *Indexer 3* fail:

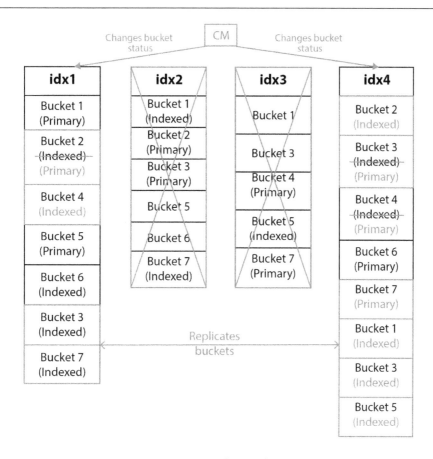

Figure 9.11 – Catastrophic failure of Indexer 2 and 3

This example was a simplistic scenario that assumed that both *Indexer 2* and *Indexer 3* failed at the same time. The exact sequence of events may not be exactly as discussed. However, the goal will be to maintain the search factor of *2*.

Scenario 5 – the cluster manager fails

A failed cluster manager is serious for the indexer cluster. As we have seen so far, the cluster manager is the brain of the indexer cluster. If the cluster manager fails, the cluster peer nodes will continue to perform indexing, replicating, and searching actions. However, the stability of the cluster can only be maintained while all the peer nodes remain healthy. If the peer goes down while the cluster manager node is down, there is no way to coordinate the bucket fixup processes that we discussed in the previous scenarios.

If a cluster manager fails but eventually comes back up, the peer nodes will reconnect to it. However, several *bucket fixup* processes will occur to get the cluster back to a valid and complete state.

Now that we have discussed how indexer clusters work, we will take a quick look at how they are configured.

Configuring indexer clusters

We can configure, manage, and view indexer clusters using a series of CLI commands. Indexer cluster configurations are stored in stanzas in the `server.conf` file on the cluster manager. Any configurations that are shared among the cluster peers are stored in the `manager-apps` directory on the cluster manager. These configurations are applied to the cluster peer nodes using CLI commands. The configurations, including apps and add-ons, are pushed to the `peer-apps` directory on the peer nodes. It is important to note that you should never directly shut down a peer node as this may result in loss of data. Instead, the Splunk admin must execute commands such as `splunk offline` and `splunk rolling-restart cluster-peers` on the cluster manager to restart the peer nodes.

Table 9.1 lists some of the more common commands used:

Command Syntax	Decsription	Where To Run the Command
`splunk edit cluster-config -mode manager -replication_factor 3 -search_factor 2 -secret my_cluster_ key -cluster_label my_cluster_label`	Enables a cluster manager with a replication factor of 3 and a search factor of 2. This assigns a Splunk secret and assigns the name of the cluster.	Cluster manager
`splunk edit cluster-config -mode peer -manager_uri <cluster manager IP address>:8089 -replication_port <replication port> -secret my_cluster_ key`	Enables a peer node and points it to the cluster manager. The command also sets the replication port and the secret key.	Cluster peer node
`splunk edit cluster-config -mode searchhead -manager_ uri <cluster manager IP address>:8089- secret my_cluster_key`	Enables the search head and points it to the cluster manager. It also sets the secret key.	Search head
`splunk list cluster-peers`	Views all the search peers.	Cluster manager

Command Syntax	Decsription	Where To Run the Command
`splunk list cluster-config`	Views the cluster configuration.	Cluster manager
`splunk offline`	Takes a peer offline.	Cluster peer node
`splunk apply cluster-bundle`	Pushes any changes to configurations to the peers.	Cluster manager
`splunk rolling-restart cluster-peers`	Restarts cluster peers in a rolling fashion.	Cluster manager
`splunk enable maintenance-mode`	Sets the cluster manager to maintenance mode, which pauses bucket fixup processes. It also prevents hot buckets while making changes, such as upgrading the cluster nodes.	Cluster manager
`splunk enable maintenance-mode`	Turns off maintenance mode.	Cluster manager
`splunk show maintenance-mode`	Shows whether the cluster is in maintenance mode or not.	Cluster manager

Table 9.1 – Configuration commands for managing an indexer cluster

Although we won't explore the *indexer clustering* dashboard in this chapter, it is a very useful dashboard for monitoring the status of the indexer cluster. It shows the state of the indexer cluster, including the following:

- **Maintenance mode status**: Whether the cluster is in maintenance mode or not
- **Search and replication factor status**: Whether the cluster is meeting its search and replication factors
- **Indexes status**: A visual representation of the indexes showing whether the search and replication factors have been met for each index
- **Bucket fixup status**: A visual listing of any bucket issues
- **Peer status**: A list of all the peer nodes
- **Search head**: A list of search heads

With that, we have explored search head and indexer clusters.

Summary

This has been an interesting chapter on increasing Splunk fault tolerance and security. Splunk indexer and search head clusters give us the ability to increase the availability of data in the Splunk deployment. The search head cluster captain coordinates how configurations and knowledge objects are shared across cluster members. A functioning search cluster captain is important for the proper running of the search head cluster and Splunk has built-in processes for ensuring that the cluster can resume after any mishaps. An indexer cluster is managed by the cluster manager. We explored different scenarios where the state of the cluster is disturbed and looked at the steps that the cluster manager takes to remedy the situation. We got a high-level overview of how search head and indexer clusters are configured using CLI commands or by modifying the `server.conf` file.

In the next chapter, we will explore data models, acceleration, and other ways to improve performance.

10

Data Models, Acceleration, and Other Ways to Improve Performance

In this chapter, we will shift gears and look at ways we can improve performance in Splunk. We will introduce concepts such as datasets, lookups, and data models in Splunk. Datasets, lookups, and data models are all logical ways of storing data in Splunk to improve search performance. In addition, data models can be accelerated – that is, data in the data model is stored with indexed fields. These additional indexed fields can be specified in searches using special commands such as the Splunk `tstats` command. The `tstats` command can be used with aggregate functions such as `avg()` and `earliest()`. We will learn different terms associated with data models such as constraints, root events, and child searches. The Splunk **Common Information Model** (**CIM**) add-on is a useful add-on that comes preconfigured with data models that, when implemented properly, improve Splunk's performance. We will explore the different data models in the CIM and explain how they work. Finally, we will summarize the topic of Splunk improvement by discussing 20 ways to improve performance in Splunk.

In this chapter, we will explore the following topics:

- Understanding data models
- Accelerating data models
- Improving performance

Understanding data models

The concept of a *dataset* is well-known in the field of data management. A dataset is a collection of data that serves a particular purpose. It's usually used to refer to data expressed in some form of a *table* with *columns* and *rows*. This could be a file where columns are defined by comma- or tab-separated values, a Microsoft Excel spreadsheet, or a SQL database table. Each *column* defines a particular variable, and each *row* represents a separate entity in the collection. BOTS dataset v1 (`https://github.com/splunk/botsv1`), which we used in the first few chapters of this book, represents a collection of datasets. We can use the **Datasets** page to view and manage datasets. There is a link to this page from the **Apps | Searching and Reporting** area.

Figure 10.1 shows the navigation menu in the **Searching and Reporting** app:

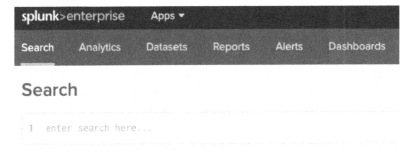

Figure 10.1 – The Search and Reporting navigation menu

Clicking on the **Datasets** link opens the **Datasets listing** page. There are three types of datasets in Splunk:

1. **Lookups**
2. **Table datasets**
3. **Data model datasets**

We will explore each of these in the next few subsections.

Lookups

Lookups in the **Datasets listing** page include lookup table files (`comma-separated value` (`.csv` files) and lookup table definitions (`.csv` lookups and **Key/Value** (**KV**) store lookups). The **Datasets listing** page does not list external lookups such as those created with Python or `bash` scripts. It also does not include automatic lookups.

Figure 10.2 shows how we can create a new lookup file by navigating to **Settings | Lookups | Lookup table files | Add new**:

Add new

Lookups » Lookup table files » Add new

Destination app	search ▾
Upload a lookup file	**Choose File** No file chosen
	Select either a plaintext CSV file, a gzipped CSV file, or a KMZ/KML file. The maximum file size that can be uploaded through the browser is 500MB.
Destination filename *	
	Enter the name this lookup table file will have on the Splunk server. If you are uploading a gzipped CSV file, enter a filename ending in ".gz". If you are uploading a plaintext CSV file, we recommend a filename ending in ".csv". For a KMZ/KML file, we recommend a filename ending in ".kmz"/".kml".

Cancel   Save

Figure 10.2 – Uploading a new lookup table

Figure 10.3 shows a listing of lookup table files from the **TA-suricata-4** app that we installed in *Chapter 3, Onboarding and Normalizing Data*:

Figure 10.3 – Example lookup tables

Figure 10.4 shows some lookup tables and definitions from the **Palo Alto Networks** add-on that we installed in *Chapter 3, Onboarding and Normalizing Data*:

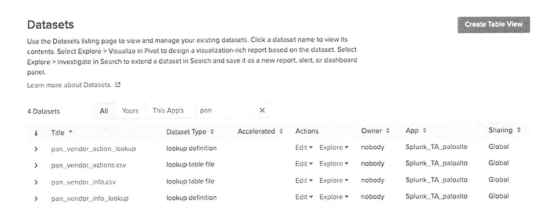

Figure 10.4 – Lookup table files and definitions in the Palo Alto Networks add-on

Now, let's look at table datasets.

Table datasets

A **table dataset** is a collection of Splunk event data that we can create by specifying a set of events via a Splunk query, existing datasets, or a collection of relevant sourcetypes and/or indexes. Table datasets allow you to create these abstractions that can be edited later by adding new fields or changing field names. Let's create a table dataset by clicking the green **Create Table View** button at the top right-hand side of the **Datasets** page. *Figure 10.5* shows the **Select an index** page:

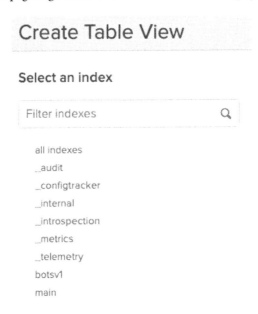

Figure 10.5 – Select an index

We will select the **botsv1** index. Upon doing so, we will be prompted to **Select one or more sourcetypes**, as shown in *Figure 10.6*:

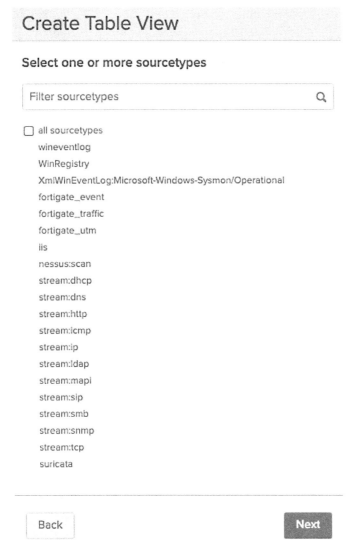

Figure 10.6 – Select one or more sourcetypes

Let's click on the **iis** and **stream:http** sourcetype and click **Next**. This brings up the **Select existing fields** option, as shown in *Figure 10.7*:

Figure 10.7 – Selecting fields

Note that the _time, _raw, and sourcetype fields are already selected. Let's select the following fields and click **Start Editing**:

1. **action**
2. **bytes**
3. **dest**
4. **request**
5. **src**
6. **url**

Figure 10.8 shows the next page. We can explore the data on this page:

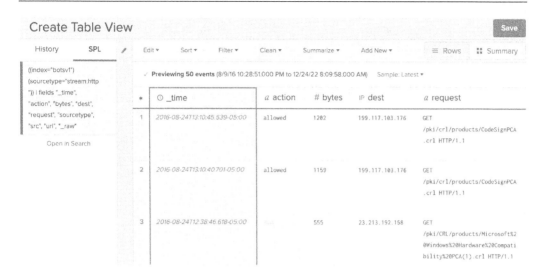

Figure 10.8 – Exploring the data

Note that the following Splunk **Search Processing Language** (**SPL**) representing the table dataset is shown on the left-hand side of the page:

```
((index="botsv1") (sourcetype="stream:http")) | fields "_time",
"action", "bytes", "dest", "request", "sourcetype", "src",
"url", "_raw"
```

Let's explore the options available at the top of the page. We can perform several tasks on the data, including the following:

- *Rearrange the columns in the table dataset* by clicking on a column, selecting **Edit** | **Move**, and dragging the column to the new position

- *Delete or rename a column* by selecting **Edit** | **Delete** or **Edit** | **Rename…**

- *Sort in ascending and descending order* by selecting **Sort** | **Sort Ascending** or **Sort** | **Sort Descending**

- *Filter data by value* by using the **Filter** menu

- *Check for null values* by using the **Filter** menu

- *Remove duplicates and type mismatches* by using the **Filter** menu

- *Clean data* by filling in `null` or empty values, and replacing or rounding values using the **Clean** menu

- *Create aggregate fields* by using the **Summarize** menu

Every new action performed on the data will be represented under the **SPL** tab on the left. Let's perform the following actions on the dataset:

1. *Sort* the action field by selecting **Sort | Sort ascending**.

2. *Filter* the dest field to only show the dest of 67.132.183.25 by clicking on a cell containing 67.132.183.25 and selecting **Filter | Equals Selected Value**.

3. *Remove* the _raw field by selecting the _raw field and clicking **Edit | Delete**.

    Figure 10.9 shows the result of these actions:

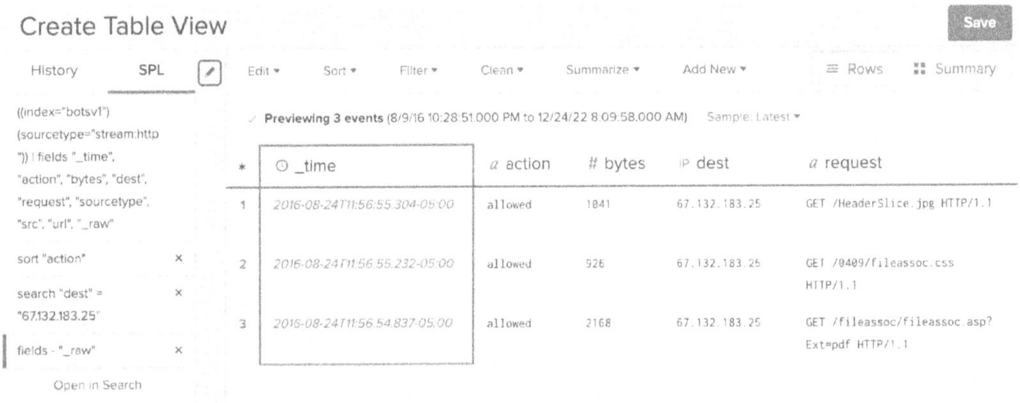

Figure 10.9 – Using the menu to create the dataset

4. Now let us create an aggregate field to show the sum of the bytes by clicking on the bytes field and selecting **Summarize | Stats**. Click + **Add functions…** and select the sum function. Then clicking **Apply**.

5. Note that the actions we performed are displayed on the left-hand side. The results of the **Summarize | Stats** operation are shown in the **Summary** tab on the top right. Clicking the **Summary** tab shows us the sum of the bytes field, as shown in *Figure 10.10*:

Figure 10.10 – Summarizing data in the dataset

We can view the resulting search query in the following screenshot. We did this by clicking Open in Search on the left, as shown in *Figure 10.11*:

Figure 10.11 – Viewing the dataset schema in the search area (with the stats command)

Click on the Back button to return to the **Create Table View**. Clicking on the **X** next to the SPL on the **Create Table View** page removes any of the actions that we have performed. For example, clicking next to `stats sum(bytes)` on the left removes the `stats` clause. Click on **Open in Search** to see the table dataset results, as shown in *Figure 10.12*:

Figure 10.12 – Viewing the dataset schema in the search area (without the stats command)

We can click **Save** once we have made all the changes that we need to the dataset. We can further explore the dataset by clicking the **Explore** menu and selecting **Visualize with Pivot** or **Investigate in Search**.

Table datasets are an easy and useful way of creating tables that can be used further in Splunk. We can also create complete table datasets without knowing SPL. Now, let's explore another powerful feature of Splunk called a **data model**.

Data model datasets

The third kind of dataset available in Splunk is the **data model** dataset. A data model is a conceptual grouping of datasets at search time. *Figure 10.13* shows the list of data model datasets on the **Datasets listing** page:

Datasets

Create Table View

Use the Datasets listing page to view and manage your existing datasets. Click a dataset name to view its contents. Select Explore > Visualize in Pivot to design a visualization-rich report based on the dataset. Select Explore > Investigate in Search to extend a dataset in Search and save it as a new report, alert, or dashboard panel.

Learn more about Datasets. ↗

454 Datasets   All   Yours   This App's   1   2   3   4   5   Next >

Filter by title, description, fields 🔍

i	Tit	Dataset Type ⇕	Accelerated ⇕	Actions	Owner ⇕	App ⇕	Sharing ⇕
>	A.	data model	ϟ	Edit ▾ Explore ▾	nobody	Splunk_SA_CIM	Global
>	A.	data model	ϟ	Edit ▾ Explore ▾	nobody	Splunk_SA_CIM	Global
>	A.	data model	ϟ	Edit ▾ Explore ▾	nobody	Splunk_SA_CIM	Global
>	A.	data model	ϟ	Edit ▾ Explore ▾	nobody	Splunk_SA_CIM	Global
>	A.	data model	ϟ	Edit ▾ Explore ▾	nobody	Splunk_SA_CIM	Global

Figure 10.13 – Data model datasets

These data model datasets are part of Splunk's internal data model datasets. But first, we will explore the **Splunk's Internal Audit Logs - SAMPLE > Audit** data model. Let's expand the dataset by clicking the > icon next to its name on the **Datasets listing** page. *Figure 10.14* shows the information that's revealed:

Figure 10.14 – The sample data model dataset

We can see that the dataset is a data model stored in the **Searching and Reporting (search)** app context. The dataset consists of the `_time`, `host`, `source`, `sourcetype`, `action`, `info`, and `user` fields. Clicking on the data model name takes us to the logs that make up the dataset.

This dataset shows Splunk configuration changes and search activity from the `audittrail` sourcetype in the `_audit` index. We can view the query that runs this dataset by selecting **Investigate** in the search area of the **Explore** dropdown at the top right of the page. This will reveal the following search query:

```
| from datamodel:"internal_audit_logs.Audit"
```

This search query uses the Splunk `from` command. This command is used to retrieve data from a dataset. The command is followed by a *dataset type*, *a colon (:)* or *space*, and a *dataset name*. The type of dataset can be **datamodel**, **lookup**, or **savedsearch**. In this case, the dataset type is a `datamodel` called `internal_audit_logs.Audit`.

We can also select **Visualize with Pivot** from the **Explore** dropdown to view the data using the **Pivot** tool. The **Pivot** tool allows us to add columns to the data, create aggregations, and express the results in different visualization formats. *Figure 10.15* shows the **Pivot** interface for this dataset:

Figure 10.15 – Pivot tool

This current view on the **Pivot** interface displays the count of all the rows in the **Audit** dataset. We can change the visualization by clicking the **Single Value icon (42)** on the left to display the count as a single value. *Figure 10.16* shows this visualization:

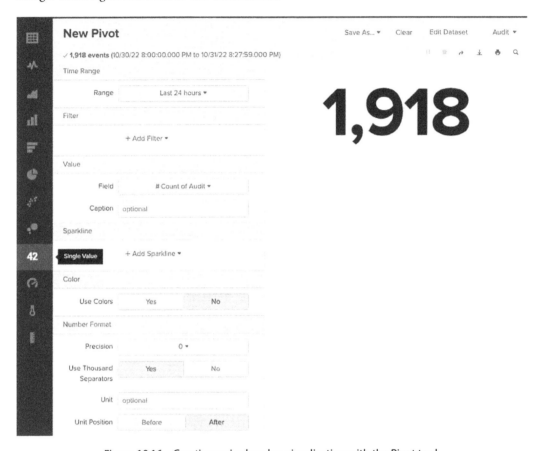

Figure 10.16 – Creating a single value visualization with the Pivot tool

Now that we've taken a quick look at the **Splunk's Internal Audit Logs - SAMPLE** table dataset, the Splunk query, and the **Pivot** tool, let's look at the data model schema. Let's access the data model by selecting **Edit Data Model** from the green **Edit** dropdown on the **Splunk's Internal Audit Logs - SAMPLE** dataset page. This opens the data model page, as shown in *Figure 10.17*:

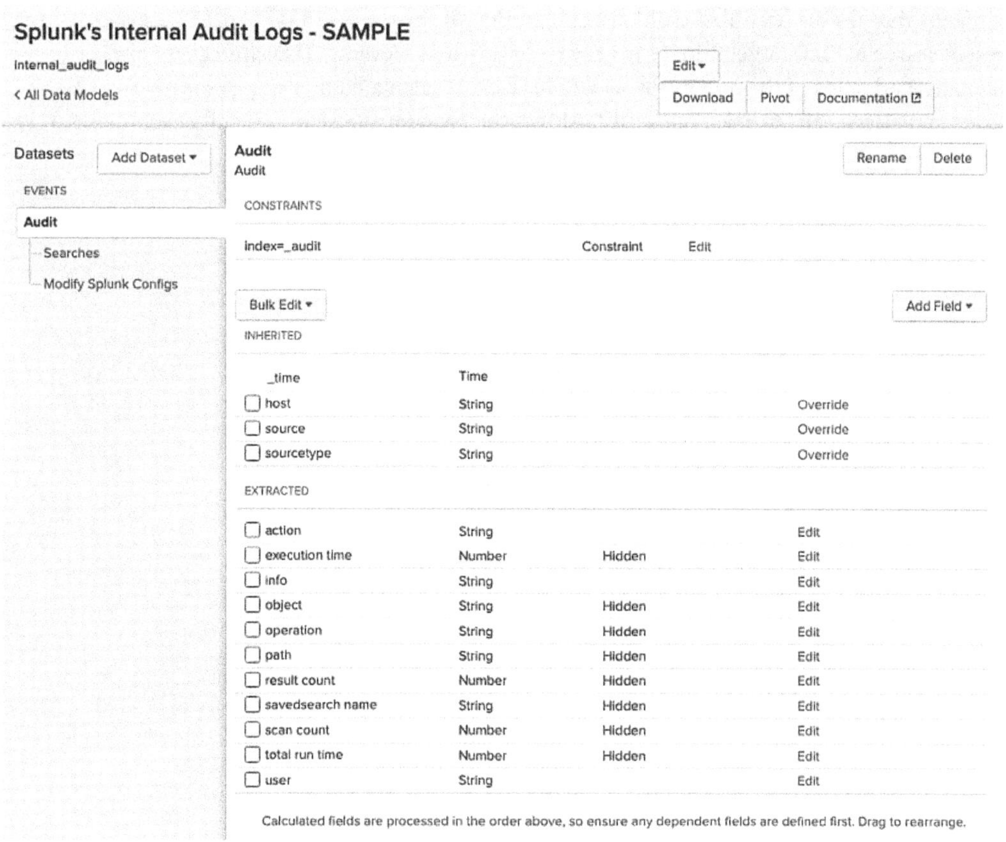

Splunk's Internal Audit Logs - SAMPLE

internal_audit_logs

‹ All Data Models

Edit ▾

Download | Pivot | Documentation ⬀

Datasets	Add Dataset ▾
EVENTS	
Audit	
Searches	
Modify Splunk Configs	

Audit
Audit

CONSTRAINTS

index=_audit		Constraint	Edit

Bulk Edit ▾   Add Field ▾

INHERITED

_time	Time		
☐ host	String		Override
☐ source	String		Override
☐ sourcetype	String		Override

EXTRACTED

☐ action	String		Edit
☐ execution time	Number	Hidden	Edit
☐ info	String		Edit
☐ object	String	Hidden	Edit
☐ operation	String	Hidden	Edit
☐ path	String	Hidden	Edit
☐ result count	Number	Hidden	Edit
☐ savedsearch name	String	Hidden	Edit
☐ scan count	Number	Hidden	Edit
☐ total run time	Number	Hidden	Edit
☐ user	String		Edit

Calculated fields are processed in the order above, so ensure any dependent fields are defined first. Drag to rearrange.

Figure 10.17 – Data model edit page

The data model page shows the set of datasets arranged *hierarchically* based on their constraints. We can see that the data model is named `internal_audit_logs` and consists of one **root event** called *Audit*, which has two **child events** called *Searches* and *Modify Splunk Configs*. The `Audit` root event has the following constraint:

```
index=_audit
```

The `Audit` root event also has several extracted fields, including `action`, `execution time`, `info`, `object`, `operation`, `path`, `result count`, `savedsearch name`, `scan count`, `total run time`, and `user`. The `Searches` child event inherits the `index=_audit` constraint from the `Audit` root event and has the following additional constraint:

```
action=search NOT dmauditsearch
```

This means that the `Searches` child event includes all the events in the `_audit` event, which represent search actions but eliminate any `dmauditsearch` events. This child event also includes all the inherited fields of the root event, as well as a set of calculated fields, including `search_id`, `search`, and `search type`. *Figure 10.18* shows the page for the **Searches** child event dataset:

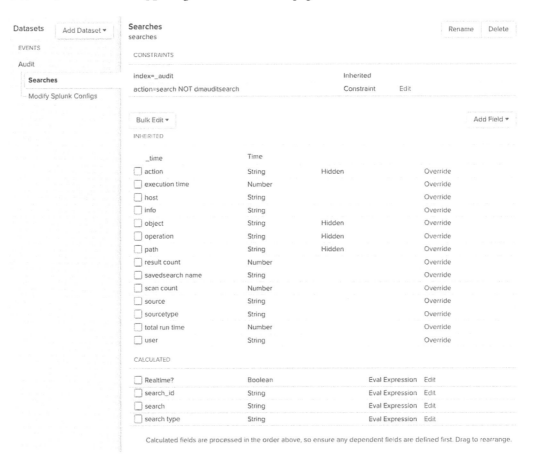

Figure 10.18 – Searches child event

The `Modify Splunk Configs` child event also inherits from the `Audit` root event. It inherits the `index=_audit` constraint and has an additional constraint, as follows:

```
action=edit_user OR action=edit_roles OR action=update
```

Note that this child event inherits the fields from the root event but has *no* additional extracted or calculated fields.

We can add additional datasets to the data model, such as another **root event**, **root transaction**, **root search**, or **child**. We can also rename or delete the parts of the data model and add fields. We can create a new event dataset by assigning the dataset a name and constraints. Clicking the Preview button displays the resulting events as shown in *Figure 10.19*:

Add Event Dataset   Documentation ↗

Data Model: Splunk's Internal Audit Logs - SAMPLE

Dataset Name   Constraints

Admin Actions   index=_audit object=admin

Dataset ID   The search must have an explicit index constraint to maximize performance.
                                      Examples:
Admin_Actions   index=main uri="*.php*" OR uri="*.py*"
                                      index=main NOT (referer=null OR referer="-")
The dataset ID can only contain letters, numbers, dashes,
and underscores. Do not start the dataset ID with a
period.

                                                            Cancel   Preview   Save

✓ 7 events (before 12/24/22 8:57:37.000 AM)   20 per page ▾

Sample: 1,000 events ▾

Event

Audit:[timestamp=09-21-2022 16:01:34.413, user=admin, action=update,path="/Applications/Splunk/etc/users/admin", isdir=1, size=416, gid=0, uid=501, modt
ime="Wed Sep 21 15:49:07 2022", mode="rwx------", hash=, chgs="modtime "]

Audit:[timestamp=07-06-2022 18:33:46.271, user=admin, action=update,path="/Applications/Splunk/etc/users/admin", isdir=1, size=384, gid=0, uid=501, modt
ime="Wed Jul 6 18:24:22 2022", mode="rwx------", hash=, chgs="modtime "][n/a]

Figure 10.19 – Adding an event dataset

Figure 10.19 shows the new **Admin Actions Dataset** which consists of all events in the _audit index where the object is admin. All root events must have an explicit index constraint such as index=_audit. Child events do not require an explicit index constraint.

The **Pivot** tool and **Datasets** pages offer us a great way of filtering and organizing Splunk data without writing SPL. However, there is an additional benefit of using data models. Data models can be **accelerated**. We will look at accelerated data models in the next section.

Accelerating data models

We have seen how data models can be created to collect datasets. These data models can be used to increase search speed when accelerated. Searching an accelerated data model returns search results faster than searching raw data in an index. Let's look at how data models are stored on disk, which makes them more easily searchable compared to regular indexes. The *Splunk Enterprise Knowledge Manager Manual* defines a data model as a search-time mapping of datasets in a hierarchical form (https://tinyurl.com/4wyyx3ft). Data models drive tools such as **Pivot** and are the backbone of apps such as Splunk Enterprise Security (`https://splunkbase.splunk.com/app/263`). The **Searches** child event dataset that we saw in the previous section under **Understanding Data Models** | **Data Model Datasets** inherited constraints from the `Audit` root event. In addition, this dataset had its own constraints:

```
action=search NOT dmauditsearch
```

These constraints include an extracted action field and a raw text search for the phrase *dmauditsearch*. *Figure 10.19* shows the `Searches` dataset in the **Splunk's Internal Audit Logs - SAMPLE** data model.

The fields that make up the dataset can be generated by choosing one of the following options from the **Add Field** dropdown at the top right-hand side of the **Inherited fields** section:

- **An auto-extracted field**
- **A calculated field** created using one of the following:

  - **Eval expression** such as `realtime` is a Boolean calculated field in the `Searches` dataset and is created using the following eval expression:

    ```
    case(is_realtime == 0, "false", is_realtime == 1, "true",
    is_realtime == "N/A", "false")
    ```

  - **Lookup**
  - **Regular Expression**
  - **Geo IP**

The auto-extracted fields can be configured in **Settings** | **Fields** | **Field Extractions**, so this option is often grayed out.

We can make changes to the different fields in the data model by clicking on the **Edit** link at the end of each field row. We want to ensure that we are happy with the structure and fields of our data model before we accelerate. An accelerated data model cannot be edited without us stopping the acceleration.

We can accelerate data models by clicking **Edit** | **Edit Acceleration** on the **Data Models** page and clicking the checkbox next to **Accelerate**. We also need to set the **summary range** of the accelerated data model by selecting **1 Day, 7 Days, 1 Month, 3 Months, 1 Year, All Time,** or **Custom**. This depends on how much data we want to summarize. It is important to consider the kinds of searches that we usually run on the data in the data model. For example, if we normally run searches over the last year, then it would benefit us to set the **Summary Range** property of our data model to *1 Year*.

What does it mean to **accelerate** a data model? How does this change the data model? The process of acceleration builds summaries of the data and stores the summaries in index buckets on the indexers. These summaries are stored in the same location as the buckets that they summarize. Accelerating a data model depends on the **high-performance analytics store** function in Splunk. *Table 10.1* illustrates the concept of the **Audit** data model:

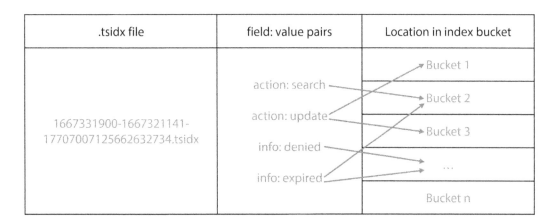

.tsidx file	field: value pairs	Location in index bucket
1667331900-1667321141-177070071 25662632734.tsidx	action: search action: update info: denied info: expired	Bucket 1 Bucket 2 Bucket 3 ... Bucket n

Table 10.1 – How .tsidx works

As *Table 10.1* shows, the `.tsidx` file contains a series of `field:value` pairs such as `action:search` and `info:denied` and the location of these values in the index. This creates a shortcut to searching Splunk indexes and improves search performance. Once the summaries have been created, Splunk runs the base searches that make up the data model every 5 minutes, generating new `field:value-index` location mappings. Splunk provides special search commands that can be used with data models. We will explore one such command called `tstats` in the next subsection.

Understanding the tstats command

The `tstats` command is a generating command used to run statistical queries against indexed fields stored in `.tsidx` files. `tstats` returns search results much faster than a regular `stats` command. Just like the `stats` command, the `tstats` command works with different functions, including the following:

- Aggregate functions such as `avg()`, `count()`, and `sum()`
- Event order functions such as `first()` and `last()`
- Multivalue-generating functions such as `values()`
- Time functions such as `earliest()` and `latest()`

Let's look at a few examples to illustrate how the `tstats` command works.

You can use `tstats` to display all the sourcetypes in the `botsv1` index:

```
| tstats count where index=botsv1 by sourcetype
```

Alternatively, you can use the following code:

```
| tstats values(sourcetype) as st where index=botsv1
```

Now, we will look at the set of data models in the Splunk CIM add-on.

Exploring the Splunk CIM add-on

The Splunk CIM add-on is a semantic model that was introduced to enforce uniform field extraction and group data into different domains. The Splunk CIM allows for search time normalization of data from multiple sources and sourcetypes. The Splunk CIM ships with a set of data models. The JSON implementation of each of these data models can be found in `$SPLUNK_HOME/etc/apps/ Splunk_SA_CIM/default/data/models`. Some of the data models included in the latest release of the Splunk CIM (at the time of writing) include the following:

- **Authentication**: This defines access activity in the logs. Examples include Windows logon/logout events, administrative access to AWS consoles, or ssh logins to Unix devices. The Authentication data model includes the `Default_Authentication`, `Insecure_Authentication`, and `Privileged_Authentication` child datasets. The fields in this data model include `action`, `dest`, `src`, and `user`.

To be ingested into the Authentication data model, an event must be tagged with the following:

- Authentication tag: authentication
- Additional tags:

  - default (`Default_Authentication`)
  - cleartext OR insecure (`Insecure_Authentication`)
  - privileged (`Privileged_Authentication`)

Let's look at some examples of the `tstats` command of the Authentication data model.

You can display the number of times that each privileged user fails (Windows EventCode `4625`) on each Windows host:

```
| tstats count from datamodel=Authentication where
Privileged_Authentication.signature_id=4625 by
Authentication.src,  Authentication.user
```

You can display the number of events in the data model for each application:

```
| tstats count from datamodel=Authentication by
Authentication.app
```

- **Change**: This defines **Create, Read, Update, and Delete** (**CRUD**) activities in the logs. Examples include adding/removing/modifying users in Windows event logs and making changes to groups in Active Directory or changes to database schemas. The Change data model includes the `Auditing_Changes`, `Endpoint_Changes`, `Network_Changes`, `Account_Management`, and `Instance_Changes` child datasets. The fields in this model include `action`, `change_type`, `dest`, `object`, `result`, `src`, `status`, and `user`.

  To be ingested into the Change data model, an event must be tagged with the following:

  - Change tag: change
  - Additional tags:

    - audit (`Audit_Changes`)
    - endpoint (`Endpoint_Changes`)
    - network (`Network_Changes`)
    - account (`Account_Management`)
    - instance (`Instance_Changes`)

  Let's look at some examples of the `tstats` command of the Change data model.

  You can get all the actions performed by a user:

  ```
  | tstats values(action) as action from datamodel=Change
  by All_Changes.user
  ```

  You can get the number of changes made by `jsmith`:

  ```
  | tstats count from datamodel=Change where Account_
  Management.src_user="jsmith"
  ```

- **Endpoint**: This defines service and process activities on endpoint devices such as laptops, desktops, and phones. Examples include running Windows `services`, installing `processes` from malicious files, and Unix daemons. The Endpoint data model includes the `Ports`, `Processes`, `Services`, `Filesystem`, and `Registry` child datasets. The fields in this `Ports` child dataset of the data model include `dest`, `dest_port`, `src`, `src_port`, `transport`, and `user`. The fields in the `Processes` child dataset of the data model include `action`, `dest`, `parent_process`, `process`, and `process_id`. The fields in the `Services` child dataset of the data model include `dest`, `service`, `start_mode`, `status`, and `user`. Just like the `Ports`, `Processes`, and `Services` child datasets, the other child datasets also have their own sets of standard fields. Unlike some of the other CIM data models, we need to specify the child dataset when searching the Endpoint data model. This is accomplished by specifying the data model (Endpoint), followed by a dot and the child dataset. For example, searching the `Ports` child dataset can be done by specifying `Endpoint.Port`.

To be ingested into the Endpoint data model, an event must be tagged with the following:

- Endpoint tag: N/A

- Additional tags:

  - listening, port (`Ports`)

  - process, report (`Processes`)

  - service, Report (`Services`)

  - endpoint, filesystem (`Filesystem`)

  - endpoint, registry (`Registry`)

Let's look at some examples of the `tstats` command of the Endpoint data model.

You can display the number of occurrences of each service:

```
| tstats count from datamodel=Endpoint.Services by
Services.service
```

You can display the number of `processes` spawned by `cmd.exe`:

```
| tstats count from datamodel=Endpoint.Processes where
Processes.parent_process_name="cmd.exe"
```

- **Network Traffic**: This defines network flow across different devices. Examples include firewall threats and flow traffic. The Network Traffic data model has one root event called `All_Traffic`. All searches are done against this `All_Traffic` root event. The fields in the Network Traffic data model include `action`, `bytes`, `dest`, `dest_port`, `rule`, `src`, `src_port`, `transport`, and `user`.

To be ingested into the Network Traffic data model, an event must be tagged with the following:

- All_Traffic tag: network, communicate

- Additional tags: none

Let's look at some examples of `tstats` searches of the Network Traffic data model.

You can display the number of external DNS requests by the `src` host:

```
| tstats count from datamodel=Network_Traffic where All_
Traffic.dest_port="53" All_Traffic.dest_zone="External"
by All_Traffic.src
```

You can display the sum of bytes to a destination host grouped by the `src` host:

```
| tstats sum(bytes) as bytes from datamodel=Network_
Traffic where All_Traffic.dest_ip="69.45.33.32" by All_
Traffic.src
```

The Splunk CIM can be configured via the setup page. This can be done by using the **Apps** page and clicking the **Set up** link under the **Actions** column. The most important step in setting up the Splunk CIM add-on is mapping the indexes to the data models. Splunk provides macros specifically for this purpose. For example, we can map the Palo Alto Networks logs to the Network Traffic data model by adding the `firewall_logs` index to the list of Network Traffic indexes textbox on the CIM setup page. We can also map logs to the CIM data model by modifying **cim_ macros** under **Settings | Search macros**. For example, we can add an index called `win_serv` containing Windows security event logs to the Authentication data model by editing the `cim_Authentication_indexes()` macro. The data must be tagged properly for you to fully get the advantages of the data model. Events can be tagged by creating event types using **Settings | Event types**. Well-configured data models help reduce search time. What other best practices can we use to improve our Splunk experience? We will explore some useful tips in the next section.

Improving performance

In this section, we will look at several best practices that can help improve our Splunk experience. We will explore useful backend and search time practices, including efficient search syntax, setting limits, and other interesting methods.

We can increase the efficiency of Splunk on the backend by implementing some simple configurations and practices:

1. Follow the memory and CPU recommendations from Splunk. Refer to the current Splunk documentation to ensure that your servers meet Splunk's recommendations.

2. Ensure that the operating system supports the version of Splunk you plan to use. Universal forwarders work on a range of operating systems. However, the current Enterprise License only works on the latest **Linux** (x86 64- bit) kernel versions, **Windows Server** (2022, 2016, and 2019), and **Windows 10** (x86 64-bit). Splunk also runs on AWS instances (as we saw in *Chapter 2, Setting Up the Splunk Environment*). Containerized solutions such as **Docker** and **Kubernetes** are also supported.

3. Ensure that you use the right filesystem, such as **Linux ext3**, **XFS**, **Windows NTFS**, or **FAT32**. Splunk has special considerations when it comes to using the **Network File System (NFS)** filesystem.

4. Follow the versioning compatibility recommendations across components from Splunk. Also, ensure that any apps and add-ons that you need to use will work in the version you are installing.

5. Ensure that the resources on the devices are set at the right limits. For example, the recommended value for opening files is `64000` for **Splunk 9.x** and the number of user `processes` is `16000`. You can change these settings by using the `ulimit` command in **nix* systems with different parameters. For example, setting the recommended value for open files can be done using the following command:

```
ulimit -n 64000
```

6. Use the deployment server and/or deployer to ensure that your configurations are consistent across groups of servers with similar purposes.

7. Consider securing your Splunk deployment by implementing basic security hardening procedures such as the following:

   A. Changing default passwords

   B. Disabling *admin* accounts

   C. Securing physical access to servers

   D. Using encryption by setting up security certificates

   E. Limiting network access to your servers using firewall rules

   F. Setting up user authentication and role-based access control

   G. Disabling REST APIs on universal forwarders to avoid unnecessary intrusion by malicious users

   H. Using secure service accounts for Splunk interactions with external systems such as databases and scripts

8. Maintain proper monitoring routines of internal Splunk logs to detect server errors and missing data.

9. Ensure that your data is normalized and that the data models are accelerated when in use.

We can increase the efficiency of Splunk during search time by implementing some simple practices:

1. Specify the automatic fields such as `index`, `source`, and `sourcetype`.

2. Do not use `index=*` and **All Time** time settings during searches on production machines.

3. Do not use real-time searches unless necessary.

4. Use the **Job Inspector** tool to inspect searches that appear to lag.

5. Use Fast Mode for faster search results but be aware that not all fields will be extracted.

6. Be specific with search criteria. For example, if you are only concerned about the `src` field, avoid including other fields in the search. Use the `fields` command to narrow down your search results.

7. Avoid using negative clauses when possible. Rather than using a negative clause such as `action!="success"`, use a positive clause by specifying `action="failure"` instead. However, be aware of the other possible options so that you don't exclude results.

8. Use OR instead of wildcards. For example, instead of saying `index=win*`, specify `index=win_ security OR index=win_system OR index=win_application` to specify different Windows indexes.

9. Try to filter data in the first part of the search (before the first pipe) using field/value pairs. For example, instead of writing `index=win_security | search EventCode=4624`, write `index=win_security EventCode=4624`.

10. Remove unnecessary fields and filter events before doing any calculations and use non-streaming commands such as `sort` and `stats` at the end of the search when necessary.

There are many other ways of improving Splunk performance through proper configuration and correct searching. You are encouraged to read through the current Splunk documentation for other helpful tips.

Summary

This chapter focused on improving search performance. We looked at different conceptual ways of storing data, including table datasets, lookup datasets, and datamodel datasets. All of these concepts, when used correctly, can increase Splunk's efficiency. We also looked at examples of each of these concepts. We explored how data is stored on disk when organized in data models and we introduced the `tstats` command for searching data models. We looked at the CIM and explored its various datasets and features. Finally, we highlighted 20 different ways we can improve Splunk performance, including from an administrative point of view and when searching.

In the next chapter, we will look at some newly introduced Splunk concepts such as federated searches.

11

Multisite Splunk Deployments and Federated Search

Splunk understands that, for some companies, the basic clustered indexer format does not always work. In some cases, companies may want to cut data center maintenance costs by moving to Splunk Cloud. In other cases, companies may want to increase fault tolerance by extending their Splunk deployment across geographic locations. Some companies may just be so large that one data center is not sufficient and so their data is spread out in different clusters. In this chapter, we will explore several alternative Splunk deployments. We will look at how Splunk Cloud differs from Splunk Enterprise. Then, we will look at how to set up multisite Splunk deployments. Lastly, we will talk about how to search across Splunk deployments using hybrid and federated search.

In this chapter, we will explore the following topics:

- Exploring multisite Splunk deployments
- Configuring federated search
- Using federated search

Exploring multisite Splunk deployments

We will explore more complex Splunk deployment in this section. We will look at the features of Splunk Cloud, including its key features and components. We will also look at how multisite Splunk deployments operate. Finally, we will look at the concept of hybrid search that allows for the integration of Splunk Enterprise and Splunk Cloud.

Splunk Cloud Platform

Splunk Cloud Platform, also referred to as *Splunk Cloud*, is a cloud-based service. Customers who subscribe to Splunk Cloud get access to a Splunk deployment where they utilize all the features of Splunk without the overhead of on-premises costs and maintenance. Unlike Splunk Enterprise, Splunk Cloud licensing is workload-based and sized for resource capacity. Customers may request exceptions to allow them to use ingest volume-based pricing.

The following list discusses some key features of Splunk Cloud:

- *Splunk Cloud only supports vetted and compatible apps as defined in Splunkbase*, but private apps are allowed.

- *There is a strong dependence on Splunk Support for installation and maintenance.* For example, customers do not have access to the **Command-Line Interface** (**CLI**). Customers reach out to Splunk Support by filing a ticket if the CLI is needed. A ticket is needed to enable real-time searches or REST API endpoints in Splunk Cloud.

- *Splunk Cloud does not accept any direct data feeds such as syslog.* The customer is dependent on the Splunk forwarder to send data to Splunk Cloud. Similarly, customers are not able to configure syslog outputs from Splunk Cloud.

- *Splunk Cloud does not support* **Multi-Factor Authentication** (**MFA**).

- *Splunk Cloud supports predefined user roles and users* such as the `sc_admin` role, which allows a customer admin to install apps, create and manage indexes, and manage users and passwords.

- *Unlike Splunk Enterprise, Splunk maintains Splunk Cloud Platform*, including security, upgrades, and patching.

- *Splunk Cloud uses SmartStore*, which is a feature that allows Splunk to use remote object storage, including **Amazon S3**, **Google Cloud Storage** (**GCS**), or **Microsoft Azure Blob Storage** (`https://tinyurl.com/2p8x8unp`). It includes a cache manager that controls which data is transferred over to remote storage. Some of the advantages of **SmartStore** include reduced storage cost, increased availability, and scalability.

- *Customers will be provided with a security key during installation.* This key is important and should be stored in a safe place.

Figure 11.1 shows the components of a Splunk Cloud deployment:

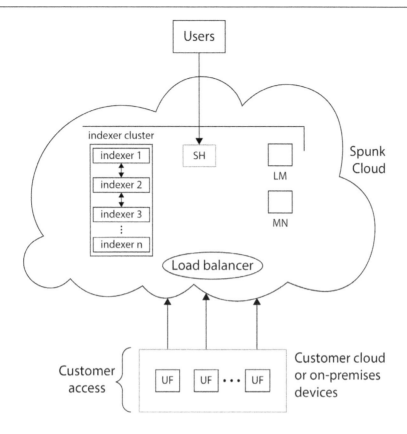

Figure 11.1 – Components of a Splunk Cloud deployment

The customer configures and manages the universal forwarders. They are hosted either on customer premises or a customer-subscribed cloud hosting platform. Encrypted data flows from the forwarders to Splunk Cloud, where it is *load-balanced* to the indexers. The customer has no access to the indexers. The search head is available to the customer for searching and some configuration of knowledge objects. The **manager node** and license manager are also hidden from the customer.

Overall, searching for data in Splunk Cloud occurs like searching in Splunk Enterprise. The average user accesses the URL of a Splunk Cloud search head using a browser.

Multisite search deployments

We looked at indexer and search head clusters in *Chapter 9, Clustering and Advanced Administration*. In this section, we will take a quick look at a different type of cluster – the Splunk multisite indexer cluster. Splunk customers may opt to configure a multisite indexer cluster because of geographic reasons or to increase fault tolerance. As the name implies, a multisite cluster consists of multiple Splunk deployments or sites that are connected. This is usually defined by geography – that is, *site*

A could be in Nashville while *site B* is in San Fransisco. Each Splunk node belongs to one of those deployments or **sites**. There are *site boundaries* that define how activities in a cluster such as searching, bucket fixing, and replication operate. For example, although site A and site B may be connected, the search head belonging to site A will not distribute searches to peers in site B.

A multisite indexer cluster consists of the following:

- *A single manager node* on *only one* of the cluster sites. The manager node is not part of the indexer cluster – that is, it does not index data like the other indexers.

- *A set of peer nodes* in each cluster site.

- *A search head* in each cluster site. In some cases, the customer may only require searching for only a select number of sites, making a search head irrelevant.

Installing a search head near the indexers reduces the need for long-distance network traffic, resulting in lower costs and faster searches. The idea of installing a search head on each site with searchable data is called **search affinity**. This is enabled by default in multisite indexer clusters but must be configured. This is accomplished by specifying a value called `site_search_factor`. Search affinity can be disabled by setting the site value of the search head to `site0` in `server.conf`. Setting the site and `site_search_factor` are just two attributes that need to be configured in a multisite indexer cluster setup.

Table 11.1 lists some other important attributes that apply to multisite indexer clusters (`https://tinyurl.com/2p8zj7zv`):

Attribute	Description	Applies to
`site`	Specifies the site name (a string of characters) of the cluster site. `site0` on a search head indicates that search affinity is disabled.	Every node
`multisite`	Indicates that the node is participating in a multisite cluster. This is a Boolean value (`true`/`false`).	Manager node and search head
`available_sites`	Name of the sites in the multisite cluster that the manager node oversees. This is a comma-delimited list of site names.	Manager node only

Attribute	Description	Applies to
`site_replication_factor`	The site replication factor, which is the multisite equivalent of the replication factor of single-site indexer clusters.	Manager node only
`site_search_factor`	The site search factor, which is the multisite equivalent of the search factor of single-site indexer clusters.	Manager node only
`mode`	The mode of the node. The mode can be manager, peer, or searchhead.	Every node

Table 11.1 – Attributes specific to multisite indexer clusters

Suppose we have a multisite indexer cluster consisting of two sites – **Site 1** and **Site 2**. A user runs a Splunk search query on the search head on **Site 1**. This search query is sent to indexers on both **Site 1** and **Site 2**, but only the indexers on **Site 1** respond with results.

Figure 11.2 shows an example of a multisite indexer cluster:

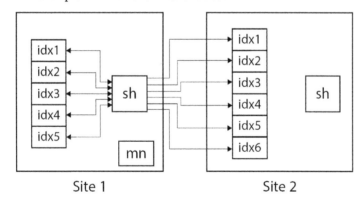

Figure 11.2 – A multisite indexer cluster

Note the bidirectional arrows between **Site 1**'s search head and the indexers in **Site 1**. Compare them to the direction of the arrows in **Site 2**. This implies that only the indexers in **Site 1** return search results but all the indexers in the multisite cluster receive the search query.

The previous scenario assumes that **Site 1** is valid. In *Chapter 9, Clustering and Advanced Administration*, we learned that an indexer cluster is valid if it meets its **search factor**. If one of the indexers goes down, the search head will get as much data from the remaining indexers in **Site 1**. However, any missing data will be retrieved from **Site 2**.

Figure 11.3 shows what happens if a node in one site goes down, making the site invalid:

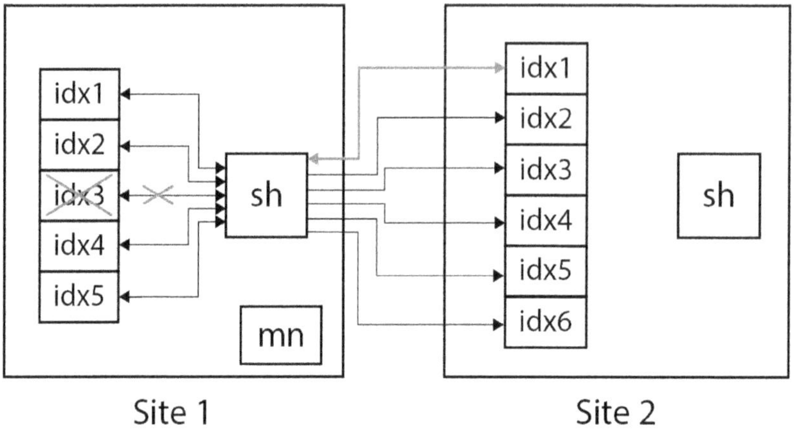

Figure 11.3 – Searching a multisite indexer cluster with a failed node

The search head sends its query request to all nodes in the multisite indexer cluster. However, since **idx3** is down, the search results will come from **idx1** in **Site 2**. Note the double arrow between **Site 1**'s search head and **idx1** in **Site 2**.

Now that we have an idea of how Splunk Cloud works and how multisite indexer clusters work, let's talk about **hybrid search**.

Hybrid search

Customers have full administrative control of their on-premises Splunk deployments. However, once a customer purchases Splunk Cloud, they lose a certain level of control. The customer may have scripts, authentication methods, apps, or even custom inputs that are not supported by Splunk Cloud. In this case, the customer may opt to have on-premises indexers and search heads that integrate with the Splunk Cloud indexer cluster. The customer can then use hybrid search to access data on both the on-premises indexers and the ones in Splunk Cloud. The following rules apply to hybrid search (`https://tinyurl.com/mwe5awub`):

*   *Hybrid search is always initiated from an on-premises search head.*
*   *The on-premises search head must be a compatible version* with the indexers in Splunk Cloud – for example, if the Splunk Cloud indexer cluster is running version 9.0.x, then the on-premises search head must be running version 9.0.x.
*   *Hybrid search does not support scheduled searches.*
*   *Premium apps such as Splunk Enterprise Security cannot be installed* on a hybrid search head.

- *The hybrid search head should also be set up to search across any on-premises indexers.*

- *Splunk Cloud support will need the public IP address of the hybrid search head* so that they can enable hybrid search. They will also need the IP address of the manager node and the security key for the Splunk Cloud indexer cluster.

- *Hybrid search requires a 1 MB Splunk Enterprise license* for the on-premises search head.

- *Configuration for hybrid search is done in* `server.conf`. An example of the configuration is given here (code retrieved from `https://tinyurl.com/mwe5awub`):

```
[general]
site = site0

[clustering]
multisite = true
manager_uri = <manager node URI in the format https://
c0m1.<stack name>.splunkcloud.com:8089>
mode = searchhead
pass4SymmKey = <security key>
```

Figure 11.4 shows an example of a hybrid search environment:

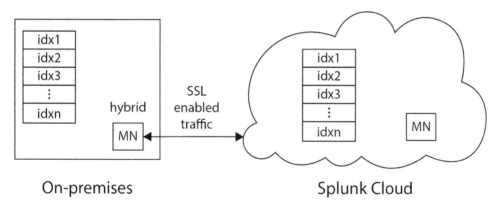

Figure 11.4 – Hybrid search

This section introduced the concept of hybrid search, which allows us to search Splunk Cloud indexers using on-premises Splunk Enterprise search heads. We will look at how federated search can be used to search across multiple Splunk platforms, including on-premises Splunk Enterprise and Splunk Cloud, in the next section.

Configuring federated search

Hybrid search allows us to search Splunk Cloud from an on-premises (Splunk Enterprise) search head. Without hybrid search, it is not possible to integrate the two technologies. **Federated search** builds on this concept to allow us to search across different types of remote Splunk platforms. Federated search allows us to use our search head to search datasets across multiple Splunk deployments, regardless of topology. Suppose our company has a Splunk deployment in *location X*, another Splunk Enterprise deployment in *location Y*, and a Splunk Cloud deployment, where each deployment contains high-value datasets. Federated search allows us to use a search head at *location X* to search the deployment at *location Y* and the Splunk Cloud deployment. In addition, federated search allows us to search from the Splunk Cloud instance to the Splunk Enterprise deployment at *location X* and *location Y*. Hybrid search allows us to search in Splunk Cloud from Splunk Enterprise. Federated search allows us to search from Splunk Enterprise to Splunk Cloud and from Splunk Cloud to Splunk Enterprise. There are two main components of federated search:

1. **Local deployment** – the location of the **federated search head** and the origin of the search.
2. **Federated provider** – the remote Splunk deployment containing the set of indexers that contains the indexed data. The federated provider includes the **remote search head**.

To set up federated search, a Splunk Enterprise `admin` user or a Splunk Cloud `sc_admin` user will first determine the federated provider hostname. This name has to be in the `format <deployment name>.yourdomain.com` for Splunk Enterprise deployments and `<deployment name>. splunkcloud.com>` for Splunk Cloud deployments. In cases where the federated provider is hosted in Splunk Cloud with a search head cluster, the format of the federated provider is `shc1.<stack name>.splunkcloud.com` and `<deployment name>-shc. yourdomain.com` if the search head cluster is hosted in a Splunk Enterprise deployment.

The Splunk `admin` or `sc_admin` user also needs to specify the provider **mode**. A federated provider works in two modes:

*   **Transparent mode** – used in situations when the Splunk customer already has one or more Splunk Enterprise search heads making hybrid search queries on indexes in a Splunk Cloud indexer cluster. Customers can continue running hybrid searches from Splunk Enterprise to Splunk Cloud without changes. To enable federated search in transparent mode, you need a **federated provider definition**.

*   **Standard mode (default)** – used if the Splunk customer does not use hybrid search but wants to connect to other Splunk deployments, including Splunk Cloud. Federated search in standard mode works from one Splunk Cloud deployment to another Splunk Cloud deployment, from one Splunk Enterprise deployment to another Splunk Enterprise deployment, from a Splunk Cloud deployment to a Splunk Enterprise deployment, and most importantly, from a Splunk Enterprise deployment to a Splunk Cloud deployment (if hybrid search is not enabled).

It is important to note that the federated search environment can either be transparent or standard. Federated search does not permit both modes at the same time – for example, *federated provider A* cannot run in transparent mode while *federated provider B* runs in standard mode.

The Splunk `admin` or `sc_admin` user also needs to specify a username and password for a **service account** on the federated provider deployment. This user needs to have a role with `read permissions` for any remote datasets that we will be searching. In addition, service accounts for federated providers running in transparent mode must also have `fsh_manage` and `search` capabilities.

So how does it work? A federated search head on the local deployment sends a request to a remote search head on the federated provider. The federated search head has a **federated index** that is a *logical mapping* to a *remote dataset*. The remote dataset can be an *event index* or a *saved search*. Note that a federated index does not actually ingest data. It is a logical data structure connecting the search head to actual remote data. The remote data can be stored in Splunk Cloud deployments or remote on-premises Splunk Enterprise deployments. This is what makes the idea of federated search so interesting. The federated search in the local deployment does not care about the Splunk platform in the federated provider environment. The federated provider could be a Splunk Cloud deployment or another on-premises deployment. Parts of the federated search are executed on the local deployment and the other parts are executed on the federated providers. The processing of the search on the remote search heads located on the federated providers helps ensure that the search results do not take up too much bandwidth.

Figure 11.5 illustrates a simple federated search scenario:

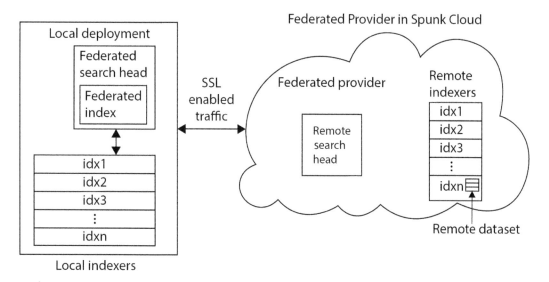

Figure 11.5 – Federated search setup

How does federated search syntax differ from regular SPL? We will see this in the next section.

Using federated search

Running federated searches varies, based on whether the federated provider is running in standard or transparent mode. Federated searches that run over transparent mode do not require any new syntax. These federated searches are run using the same syntax as regular local searches. However, federated searches executed on standard mode federated providers require additional syntax. If this syntax is not used, the search will be executed on the indexers in the local deployment only. Before we can run a federated search in standard mode, we must ensure that a user with the *admin* role creates federated indexes on the federated search head in the local deployment. Remember that this is a logical index and does not actually ingest data. In addition, you need to ensure that the knowledge objects in your search, such as lookups, are present both on the local search head and the federated search head on the remote deployment. The following examples show how to run federated searches on different types of remote datasets.

Searching remote indexes

We need to use the `search` command when conducting a federated search on an index. For example, suppose the `botsv1` index is stored in a remote dataset. We would configure a federated index on the local search head that maps to the `botsv1` index on the federated provider. To search this remote index, we would specify the following query:

```
search index=federated:botsv1
```

Note that, in this case, the name of the federated index is the same as the remote dataset/index.

Searching remote saved searches

Instead of using the `search` command when searching remote saved searches, we use the `from` command. It is preceded by the pipe symbol (`|`). For example, if we wanted to search the results of a remote saved search that is mapped to a federated index called `malicious_agents`, we would specify the following:

```
| from federated:malicious_agents
```

Next, let's see how we would search a remote data model.

Searching remote data models

The syntax used for searching remote data depends on whether we are searching an accelerated data model or not. If we are searching an unaccelerated data model, we would use the `from` command, like the one used for searching remote saved searches. However, if we are searching an accelerated data model, we would use the `tstats` command. For example, suppose we have an unaccelerated data model called **Malicious Activity** that is mapped to a federated index called `malicious_activity`; we would specify the following:

```
| from federated:malicious_activity
```

However, if the `malicious_activity` data model was accelerated and we wanted to count the number of events, we would use the following syntax:

```
| tstats count from datamodel=federated:malicious_activity
```

That concludes this section on federated searches. Now, let's summarize the chapter.

Summary

In this chapter, we covered different types of deployments. We looked at how Splunk Cloud differs from Splunk Enterprise by pointing out some additional benefits (such as lower cost) and some constraints (such as reduced administrative control). We then discussed multisite indexer clusters and how they function. We looked at how hybrid search allows us to search from a search head in a Splunk Enterprise deployment to an indexer cluster in a Splunk Cloud **deployment**. Finally, we looked at federated search, which improves on hybrid search by allowing us to search different Splunk environments.

In *Chapter 12*, *Container Management*, we will look at how we can use containers such as **Kubernetes** and **Docker** with Splunk.

12

Container Management

We discussed different configurations available for extending Splunk deployments across multiple clusters geographically and otherwise in *Chapter 11, Multisite Splunk Deployments and Federated Search*. These types of deployments are becoming more prevalent as the rise in globalization and data production increase. Organizations want to ensure that data is available to consumers. In this chapter, we will look at one last technology that organizations can use to deploy Splunk efficiently. **Containerization** is the term used to refer to hosting multiple isolated software units that share the same **Operating System (OS)** kernel. We have already seen one cloud-based container environment when we installed Splunk Enterprise on AWS instances in *Chapter 2, Setting Up the Splunk Environment*. We will look at some basic information about containers in this chapter. We will also look at spinning up Splunk in **Docker** containers. There, we will learn about the **Splunk Operator for Kubernetes**. Finally, we will look at how data is stored in a container and whether we should be concerned about its security.

In this chapter, we will explore the following topics:

- Understanding container management
- Deploying Splunk in Docker
- Getting started with Splunk Operator for Kubernetes
- Exploring container logs using Splunk

Understanding container management

The AWS instances we spun up in *Chapter 2, Setting Up the Splunk Environment*, were **cloud-based containers**. In this section, we will look at containers in general. What is a container? A **container** is a software development concept that allows multiple isolated processes to share the same OS kernel. The idea of multiple isolated processes sharing a host (virtualization) is not a new one. Organizations have used virtual machine technology in various forms for decades. For example, IBM introduced virtualization concepts with the CP-40 in 1967. **VMware**, one of the well-known virtual machine platforms, was patented in 1998.

Containerization, as we know it today, was introduced in 2013 with the development of **Docker**. A Docker container is a **Platform-as-a-Service (PaaS)** offering where software is packaged with all the libraries, code, tools, and configuration files that they need to run isolated on a host. Containers such as Docker share the host's OS kernel. The `chroot` command was one of the pivotal commands in Unix that made containers possible. This command sets the root directory for a new process and its children, making it possible for multiple isolated processes to run within a host. Containers such as Docker utilize features of the Linux kernel such as **Linux Control Groups (cgroups)** and **namespace isolation**. **cgroups** control the use of resources such as CPU, memory, and disk **Input/Output (I/O)** by groups of processes. Splunk running in one container cannot use the resources of Splunk running in another container. **Namespace isolation** is used to ensure that containers do not have visibility into other containers. Splunk running in one container cannot see other Splunk instances running in another container. Docker works on other non-Linux environments such as **Microsoft Windows** and **macOS**. However, Docker containers in these environments rely on Linux VMs running on top of the OS. We will focus on Linux-based installations in this chapter.

Figure 12.1 shows the difference between virtual machines and Docker containers:

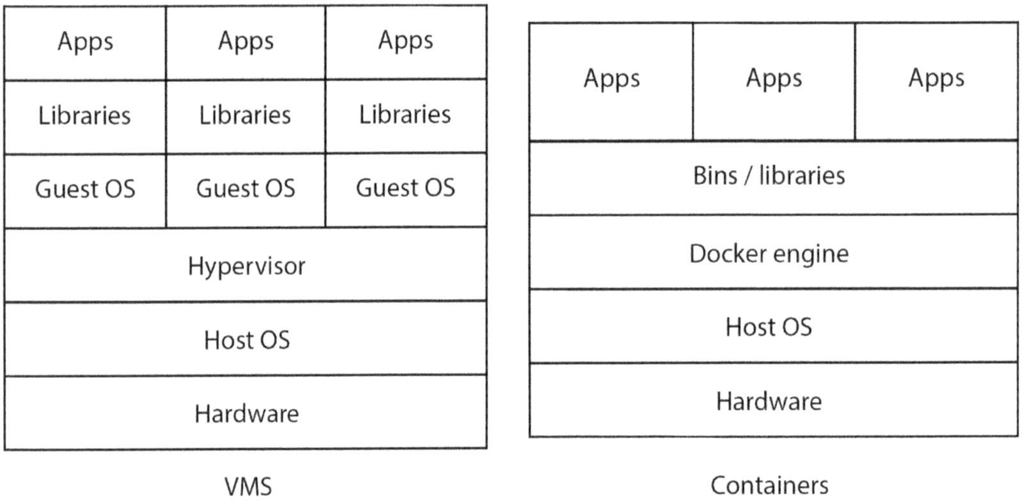

Figure 12.1 – Virtual machines versus containers

Why would we want to utilize a container? There are several reasons why a Splunk admin would decide to run Splunk in a container, including increased portability and flexibility and reduced cost. Containers also take less time to deploy after the initial setup. In *Chapter 2, Setting Up the Splunk Environment*, we spent less time installing the Splunk indexer and search head compared to the Splunk universal forwarders. We used AWS instances with Splunk Enterprise pre-installed to spin up the indexer and search head while we had to manually install the universal forwarder since a pre-installed AWS instance was not available. Now that we have an idea of what containers are, we'll deploy Splunk in a Docker container in the next section.

Deploying Splunk in Docker

In this section, we will install a small distributed Splunk deployment, including a standalone Splunk instance and one forwarder. Ensure that you have the proper system requirements to install Docker, as listed at `https://docs.docker.com/engine/install/`, then install Docker on your host machine. We will rely heavily on the instructions provided by the Docker-Splunk documentation (`https://splunk.github.io/docker-splunk/`) in this section.

Figure 12.2 shows the setup that we will deploy:

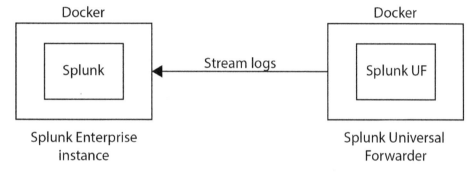

Figure 12.2 – Splunk deployment using Docker

Let's install Splunk in Docker using the following steps:

1. Install the latest Splunk Docker container from Docker Hub by using the `docker` command and specifying `splunk:latest` (latest full Splunk Enterprise) or `universalforwarder:latest` (latest Splunk Universal Forwarder):

    ```
    $docker pull splunk/splunk:latest
    $docker pull splunk/universalforwarder:latest
    ```

2. Create a Docker network using the `docker network create` command:

    ```
    $docker network create --driver bridge --attachable
    splunk_network
    ```

    This command creates a network using the **bridge** driver. `--driver` accepts either `bridge` (default) or `overlay`, which are built-in network drivers. We have specified the `--attachable` flag so that we can manually attach containers to the network. Lastly, we named the new network `splunk_network`.

3. Start up the Splunk Enterprise instance using the docker run command:

    ```
    $docker run --network splunk_network --name splunk_sa_
    instance -p 8000:8000 \
    -e "SPLUNK_PASSWORD=<my admin password>" \
    -e "SPLUNK_START_ARGS=--accept-license" \
    -it splunk/splunk:latest
    ```

    Here, we used the --network flag to specify the splunk_network network that we created in *step 2* as the name of the network. Then, we used the --name flag to assign a name to our new instance. The -p flag specifies 8000:8000, which maps the host's 8000 port to the new container's 8000 port. We also used the -e flag to specify the admin password to be used on the new Splunk instance and to accept the Splunk Enterprise license. Finally, we specified that we would like to spin up this new Splunk Enterprise instance in a Docker container using the Docker image we downloaded in *step 1*. With just this one command, we have deployed a standalone Splunk instance in Docker and connected it to our Docker network. We can access Splunk Web in the Docker container just like we did before – that is, by navigating to http://localhost:8000 using a browser. We use the user admin and the password specified in the docker run command to log in.

4. Start up the Splunk Universal Forwarder using the docker run command:

    ```
    $docker run --network splunk_network --name splunk_uf_
    instance \
    --hostname splunk_uf_instance \
    -e "SPLUNK_PASSWORD=<my admin password>" \
    -e "SPLUNK_START_ARGS=--accept-license" \
    -e "SPLUNK_STANDALONE_URL=splunk_sa_instance" \
    -it splunk/universalforwarder:latest
    ```

    This command launches the Splunk Universal Forwarder instance in a Docker container and connects it to the splunk_network network. We specified the server name and the hostname using --name and --hostname, respectively. We also specified the admin password and accepted the license, as we did in *step 3*. Note that there is one extra -e flag, which specifies that our new Splunk Universal Forwarder instance should forward logs to the splunk_sa_instance instance that we spun up in *step 2*. Finally, we specified that we would like to use the Docker image that we pulled down in *step 1*. You may be wondering why we did not use the -p 8000:8000 flag when spinning up the Splunk Universal Forwarder. This is because Splunk Universal Forwarders do not have a Splunk Web interface. Try out the installation by navigating to http://localhost:8000 in your browser and running a Splunk query.

This was a very simple example, but the results yielded a fully functioning Splunk deployment containing two nodes. We can create more advanced configurations such as heavy forwarders, deployment servers, and even indexer and search head clusters. However, these topics are beyond the scope of this book. Instead, we will move on and look at deploying Splunk using **Splunk Operator for Kubernetes**.

Getting started with Splunk Operator for Kubernetes

Kubernetes, sometimes referred to as **K8s**, is an open source framework for deploying and managing applications in containers. Splunk has a project like Docker-Splunk called **Splunk Operator for Kubernetes** (`https://splunk.github.io/splunk-operator`). First, let's look at some important keywords when dealing with Splunk in a K8s environment (`https://kubernetes.io/docs/concepts/overview/components`):

- **Node**: A virtual or physical machine. A **Node** contains the services necessary to run Pods. A Node contains several components, including the **kubelet**, the **container runtime**, and the **kube-proxy**:

  - **Kubelet**: An agent that runs in a Node to ensure that the Node is part of the Pod

  - **Container runtime**: The software responsible for running a container

  - **kube-proxy**: A network proxy containing network rules that's installed on each Node in the cluster

- **Control plane**: The part of the K8s framework that makes global decisions about the cluster. This includes activities such as scheduling and managing cluster components. The control plane consists of several components, including:

  - **API server (kube-apiserver)**: Exposes the frontend of the K8s control plane.

  - **etcd**: A key-value store for all cluster data.

  - **kube-scheduler**: Assigns newly created Pods to Nodes. The assignment is based on factors such as resource requirements, hardware and software constraints, and data locality.

  - **kube-controller-manager**: Runs controller processes.

- **Pod**: A set of running containers in a cluster.

- **Kubectl**: A command framework used to execute and modify Node objects.

Figure 12.3 shows a simplified K8s cluster:

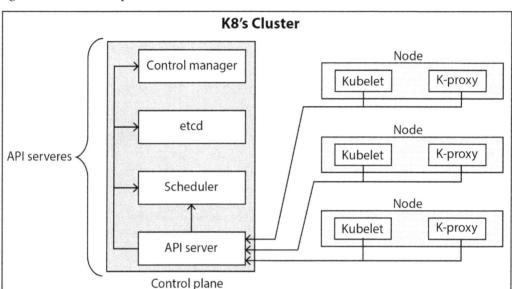

Figure 12.3 – A simple K8s cluster

We will rely strongly on the instructions published at `https://tinyurl.com/34rp7t95` as we navigate the installation of Splunk in a K8s environment. We will use the same Docker instance that we installed in *step 1* of *Deploying Splunk in Docker*:

1. Install Docker by following the steps at `https://docs.docker.com/engine/install/`, as indicated in the *Deploying Splunk in Docker* section.

2. Install the `kubectl` command-line tool (`https://kubernetes.io/docs/tasks/tools/`). This tool is like the Docker command-line tool and will allow us to run commands on K8s clusters.

3. Install and start Splunk Operator for Kubernetes for a specific namespace. We will use the instructions in the Splunk Operator for Kubernetes GitHub `README.md` file to complete the installation (`https://github.com/splunk/splunk-operator/blob/develop/docs/README.md`):

    ```
    kubectl apply -f https://github.com/splunk/splunk-
    operator/releases/download/2.1.0/splunk-operator-
    namespace.yaml
    ```

4. Use the `kubectl get pods` command to determine whether the container is up and running:

    ```
    kubectl get pods
    ```

5. Create the Splunk Enterprise deployment called `splunk_sa_instance` using the `kubectl apply` command:

    ```
    cat <<EOF | kubectl apply -n splunk-operator -f -
    apiVersion: enterprise.splunk.com/v4
    kind: Standalone
    metadata:
        name: splunk_sa_instance
        finalizers:
        - enterprise.splunk.com/delete-pvc
    EOF
    ```

6. We should see the new Splunk standalone device called `splunk_sa_instance` when we run the `kubectl get pods` command again:

    ```
    kubectl get pods
    ```

7. Open port `8000` for Splunk Web access:

    ```
    kubectl port-forward splunk_-s1-standaline-0 8000
    ```

8. We will need the Splunk Enterprise admin user and password to access Splunk Web. The passwords can be found using the `kubectl get secret` command, as follows:

    ```
    kubectl get secret splunk-default-secret -o yaml
    ```

    We can decode the secret using the following command, which yields the secrets associated with the deployment, such as the indexer cluster secret, pass4SymmKey, password, and search head cluster secret:

    ```
    kubectl get secret splunk-default-secret -o
    go-template='{{range $k,$v := .data}}{{printf "%s: " $k}}
    {{if not $v}}{{$v}}{{else}}{{$v | base64decode}}{{end}}
    {{"\n"}}{{end}}'
    ```

9. We can now log into Splunk Enterprise using Splunk Web at `http://localhost:8000`.

We now have a Splunk Enterprise instance running in a K8s environment. Again, this is only the initial setup phase of the deployment. Please refer to the Splunk Operator for Kubernetes documentation (`https://splunk.github.io/splunk-operator/`) for further instructions. We will look at monitoring containers in the next section.

Exploring container logs using Splunk

Since the focus of this book has been exploring data using Splunk, let's briefly talk about monitoring containers. Containers can introduce increased complexity in monitoring. Although they have positive attributes such as scalability, flexibility, and lower cost, troubleshooting can be very tricky. We'll focus on Docker in this section. By default, Docker logs are stored in `/var/lib/docker/containers/<container_id>` on the host where `container_id` is running. In a simple scenario, we can use the following Docker command to fetch logs from a container:

```
docker logs <container_id>
```

We can determine the `container_id` property by using the `docker ps` command to list all the running containers. The `docker logs` command retrieves batches of container logs that are available at the time of execution. This method works for troubleshooting or monitoring small deployments. However, it will not work for situations where containers are dynamically added to the cluster or where the number of containers is very large.

Splunk has several solutions for monitoring container logs in larger environments. The Splunk **HTTP Event Collector** (HEC) uses the concept of an **API token** to send logs into Splunk. Let's configure an HEC input using the following steps:

1. Navigating to **Settings** | **Data Inputs** | **HTTP Event Collector** | **Global Settings**.
2. Next, enter a **Name** for the HEC input and select a **sourcetype** and **index** on the next screen.
3. Review the settings and click the **Submit** button to generate the new **HEC token**.

We will use the token seen in the **Token Value** text box to set up log forwarding to Splunk in a Docker container.

Figure 12.4 shows the creation of a new token called `docker_token`:

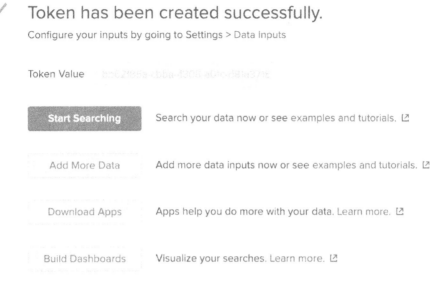

Figure 12.4 – New HEC token called docker_token

Next, we will spin up a new Docker container using the `docker run` command. We will use a series of `--log-driver` and `--log-opt` flags to tell the new container to send its new logs to Splunk. For example, suppose we have a Docker container called `docker-test`. We would use the following command to send logs to Splunk:

```
docker run --log-driver=splunk \
        --log-opt splunk-url=http://localhost:8000 \
        --log-opt splunk-token=bb62f85a-cbba-4308-a01c-
d81a3718e74f \
        --log-opt splunk-format=json \
        --log-opt tag="{{.ImageName}}/{{.Name}}/{{.ID}}"
        docker-test
```

In this example, we have specified that we are using the `splunk` log driver that is included in every Docker installation. We specify the *URL* of the Splunk instance where we generated the HEC token. In this example, Splunk is running on the same host as the Docker container. We specify the *HEC token* that we generated (see *Figure 12.4*) in Splunk. We also instruct Docker to send container logs in *JSON* format and to include information about the container, such as the *image name*, the *container name*, and the *first 12 characters of the container ID*.

The Docker documentation on logging to Splunk (`https://tinyurl.com/yhj349c5`) details several advanced options that we can specify with the `docker run` command. However, these topics are beyond the scope of this book. For more complex deployments, where the number of containers is large, we can incorporate Splunk logging into our more advanced Docker configurations. However, the principle remains the same. We can also use Splunk TAs and apps such as **Splunk Connect for Docker** to monitor containers. This certified Docker logging plugin uses HEC data inputs and is available on **Splunkbase**.

We introduced this section by talking about logging in terms of troubleshooting. However, logging is very important for monitoring the security of containers. Organizations that are new to containers may deploy them with misconfigurations, which may make the systems vulnerable to attack. Some of the issues include vulnerabilities from using publicly available images and insecure authentication measures such as failing to change default admin passwords. Some best practices for ensuring that our containers are safe include downloading only trustworthy images, patching, auditing, setting proper privileges, and monitoring traffic to and from the containers. Refer to `https://tinyurl.com/3kswaa9r` for further information on container security.

We covered logging and security in this section. Now, let's summarize what we've learned.

Summary

Although containers, namely Docker, have been around since 2013, they are only recently being accepted as a solution in modern organizations at a large scale. Container technology offers organizations flexibility and scalability at a lower cost. In this chapter, we looked at how Docker and Kubernetes work. We also looked at the basic installation and deployment steps for each tool. Finally, we ended the discussion with information on logging and securing containers.

We've also reached the end of this book. We looked at the different components that make up Splunk, including indexers, search heads, and forwarders. We installed and configured a simple Splunk deployment in AWS. We used different methods, including the configuration files and Splunk Web, to onboard and normalize data into our environment. Next, we used the Splunk BOTS v1 dataset to learn SPL, including using different types of commands, lookups, and macros. We used the data in the BOTS v1 dataset to create tables and charts and incorporated the results into dashboards. Then, we covered a few topics surrounding Splunk administration. We talked about licensing and how Splunk stores data in indexes and buckets. We looked at how Splunk availability can be improved by using indexer and search head clusters. We also looked at creating Splunk users and roles. Next, we explored how data models help increase the speed of Splunk searches and discussed two different technologies that have more recently been adopted in organizations that use Splunk. Multisite Splunk deployments and federated search increase fault tolerance and allow companies that are spread out geographically to integrate their multiple Splunk sites. Finally, this chapter introduced us to the concept of hosting Splunk in containers, as well as using Splunk as a logging repository for containers. I hope that this information was useful to you!

Index

`Packt.com`

Subscribe to our online digital library for full access to over 7,000 books and videos, as well as industry leading tools to help you plan your personal development and advance your career. For more information, please visit our website.

Why subscribe?

- Spend less time learning and more time coding with practical eBooks and Videos from over 4,000 industry professionals

- Improve your learning with Skill Plans built especially for you

- Get a free eBook or video every month

- Fully searchable for easy access to vital information

- Copy and paste, print, and bookmark content

Did you know that Packt offers eBook versions of every book published, with PDF and ePub files available? You can upgrade to the eBook version at `packt.com` and as a print book customer, you are entitled to a discount on the eBook copy. Get in touch with us at `customercare@packtpub.com` for more details.

At `www.packt.com`, you can also read a collection of free technical articles, sign up for a range of free newsletters, and receive exclusive discounts and offers on Packt books and eBooks.

Other Books You May Enjoy

If you enjoyed this book, you may be interested in these other books by Packt:

Stefanie Molin

ISBN: 978-1-80056-345-2

- Understand how data analysts and scientists gather and analyze data
- Perform data analysis and data wrangling using Python
- Combine, group, and aggregate data from multiple sources
- Create data visualizations with pandas, matplotlib, and seaborn
- Apply machine learning algorithms to identify patterns and make predictions
- Use Python data science libraries to analyze real-world datasets
- Solve common data representation and analysis problems using pandas
- Build Python scripts, modules, and packages for reusable analysis code

Gururajan Govindan, Shubhangi Hora, Konstantin Palagachev

ISBN: 978-1-83921-138-6

- Get to grips with the fundamental concepts and conventions of data analysis
- Understand how different algorithms help you to analyze the data effectively
- Determine the variation between groups of data using hypothesis testing
- Visualize your data correctly using appropriate plotting points
- Use correlation techniques to uncover the relationship between variables
- Find hidden patterns in data using advanced techniques and strategies

Packt is searching for authors like you

If you're interested in becoming an author for Packt, please visit `authors.packtpub.com` and apply today. We have worked with thousands of developers and tech professionals, just like you, to help them share their insight with the global tech community. You can make a general application, apply for a specific hot topic that we are recruiting an author for, or submit your own idea.

Share Your Thoughts

Now you've finished *Exploring Data with Splunk*, we'd love to hear your thoughts! If you purchased the book from Amazon, please click here to go straight to the Amazon review page for this book and share your feedback or leave a review on the site that you purchased it from.

Your review is important to us and the tech community and will help us make sure we're delivering excellent quality content.

Download a free PDF copy of this book

Thanks for purchasing this book!

Do you like to read on the go but are unable to carry your print books everywhere? Is your eBook purchase not compatible with the device of your choice?

Don't worry, now with every Packt book you get a DRM-free PDF version of that book at no cost.

Read anywhere, any place, on any device. Search, copy, and paste code from your favorite technical books directly into your application.

The perks don't stop there, you can get exclusive access to discounts, newsletters, and great free content in your inbox daily

Follow these simple steps to get the benefits:

1. Scan the QR code or visit the link below

https://packt.link/free-ebook/978-1-80324-941-4

2. Submit your proof of purchase
3. That's it! We'll send your free PDF and other benefits to your email directly.

CPSIA information can be obtained
at www.ICGtesting.com
Printed in the USA
JSHW061419250623
43705JS00001B/1

9 781803 249414